PENGUIN BOOKS

LET'S CALL HIM VASU

Shubhranshu Choudhary is a journalist. He has worked for over two decades with media organizations like the BBC and the *Guardian*. Currently, he devotes his time to an experiment to create a model for democratic media. In the process, he has created the world's first community radio on the mobile phone called CGnet Swara.

SHUBHRANSHU CHOUDHARY

LET'S CALL HIM VASU

WITH THE MAOISTS
IN CHHATTISGARH

PENGUIN BOOKS

An imprint of Penguin Random House

PENGUIN BOOKS

USA | Canada | UK | Ireland | Australia
New Zealand | India | South Africa | China | Singapore

Penguin Books is part of the Penguin Random House group of companies
whose addresses can be found at global.penguinrandomhouse.com

Published by Penguin Random House India Pvt. Ltd
4th Floor, Capital Tower 1, MG Road,
Gurugram 122 002, Haryana, India

First published by Penguin Books India 2012

Copyright © Shubhranshu Choudhary 2012

10 9 8 7 6 5 4 3

ISBN 9780143067573

Typeset in GoudyOlSt BT by R. Ajith Kumar, New Delhi

Printed at Repro India Limited

www.penguin.co.in

For the Adivasis of Dandakaranya,
who have suffered so much . . .

CONTENTS

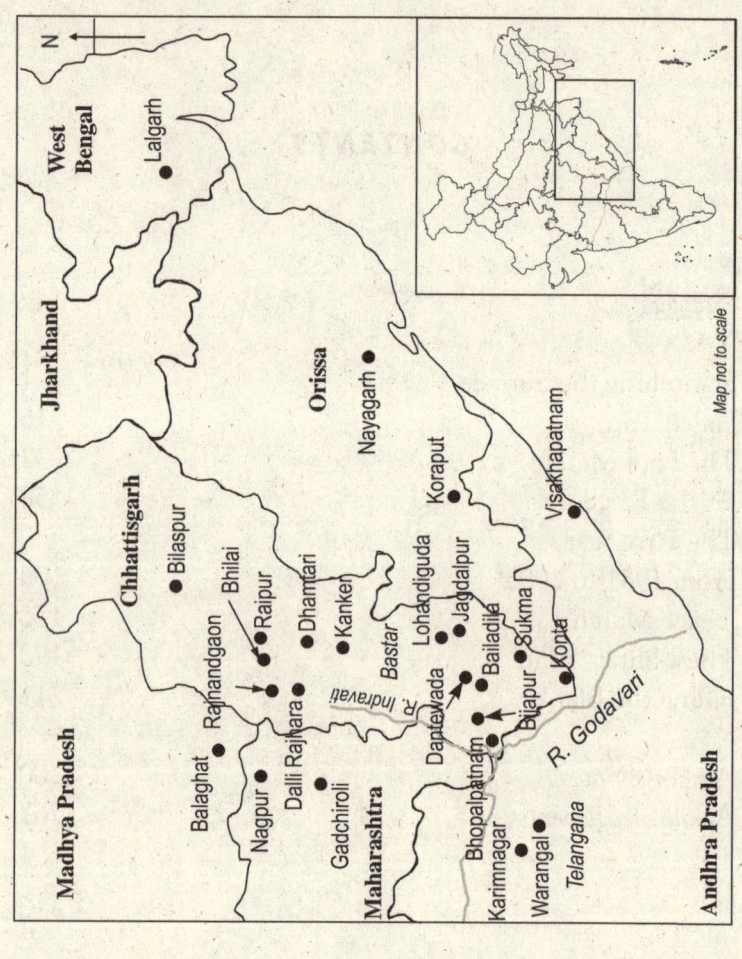

PROLOGUE

Let's call him Vasu.

He was my first Maoist contact. A dark, stocky young man who spoke Hindi with a Hyderabadi accent, he was introduced to me as a student. Vasu was new to the small town where I worked as a trainee journalist for a newspaper. In a spirit of casual friendliness, I invited him to join me at the Indian Coffee House, where I used to hang around on Sunday mornings.

Vasu never missed a Sunday. He was a serious, well-read young man who spoke knowledgeably on Marxism, and often he would recommend books to me. Ignoring my less than enthusiastic response, Vasu brought a couple of heavy-looking volumes to my room one day.

'You know my schedule, Vasu,' I told him. 'I start work at 10 a.m. with the morning meeting, and by the time I go to bed after the paper goes to press, it is 4 a.m.'

He only smiled, and promised to return. To my embarrassment, he did, before I had had a chance to open the books he left for me. Vasu was clearly made of sterner stuff than I had foreseen.

'I will come to read you a few pages every morning, when you wake up,' he insisted.

I gave in to him only because I felt that as a journalist, I ought to be open to whatever came my way. From then on, I found myself being woken up to the unmusical bell of Vasu's rickety, second-hand bicycle. Often, he would read Marx aloud to me while I was still in bed.

One day, my room-mate observed that Vasu was remarkably punctual. 'You can set your watch by his entry,' he said.

Indeed, Vasu's disciplined approach and commitment were hard to ignore.

And then he added, 'This Vasu . . . he talks like a Maoist.'

I laughed it off as a stray comment at the time, but the remark stayed in my mind.

One morning, when Vasu and I were alone in the room, I ventured a question: 'I won't ask what your real name is and where you live, but are you a Naxal?'

I'd used the popular term for underground Maoists, a word that no one would like to be associated with publicly. This was a cue for him to go into fervent denial. But Vasu simply smiled, and nodded in affirmation.

'I have been sent to Raipur to develop the Party in urban areas.'

I was a little shaken. There were so many journalists to whom I had introduced Vasu, including my room-mate. Why had he chosen to confide in me?

***

Manendragarh is a small town in the Koriya district of Chhattisgarh. A mining settlement during the British Raj, it was the last stop on a track laid to transport coal. My father had arrived there to work for the Indian Railways. He was from a refugee family who had fled East Pakistan after the Partition. In the classic style of India's democratic re-colonization, the Indian Railways employed educated middle-class Indians. In independent India, we were the new colonizers of the original inhabitants, the Adivasis. In these undeveloped locations in the heart of India, the Indian Railways built and maintained their own residential quarters. Although there were no fortifications, the class difference between the locals and the transplants was as good as any wall.

It was in this Railway Colony of Manendragarh, typical of its time, that I grew up. I remember the club where we celebrated Durga Puja every year—an imposing colonial building. The ballroom, once frequented by the British sahibs, had been converted into a table-tennis hall. On shelves that had once held bottles of whisky, now rested novels in Indian languages.

I do not remember interacting with the tribals. There was a tribal woman who came home every morning to deliver milk, and a man who tended to our garden on occasion. But we had nothing to do with them socially, even though the school in which I studied—the only one in town—was run by the tribal welfare department of the state government. The tribal children occupied the back benches of the classroom and lived in a hostel assigned specially to them.

I visited the hostel a couple of times with a classmate,

and remember thin, dark children: alien beings who seemed lost in the huge spartan dormitory, laid out with rows of iron cots. Their government-supplied khaki shorts were usually a couple of sizes larger than required. Their crumpled, white, half-sleeved shirts were tight around the armpits, and with their thin chests and stiff shoulders, they looked more like stunted adults than playful children. Though we saw each other every day in class, our lives ran like railway tracks: parallel but always separate.

I did not keep in touch with any of them.

There was no reason to.

My real friends were children of government employees or of local shopkeepers. We were the new Indian middle class, with a voracious appetite for self-advancement: ambitious, not too highly educated, very hard-working individuals who had migrated from various places within the country, and naturally coalesced in and around the new colonies created by the Indian administration. We learned the ropes, built contacts and got well-paid jobs or became mid-level businessmen. We knew exactly how much grease was required at which groove in the machinery to keep the wheels of progress turning. The natural bounty of places like Chhattisgarh provided just the nourishment we demanded.

For the tribals, however, all that had changed was the colour of the sahib.

***

I do not know why Vasu had chosen me, but as it turned out, I left Raipur a few months after I met him.

By 1990, I had made my way to Delhi. The business of daily news kept me on my toes . . . never visiting the same place twice, hopping from cyclone to earthquake, from civil war to political coup. Soon I began to realize that I had become a 'vulture' journalist.

By 2004, having had enough of the carrion, I started to find my way back to Chhattisgarh, where life had begun for me. The quiet, beautiful, thickly forested hills that I had left behind had been carved into a new state—ostensibly because of its 'tribal' demography. It had also become, in the words of the Indian prime minister, the epicentre of 'the gravest threat to India's internal security'.

Over the years, Vasu had kept in touch. Communication between us remained a little odd and always unidirectional. I had learned not to ask him questions that I knew he would not want to answer. It was this tacit understanding that helped us maintain a workable professional relationship. It suited us. Thanks to my job with the BBC, I owned a mobile phone long before they became ubiquitous in India. I could make out from the display on my phone that Vasu called me from a different number each time: clearly, he was using public telephones.

There was one request he would make to me persistently: he wanted me to take leave of absence from my job and accompany him to the jungles. 'Stay with our comrades for a few months and write a book about our movement,' he would say.

I always declined, since the Naxals had not been a big enough story for anyone until 2005, and certainly not so for an international news channel. I was kept busy covering

Kashmir, the North-East and the other insurgencies across South Asia that dominated the media scene at the time.

A reasonable degree of affluence affords a man some time to think. As the pressures of building a career in the media started to ease and the noise level in my life reduced, I started to reflect on the shallowness of modern media. I began to see that the limited objective of keeping the world 'informed' took away substantially from understanding how and why events shape up the way they do.

In 2005, I started travelling around Chhattisgarh. Now, I had the time to listen to the people I met, and began to see my own life reflected in the events in Chhattisgarh. With my ear close to the ground, I heard new voices.

'The Tatas are coming; something bad will happen here,' said one. The tone reminded me of a movie where an old man in Africa prays that no oil be found on his land.

'Your newspapers write only *your* stories,' said another.

'You don't talk to us,' said a third.

I could sense their alienation. After all, even I spoke to the tribals through translators. I did not know their language, and neither did any of the other scribes. There was no tribal journalist in a state that had been created on the basis of its sizeable tribal population. I was beginning to understand that a majority of readers, writers and owners of newspapers were on the other side.

My travels gave me ideas for my weekly column in a newly launched local newspaper. What I wrote was mostly criticized, but I got enough positive feedback from people who were interested in my stories to keep me going. Eventually, I found the best space for most of what I wanted to say on the Internet through CGNet, a discussion forum I launched.

Around that time, mainstream newspapers published reports of 'a spontaneous uprising' by the people against the Maoists. They called it 'Salwa Judum', literally meaning 'Peace March'. The leader of this 'peaceful' movement was surrounded by gun-toting guards. Photographs showed truckloads of tribals in a remote area being moved to the 'safety' of roadside camps: not exactly a picture of spontaneity. Clearly, someone was organizing and paying for the movement. The police had devised a strategy where they secretly compared Maoists to fish that survived in the water of local support. And they planned to remove the water. With this aim in mind, the state started the process of establishing roadside camps, ostensibly to give shelter to tribals fleeing from the Maoists. New lines were drawn to define sides.

The Chhattisgarh Special Public Security Act was passed. According to this law, the 'glamorization' of Maoists by a journalist was punishable. The mainstream media, though, had already chosen where to position itself. A column that I had been writing for two years was stopped without explanation. I could not travel in Chhattisgarh without being stopped and questioned. Friends who helped me found themselves harassed by the government.

The Internet had, by now, kick-started the free flow of information. International media and human rights organizations began to pick up news from CGNet, which was acquiring information directly from the ground. All this took considerable legwork and a lot of time, but once the national press got down to covering the reality of the Salwa

Judum, I felt it was time to do what Vasu had always asked me to do: write his story, understand his people. The same people who were said to constitute the greatest internal security threat to India.

In my head, I heard the voice of Fred Scott of the BBC, my cameraman guru: 'If you want your story to be complete, move your ass, and get another angle.' So I decided to move behind enemy lines, place the camera on the shoulder of the Naxal, and look at the world through Vasu's eyes.

Vasu, though, had disappeared. It took me time to find new contacts in his shadowy world, but eventually, I did.

I took a deep breath and dove headfirst into the jungles, travelling extensively with the leaders and cadres of the Naxal movement, listening to them, trying to understand their motivation and aspirations, just as Vasu had suggested so many times. It took many months of trudging through some of the most brutal terrain in India, wading through translations from the prevalent Gondi spoken by the guerrilla fighters in the region.

Through the stories I heard, I have tried to piece together the history of the Naxal movement in the central tribal region through the 1980s up to the present. I do not aim to provide a 360-degree panoramic view of everything related to left wing extremism. For me, this book is just a step forward in the larger effort that is required to understand the 'why' of the 'Naxal problem'.

1

SCRATCHING THE SURFACE

I was cooking dinner when the phone rang. The voice sounded old and the accent was distinctly South Indian. The man did not reveal his identity and the conversation was trivial.

I sensed he belonged to one of the banned organizations, perhaps the Andhra-based Maoists, but my cell phone display showed that the call came from West Bengal. I knew my phone was being tapped since my days in the BBC, when I would get similar calls from Islamic militants or from one of the North-Eastern groups. My communication with the Maoists having dried up with Vasu's disappearance, I was keen to open fresh channels.

I was familiar with the drill, and called the man back from a public phone.

He said he was Prashant. 'You covered a Bhumkal Day function in 2004.'

For some years now, the Maoists have been commemorating 10 February—the day the tribals of Bastar in south

Chhattisgarh revolted against the British and took control of their homeland for a few days in 1910—as Bhumkal Day. As a day celebrating Adivasi pride in the forest of Dandakaranya in tribal central India, Bhumkal Day showcases Maoist strength in the region. I remembered a trip I had once made to cover the event for a BBC documentary.

'Would you like to do it again this year?' Prashant wanted to know.

I had other plans for that week, but bit the bullet nevertheless, and pitched my idea of a book to him.

Though much has been said and written about the Maoist movement in Andhra Pradesh and Bihar, their Dandakaranya story has not been explored in detail. Spread over five states, the Dandakaranya forest, initially a hideout for fleeing Maoists, is now the headquarters of the Naxal movement. Once the setting for the Hindu epic, Ramayana, these forests are now the backdrop for a different kind of conflict. I wanted Prashant to arrange my access into the forest. Without permission from the Party to access the region, the book would be a non-starter.

He said he would send someone to discuss the details of the book once I was free of my current commitments. But I heard nothing from him until a couple of days after the appointed date, when I got another phone call. This time, it was a male voice with a Bengali accent. He said he was Anil.

'Can we meet at Nehru Place?' he asked, naming a shop. 'I want to get my laptop repaired.' He said he did not have a cell phone and did not need one either, as he would recognize me anyway.

I had met many Maoists at nondescript places like chai

shops and bus stations, but Nehru Place was a surprise. Touted as Asia's biggest IT market, Nehru Place in Delhi is Disneyland for the average geek. Reminiscent of the souks of Arabia with a silicon twist, it is home to dealers of everything IT, from pirated software to networking equipment, from cell phone jailbreakers to data-recovery experts.

Maoists and computers did not coexist in my imagination, which still had the picture of Vasu and his broken-down bike imprinted on it. I remember he had once asked me for advice on the purchase of a movie camera, which I discouraged, because it seemed like a waste of the obviously limited resources at his disposal. Also, here was a Bengali comrade. It was unexpected. I felt outdated.

I reached the shop at the appointed hour. Nehru Place was its usual bustling self. Anil must have been on the lookout, for he materialized out of nowhere. Just as we were shaking hands, a cell phone rang in his bag. 'I lied to you,' he said apologetically. 'The Party has banned the use of cell phones these days. It is dangerous. Many of our comrades have been arrested in the last few months because their phones were traced. Only a few of us are allowed to use them.'

Amidst the jostling crowds, with little boys hawking cheap pirated music, I tried to convey the importance of what I wanted to do. The book would study the Naxal movement by relating the stories of a few people directly or indirectly linked to the Maoist Party. For this, I would need a long and detailed conversation with him to explore possibilities. 'It is too crowded to do this here,' I told Anil.

'So will you make me a character?' he asked, sounding suspicious.

I explained that we needed to look for a quieter place to talk.

I knew I had to tread very carefully. It was the groundwork for the long-term relationship required for a project of this size. With Vasu, it would have been relatively easier because he knew me. He knew that I had the experience not to commit to what I may not be able to deliver, and the drive to get all I needed to tell a story appropriately.

Anil agreed to drive with me to the Coffee House in Connaught Place. Negotiating the Delhi traffic in my non-air-conditioned, battered Maruti, I explained how my book would pan out. I would probably interview hundreds of people over the next few years, and only a few of them would make it to the book. 'Maybe you will be one of the characters,' I told him. 'I want to probe the reasons for people taking up arms and joining the Maoists. The characters will help tell the story of the movement, as participants in this play that is being enacted in the theatre of central India, and maybe I can start with you.'

'I work as a personal courier for the Politburo,' Anil told me. The Politburo is the highest decision-making body in the Communist Party of India (Maoist)—the Party also known simply as Maoists, Naxals or Naxalites.

'They need to decide whether you will be given access for the book or not. The man who called you is a Politburo member. He told me that you had interviewed him a few years ago.'

'But I do not remember having interviewed anybody called Prashant.'

Anil smiled. 'Oh yes! He was called Ramji then, and his

name was changed again to Kishenji when he moved to Bengal. He is older now, so maybe you could not recognize his voice either.'

Kishenji is one of the much-written-about leaders of the Party in Bengal, especially in connection with the events that unfolded in Lalgarh in 2009, following an assassination bid on the then chief minister of West Bengal.

It is difficult to have an enduring relationship with Maoists or, for that matter, with any member of an underground organization. You never have a number you can call or an address to which you can write, and they change names frequently. It is safer for them, and for me, not to share those details. I did recall Ramji as a middle-aged man who had come to see me at the BBC bureau with Nishant, a student at Delhi University and my Naxal contact at that time. I had done a short radio interview with Ramji in Hindi, as the BBC was not interested in putting him on television. Shortly after that interview, I heard that Nishant had died in a police firing in Orissa. I feared that Vasu might have met the same fate.

However, for the time being, it was enough for me that Anil was willing to talk. Someone who has been operating undercover, working under levels of well-enforced hierarchy, is not prepared to open up to an outsider, however understanding and accepting the latter's approach. I wanted to use this opportunity to make an impact on him so that my intent could be appropriately understood by the powers that be. I knew that very lengthy chats would be required just to scratch the surface of this story, because its protagonists are people trained to keep themselves hidden. Over coffee, Anil started talking.

'Kolkata was the stage for the earlier communist uprising of the Party in West Bengal in the late 1960s, and students were its main actors. The movement started in 1967 in Naxalbari in northern Bengal—the name Naxal comes from Naxalbari—and was ruthlessly crushed by 1972. Following the defeat, many of our leaders moved to other states, like Bihar or Andhra Pradesh, and formed new factions. Ramji, Prashant, Kishenji, however you like to think of him, is originally from the People's War Group of Andhra Pradesh.'

I asked Anil if he had studied in Kolkata.

'Yes, my parents live there. I was studying physics honours at Presidency College before I joined the Party. My first assignment for the Party was in Dandakaranya, in 1998. I arrived in Raipur, which was then in Madhya Pradesh, from where I was to be taken by a local contact to the Bengali areas of Bastar. Many refugees from Bangladesh had been settled there by the Centre, and since I knew Bengali, the Party felt I could be useful living amidst them.'

Anil did not appear to be in a hurry, and I found myself drawn into the conversation. We ordered some masala dosa and idli.

'Is this a tag from IndiGo airlines?' I asked, pointing to his bag.

'Yes. I got delayed contacting you because I had to finish some work in the interiors and then catch a flight to Delhi.' He sounded apologetic.

Nehru Place, Bengali cadre and IndiGo airlines. The Party is definitely changing, I thought.

Anil continued, 'Once I reached Raipur, however, my contact dropped me off in a remote Adivasi village instead of the refugee settlement. Comrade Kosa, who received me, had to leave on some urgent work right away. He promised to be back soon. You know Kosa is the secretary and heads what our Party calls the "Dandakaranya State".' Anil smiled at the memory as he dug into his idli.

'Kosa did not return for ten days. I would watch the villagers farm and do their household chores and curse myself. I could not even speak to them as we did not know each other's language. No one there spoke Hindi either. I felt that I must have been insane to have believed that a revolution could happen from there. It was as if we were in the fifteenth century! The people were primitive and not conscious of their lot—I wondered why I was wasting my time there.'

'And you are still there. Why are you still wasting your time?' I asked him, trying to gauge how he would handle tougher questions.

'I know the revolution will not begin in my lifetime. But I cannot think of anything better to do. I know this is the right path and that I should make my contribution to build a better world for the future. Dandakaranya is a different world ... very isolated ... and for generations, all that people have been exposed to is the Party. Just as people in the cities dream of becoming Amitabh Bachchan, children in Dandakaranya want to take up arms and join the Party.'

'I want to meet Comrade Kosa,' I told Anil. 'I have heard from Vasu that he is the only one left on the ground from the first batch that was dispatched to Dandakaranya in 1980 to develop the area.'

'Well, I have heard of the seven batches of seven members

each that were sent out by Kondapalli Sitaramaiyyah, our leader, popularly called KS, but I am not sure if Kosa is the only survivor.'

I pressed on. 'Kosa would be able to recount everything that has transpired in central India in the last thirty years. I need him to tell the whole story. Also, I want to find Vasu, if he is still alive.'

Anil did not know anyone by that name, but promised to check for people matching the description I gave him. I was counting on Vasu's having acquired a new name.

I felt the ice between Anil and me had thawed well enough, and decided it was time to push him a bit.

'Too much philosophy. Can we talk of some real situations? Maybe you can tell me about the Binayak Sen case.'

Social activist Dr Binayak Sen had been arrested for an alleged link with Maoists. At the time when my conversation with Anil took place, there was an extensive campaign to secure his release, with even some Nobel laureates joining in, writing to the prime minister pressing for his release.

'Did he really help courier messages for you?' I asked, not expecting any response. To my surprise, Anil answered with alacrity. 'Oh yes, of course.'

I did not believe Anil was aware of the facts, so I asked him, 'And what about Piyush Guha, who has been arrested for being Dr Sen's conduit?'

'Piyush was a courier for our leader Narayan Sanyal, just as I am a courier for Prashant. Dr Sen used to meet Narayan-da in Raipur jail. Narayan-da was one of the leaders who moved to Bihar after the Party was disbanded in 1972. He was the founding member of the Communist Party of India

(Marxist-Leninist) Party Unity, one of the many factions our leaders formed.'

'Oh yes, there were a lot of factions. I counted up to thirty-two—some were parties with single-digit members,' I interjected.

'Yes, that is a big problem,' Anil said with a smile to acknowledge the dig. 'We had so many parties, almost equal to the number of leaders. Slowly, they have started to come together now. Narayan-da's Party Unity merged with my Party, CPI (ML) People's War, in 1998. Piyush was a full-time member of Party Unity. Later he became a part-timer, but he always worked harder than full-timers. Narayan-da set up a business for Piyush as a tendu leaf contractor as a cover for his work as a courier.

'When Narayan-da needed funds for his legal expenses after his arrest, Piyush collected Rs 50,000 from Sabyasachi Panda, the Orissa secretary of the Party, and went to deliver the money to Binayak Sen in Raipur. He spoke to Binayak-da over the phone—I think the phone was tapped. The police picked Piyush up from the hotel at which he was staying. By the time Dr Sen and Mrs Sen reached the hotel, Piyush was gone. The hotel manager denied that anyone by the name of Piyush had stayed there.

'After that incident, Binayak-da happened to go to Kolkata on work. When we did not hear from Piyush for a few days, we got worried. I went to meet Binayak-da at his mother's house in Kalyani and asked him to go back to Raipur to look for Piyush. He agreed. That is the story of my first meeting with Binayak-da.'

It was an interesting angle, but I could hardly put it down

in writing without confirmation from other sources. At a later date, I had the opportunity to meet Sabyasachi Panda, then head of the Maoists in Orissa. I asked him why he had sent Rs 50,000 to Dr Sen. Perhaps I caught him by surprise with the way I framed the question, or perhaps he assumed I was privy to that information. Whatever his reason, he acknowledged having lent the money to Piyush for Narayan Sanyal. I asked him if he ever got the money back. Piyush had been arrested before he could deliver or return the money, he replied. He also said he had apprised the Party's Central Committee of the course of events.

Later, when I contacted Dr Binayak Sen for his version of the story, his lawyer called back to say, 'All this is hearsay and has no truth in it.'

I continued my chat with Anil. 'How many Bengalis work for you in Chhattisgarh?' I asked him in Bangla, looking for a denial rather than an answer. But he surprised me again.

'I will not say Binayak-da worked for the Party, but yes, Jeet Guha Niyogi was a member, if you count him as a Bengali. Binayak-da was an old friend of Narayan-da's and only helped him at a personal level. Jeet, however, was probably placed quite high up in the Party—an area committee member or something. And his sister, Mukti Guha Niyogi, spent some time with us in a squad in Dandakaranya. She has also worked for us in the colleges of Raipur as an overground member.'

I must admit that Anil's claims disturbed me.

A few weeks earlier, I had written an article titled 'Kya mangta, Niyogi ya Naxali', which translates as, 'What do we want: Niyogi or Naxals?' The Niyogi to whom I referred was Shankar Guha Niyogi—Jeet and Mukti's father—a well-known trade union leader who had dissociated himself from Naxals in their early years and led a Gandhian non-violent trade union movement in Chhattisgarh. The movement had fostered hope but was brutally suppressed, with many of its workers dying at the hands of the police. Finally, Niyogi himself was killed by goons hired by local industrialists. After Niyogi's death, his organization splintered. It was in a hospital set up by Shankar Guha Niyogi for iron-ore miners in Chhattisgarh that Dr Binayak Sen had come to work.

Now, Anil's claims confirmed a hypothesis of mine, which did not bode well for any democracy—that some activists are losing hope of ever bringing about change through peaceful protests.

'I think Jeet and Mukti have both resigned from the Party now, but you should check with our leaders in Dandakaranya,' Anil added.

'Of course,' I said.

Jeet now works for the Bhilai Steel Plant and Mukti is the mayor of Dalli Rajhara town. She stood for election on a ticket from the Congress party.

I found that no other faction of the Chhattisgarh Mukti Morcha, floated by Shankar Niyogi, has links with the Maoists, except the one headed by Niyogi's family.

'Tell me one thing,' I pressed on. 'After 1980, the Party has been run mostly by comrades from Andhra Pradesh. But the call I got was from Bengal. You too are from there. Is the intellectual leadership shifting towards Bengal?'

'I would not say that yet. But yes, after the police repression in Andhra, recruitment there has dried up completely and West Bengal has come up as an alternative. Though recruitment is not huge in terms of numbers, we get a steady flow of entrants—educated youth from Kolkata colleges—who are becoming full-timers. History seems to be repeating itself.'

I thought he would laugh when I asked him if the many arrests being made in Chhattisgarh at the time—a journalist, Praful Jha, had also been picked up—had a Bengali connection too. But the Bengali connection to Maoists is no laughing matter, it seems, as my shot in the dark hit its target.

'Oh yes. It was indeed a Bengali who was responsible for all the arrests. His name was Sumit and he too was a member of Party Unity in Bengal, to start with. Like me, he was sent to the Bengali areas of Bastar around 1998. Later, he was shifted to the Manpur area in nearby Rajnandgaon, where the Party established him as an RMP doctor (Registered Medical Practitioner) even though he had no medical training. It was a cover for Party work. Sumit even married a tribal girl, Jamuna.

'Later, Sumit became a police informer. Kosa had left the forest for some official work, and Sumit ferried him back to his hideout on his motorcycle. As he rode back after dropping off Kosa, he was arrested. He had Rs 10 lakh, which was the Party's money, in the carrier of his bike. Vinod Choube, the superintendent of police (SP), made sure that Sumit's arrest did not show up in the records, and that he was not presented in court. Instead, Sumit was given a severe beating, after which he agreed to become an informant. Based on his tip-offs, the police arrested fifteen people, including Praful Jha, though he has no connection with our Party. Sumit's arrest was a major blow to our overground work in the state.'

Anil continued his revelations, rather recklessly, I thought. 'A woman called Malti was also arrested. Sumit was with the police party when they arrested her: he identified her from the cover of a police jeep. From the descriptions of Vasu that you have given me, Malti might have been his wife.'

I had been told by some overground workers that Vasu had been arrested in Maharashtra. I had even looked for him in the jails that I visited there, an uphill task when one does not know a person's real name.

'If Vasu is the same man I think he is, then he is not in jail,' said Anil. 'I know for sure that Malti's husband eluded arrest because he was on an assignment for the Party.'

If what Anil said was true, I could meet Vasu again. As I held that thought, Anil went back to Sumit's story. 'Sumit was the first serious attempt by the Chhattisgarh police to send their infiltrators into the party, Andhra style. That's how they finished us in Andhra. We cannot allow that to happen again.'

'What happened to the money Sumit was carrying?' I remembered suddenly.

Anil raised his eyebrows in mock surprise, and reminded me that the arrest had not been made public by the police. I felt suitably chastised for my naivety.

'Sumit turned up a few months after his arrest. He sent a message that he had escaped and wanted to rejoin the Party. But the Party had been conducting its own investigation during the time he had gone missing. We found out that the police had arranged for him to "assist" another doctor in Madhya Pradesh for some time. When he came to us, the

Party grilled him intensively about the details of his bank
account and SIM card. His SIM card had been given by SP
Vinod Choube, who also deposited money in his State Bank
of India account in Rajnandgaon. Sumit finally gave in and
admitted that the police had sent him to be a covert operator.
His interviews were recorded on video.'

'So what happened to Sumit?'

'The Party gave him the death sentence.'

Later, the Maoists also killed SP Choube along with
twenty-eight other policemen in a daring attack in Manpur.

Anil had brought me up to speed rather quickly. Although
I had been in touch with contacts from across the Party ranks,
and had also reported on the movement for television, I did
not realize how powerful the Maoists had grown outside
Andhra and Bihar. I felt that I now had a good handle on
the escalation of Party activity in Chhattisgarh. On the
other hand, the police force of the state, which I had taken
to be meek and slightly ineffective, was pulling off daring
acts—infiltrating enemy camps takes a lot of preparation.

Anil's stories gave me a glimpse of the changing scenario
of Maoist activity in Chhattisgarh. The movement would
mature in 2004, with the coming together of the two streams
of the Party, one from Bihar and the other from Andhra.
Dandakaranya now was more than just a place for Maoists to
hide when members faced rough weather in the main areas of
their operation, which is how it had been planned in the early
1980s. So deep had they dug their heels into this forest that
the Centre first needed to focus on clearing Chhattisgarh of
Maoists before it could allow powerful corporates to exploit
its mineral wealth. The creation of the Salwa Judum militia

with the help of Congress leader Mahendra Karma seemed part of the same scheme.

The dynamics at work in the state would need to be explored at length in order to be understood. But one thing was clear enough—Dandakaranya had become a dangerous place.

2

FAILED TRIP

The permission from the Politburo took a long time to arrive. There was little else I could do but wait. If I have learned anything over the years of following this story, it is that one must be patient and take failure in one's stride. I have also learned that it is best not to draw conclusions about the tribal world with my urban understanding. The wait itself proved instructive about what was happening—one just had to pay attention.

Finally, I received a letter from Anil, directing me to wait near the Chitrakoot Falls at 9 a.m. on a designated date. He also named a three-star hotel in Chitrakoot where we could stay. Having learned from experience that such clandestine meetings often had to be played by ear, I told my photographer, Mustafa, about the appointment, warning him that things might not work out as planned.

Anil's letter had spelt out detailed instructions—one of us was to hold a camera in one hand and a spectacle case in the other. Our contact would be identified by a copy of *India*

Today in his hand. We waited near the Falls at the appointed hour, Mustafa growing increasingly apprehensive that we might be at the wrong location. Waiting for a Maoist contact at the wrong place on an earlier occasion had made him wary.

I expected that we would be taken to some nondescript village by road, before entering the forest on foot. That had been the modus operandi each time I met with Maoists, because their strongholds, where they allowed journalists, were always deep in the forest. I had even hired a taxi.

Soon enough, I spotted a man in an off-white safari suit in a Shiva temple near the Falls. Moving closer, we saw the copy of *India Today* and knew we had our man. He introduced himself as Gopinath and said, 'We will walk from here. Let us cross the river first.'

I did not believe him.

'Naxals have no presence in this area, do they?' I asked.

'Things have changed here since the Tatas' arrival.' Gopinath seemed to be mocking us. We were supposed to be journalists, after all.

I remembered that the Maoists had blown up a police vehicle in this very area when the then President Pratibha Patil visited the Chitrakoot Falls in 2008. I had dismissed it as a stray attack then. A mistake on my part, just as overlooking other telltale signs had been. On my earlier visits, I had heard the youth in these villages express a desire to become Naxals. They had shared their distress at being cheated by journalists, leaders, the police and the administration, all for the benefit of industrial houses. But could things have changed so much in such a short time? Could the Maoists have taken root in an area so rapidly?

We let the taxi go and crossed the Indravati on foot. Two motorbikes waited for us on the other side. One belonged to Gopinath, who, we learned, used to be a sarpanch. The second belonged to another sarpanch.

'Won't people notice us if we ride with you?' I asked Gopinath.

'No. I have told the villagers that you are sahibs from the agriculture department.'

I wondered how convincing it would be to have sahibs from the agriculture department carry big cameras, but we were already on the road.

'This is a new road.' Gopinath had to shout to be heard over the sound of the wind as he rode down a narrow road. 'The chief minister himself came to inaugurate it a few weeks ago. Work on the Bodhghat Dam will start soon.'

The Bodhghat project had been dropped in the 1990s when it did not get clearance from the environment ministry, but could come through now that industry Goliaths were interested.

'All these villages will be submerged once the dam is built,' Gopinath said.

We had crossed the river in ankle-deep water. I wondered about the future of the Indravati once the industries channelled all the water away. The Chitrakoot Falls could well be reduced to a seasonal phenomenon in the years to come.

After a short ride, we started walking.

'I will escort you to the next contact by evening; I do not know where you will be taken next.'

I asked him how a sarpanch was working with dadas or elder brothers, as the Maoists are called.

'I also work with the Congress,' he assured me. 'We need to work with everyone. You never know who will become powerful. But only the dadas can save us from Bodhghat and the Tatas. If a Tata plant comes up on the other side of the river as planned, then all the people from there will shift to our area. And if the Bodhghat Dam is built, our entire settlement will have to go. Only the Tata plant will remain.'

I prodded him on the speed with which the Maoists had spread out in the area. He agreed, and conceded that the dadas had had no hold on the area until a year and a half earlier. 'They did try to get a foothold here many years ago, in 1996, I think. But they did not stay. They began to return after the Tata project was announced.'

A walk provides the best opportunity to soak in local colour and get nuanced insights into the lives of the residents. Ambling on, I asked Gopinath why he, despite being a tribal, had been waiting for us in the temple of a Hindu deity.

'I worship Lord Shiva along with our venerable king Pravir every day. You know the king who was killed by the police?'

I nodded. If you go to Jagdalpur for research, you cannot but hear of Pravir.

'Also, my life changed after I met Bihari Das. He was an avatar of King Pravir.'

From my research, I knew of Bihari Das as a Hindu proselytizer who rode on the wave of tribal devotion to their old king and directed his 'subjects' as he deemed fit. I thought it was clever, because King Pravir Chandra Bhanjdeo had been a central figure in the politics of Bastar after Independence. As his 'reincarnation', one could be assured of instant acceptance. All candidates nominated by Pravir would invariably win the elections in Bastar, till the time that he was murdered in his palace in 1966. Newspapers quoted the tribals as saying that they would vote for anyone the king pointed to, even if it were a lamp post or his dog.

The ancestors of King Pravir had injected their form of Hinduism into the tribal society of Bastar by introducing their own deity, Danteshwari. They had started a special Dussehra function centring on the king, deifying him. The Congress watched the tribals deify their king with unease. After all, all political parties, except the CPI, were run by upper-caste outsiders.

'What about the new king?' I asked him, not revealing that I had already met Kamal Bhanjdeo before coming to Chitrakoot. 'Isn't he attending the anti-Tata rallies these days?'

'Yes, this one does look different.'

Kamal Bhanjdeo is a young man of twenty-four; an alumnus of the London School of Economics. Gopinath, however, was talking about something else: 'We feel that Kamal might actually do something for us.'

Gopinath had in mind Kamal's grandfather, King Pravir's brother—a man who had been appointed a figurehead king by the Centre after Pravir was removed from the throne.

I probed him to get a sense of the local politics. 'I hear that Kamal held a procession on Dussehra just like the ones King Pravir used to hold, after more than four decades. Do you think that the new people from Andhra, these dadas, are teaming up with the old Andhraites?'

My reference was to the Bhanjdeos' Warangal ancestry. In a battle with the last tribal kings in Chitrakoot in 1324, the Andhraites had taken over Bastar. Pravir was anointed king of Bastar by the British days before Independence in 1947, an event historians link with Pravir's handover of the Bailadila Hills to the Nizam of Hyderabad through a ninety-nine-year lease. The people of Jagdalpur in Bastar had protested the signing of the lease, fearing that it was a plot to cede Bastar to Hyderabad, and declare the latter a free nation. But when the king agreed to make Bastar a part of India on 15 December 1947, the lease was rendered null and void.

The Bailadila Hills had become a prized geographical location ever since the British discovered iron ore of a high quality in its recesses.

In the years following Independence, Pravir aligned himself increasingly with his people, the tribals. This was not easy for the Congress to digest. The local Congress party was run by outsiders, who did not want a king as staunchly supported by local residents as Pravir was, ruling over Bastar, the place they had made their home. To make matters worse, in a public meeting on 13 December 1960, Pravir spoke of the possibility of joining the communists. He was arrested shortly after, and his brother, Kamal's grandfather, tellingly called Sarkari Raja by the people, was declared king. The tribals demanded that Pravir be reinstated, but it was not to be.

On 31 March 1961, twelve tribals were killed in police firing in Lohandiguda near Chitrakoot, where a crowd had assembled demanding the release and reinstatement of Pravir as king. Lawyers representing the tribals claimed that the number of dead Adivasis was more than fifty. In independent India, this was the first time that tribals had been killed by police in Bastar. Pravir was reinstated after the killings, but his relations with local Congress leaders worsened. Five years later, he was gunned down by police in his palace. There were whispers that orders to kill Pravir had come from top bosses in the Congress.

I had met Kamal Chandra Bhanjdeo in his palace in Jagdalpur on an earlier trip. When Kamal appeared before us, resplendent in his formal attire, with the chief priest in attendance, a portrait of King Pravir loomed large in the background. It appeared, from the way he spoke, that he wished to emulate Pravir and not his own grandfather. I talked to Kamal about the proposed steel plant of the Tatas in Lohandiguda. 'It cannot be good for my praja (subjects),' he said. 'My family has paid dearly for opposing industrialization. I have no closure yet on the mysterious death of Maharani Komal, King Pravir's mother. She too was against giving Bailadila to the British.'

Kamal has taken a public stand against the Tata plant, which would use iron ore from mines in Bailadila. He explained, 'King Pravir changed his mind when he understood that mining would bring outsiders into Bastar—that it would then no longer belong to the tribals. He wanted industrialization to start only when the tribals were educated and could work in the mines themselves.'

In our meeting, Kamal came across as self-assured, prosperous, slightly spoilt even, as any other young man in his privileged position would be. I thought he wanted to milk political mileage out of the tribal devotion to King Pravir, in whose image he is moulding himself. His claim that the people are turning to the palace again after four decades is true, though. The crowds in the traditional celebration of Dussehra are back, and support for the young King Kamal is growing—visibly so—amongst the tribals.

With Pravir's murder, the Congress had got rid of a thorn in its side. But its leaders had still to gain the kind of comprehensive control over Bastar that they coveted. As all parliamentary seats were reserved for the tribals, the Congress had no choice but to negotiate with them. They cleverly used Bihari Das, who declared himself an avatar of King Pravir, as their mascot during the elections. The 'creamy' layer within the tribals was responsive to their overtures and an uncle of Mahendra Karma's became a Congress candidate. These tribal representatives, more often than not, served as mere rubber stamps for the outsider upper-caste Hindu business community that controlled the economics and politics of the region.

The mainstream communists also tried to grab a slice of the pie in the 1960s, through unsuccessful land movements and a strong trade union in Bailadila. In the leadership vacuum after King Pravir's death, they were the only mass-based Party in Bastar for a long time. But unfortunately for them, votes came from the barrels of country liquor to which moneyed parties had greater access.

Sudhir Mukherjee, a Bengali communist, spotted the rebel tribal, Mahendra Karma, in a tribal hostel in Jagdalpur and took him under his wing. Karma's father was a tribal chieftain. It is said that he had sided with the British during the Bhumkal rebellion, though I have not found any documentary proof of the claim. Karma's uncle was a member of Parliament from the Congress party.

Karma was quite the angry young man. When he became a communist member of the legislative assembly in 1980, his speeches were so fierce that often, he had to be physically carried out of the assembly by marshals. However, Party policy did not serve his personal goals in the long run; the rules were too restrictive. Even his salary as an MLA was taken away, leaving him with a stipend—a meagre one, at that—which made him abandon the Left.

The communists say that just like other upper-class tribal leaders, Karma soon succumbed to the corrupt way of life and its attendant perks, such as better prospects for himself. They found it impossible to tolerate his greed, and were forced to throw this otherwise promising young MLA out of the Party in the late 1980s.

Karma was quick to learn the ropes in the Congress. Soon enough, in the early 1990s, he was implicated in the 'Malik Makbooja' case. The term, which means 'possessed by the owner', implies that the owner of a plot of land also owns the trees growing on it. When those trees are teak, they are far more valuable than the land itself. In Bastar, only a tribal could buy land from another tribal. Like other tribal politicians, Karma tricked the tribals into selling him their land—along with a thriving crop of teak trees—at throwaway prices. The tribals were clueless about the price that teak commanded in the market. Indeed, they did not know the value of money itself. A former associate of Karma's told me they used to pay the tribals in bundles of Re 1 notes, to fool them into thinking they were getting substantial money for their land. The Bharatiya Janata Party (BJP), which was in power at the time, came to Karma's rescue, and it looked like a new bond had been forged.

The Maoists, who too had their eyes trained on Bastar, made an entry into its political scene by shooting Karma's cousin, Kalma Deva, in 1987. With the strength of their guns, the Maoists aimed at creating a parallel power structure, challenging traditional leaders through village-level groups called sanghams. Kalma's murder was their first political killing. Over the years, the Maoists would become a force to reckon with, and all other parties—Left, Right and Centre—would accept the leadership of Mahendra Karma.

In the midst of it all, Kamal has kept his palace doors open, playing a wait-and-watch game.

It is no wonder that Gopinath knows he must maintain *his* relationship with all parties. The stakes for each player may be different, but they are all in the game.

Exhausted after trekking up two hills, we decided to rest in the ample shade of a mango tree. Gopinath walked ahead to check for a message about the next contact. I could see that we were close to a village. As we waited, some villagers brought mats for us to rest on. An old man started to chat, but all I understood were the words 'Mahendra Karma' and 'Raipur'. Gopinath returned shortly—there was no message for us yet. I asked him to translate what the old man was trying to tell me.

'He says that he had seen people like you—who wear pants—when he went to Raipur,' Gopinath translated with a grin, and then explained, 'Many people were taken to the city for a rally by Mahendra Karma when he was protesting against the Bodhghat Dam.'

As Mahendra Karma supports the Bodhghat project now,

I wanted to know how long ago the rally had been held.

'When my beard was not white,' he said, smiling through a beard that bore no trace of black. It was a yardstick difficult to convert into years!

We continued to wait under the tree until darkness fell. I must have dozed off, because my next memory is of opening my eyes to see a pair of brand new Woodland sandals. They belonged to a man clad in pants just like us. I got up hurriedly, assuming he must be a high-ranking Maoist leader.

He introduced himself as Eknath.

My mocking query about the cost of his expensive-looking footwear did not win me any brownie points.

'Maybe 300 rupees,' he said.

Mustafa disputed that claim immediately. While we were still arguing about the cost of his sandals, Eknath took a letter out of his pocket. I could tell from the way it was folded and stapled that it was from the Maoists. They always fold paper as many times as is physically possible before stapling it.

'Not again!' I thought with dismay as I read the contents.

The letter stated that, owing to unavoidable reasons, the leaders had been forced to return, and would not be able to meet us. They would be in touch for the next appointment. It was signed by a certain 'Comrade Raju'.

Eknath offered to make arrangements for our stay in the village that night. We must have looked as crestfallen as we felt, for he offered to check if Ramu dada, the local commander, was nearby, and if he would meet us the next morning.

Gopinath whispered to me, 'Ramu dada's team killed the

man who was forcing people to give their land to the Tatas. It will be useful for you to meet him.'

I ran my eyes through the letter once again. I felt like I had missed something in the first three readings. And then I got it: the handwriting was familiar. It was Vasu's!

Eknath stood by his claim that the letter was written by Comrade Raju, but my mind was racing. Maybe Vasu is called Raju now, and is into direct action. That would explain his silence.

'How long has Raju been working here?' I asked with a sense of urgency.

'We created the East Division two years ago. Raju has been looking after it since its inception.'

Two years ago was about the time Vasu had gone silent.

Excited now, I asked Eknath if I could send a letter to Comrade Raju and he agreed to try to have it delivered.

By the time we were taken to a house in the village, it was pitch dark. Someone was already preparing food for us. Having got over my remark about his sandals, Eknath loosened up. He told me he was a Raj Gond tribal from the Gadchiroli district of Maharashtra.

'My younger brother is also in the Party. I have another brother who stays at home and takes care of the family. I married within the Party. My wife, Sunita, is in another division and I see her once in six or seven months. We decided not to have children, so I had a vasectomy. Kosa dada first came to my village in 1980. I was very impressed by the Party's fight for the poor and decided to join in 1983, when I turned eighteen,' he said.

Eknath had been working for the Party for more than

twenty-five years. I wanted to know if he had any hope of bringing about change.

'The revolution will come—maybe in the next generation.' He did not smile as he said it.

I wondered what that meant to a man who had spent his entire life working towards something he has neither seen nor hopes to see.

After a whole day of walking, I was happy just to sit down and be able to eat, though I could hardly see the food we were served in the dim light of the lantern. Eknath left, bearing my rather long letter to Vasu, or the man who I hoped was Vasu. (Mustafa was surprised at the length of the letter I wrote by torchlight.)

After Eknath left, I strung up my mosquito net between a tree and a bicycle. I had learned my lesson after a bout of malaria on a previous trip had landed me in hospital. We were in the most prosperous home in the village, but I was the only one using a mosquito net. Clearly, the Maoists had not been here long. Here, the Maoists and the Non-Government Organizations are united on the issue of malaria. Both claim that, on an average, three to four people die of malaria in each village in Bastar every year. Paramilitary officials posted in Bastar say that malaria has claimed more of their troops than guns have. However, official records have not reported a single death by malaria in Chhattisgarh in the last couple of years. Malaria, after all, is difficult to detect, and no one tests blood samples anyway.

In the morning, Gopinath was bright and chirpy. Apparently, he had slept as well as I had, even without a mosquito net. In the daylight, I could see the house in which we stayed—it was a mud hut. 'This house belongs to the richest man in the village,' said Gopinath. 'He has land deeds for eight acres, no less.'

The man of the house was already explaining. 'Despite all this land, my family does not grow enough food for the whole year. We sell tamarind at Rs 7 a kilo to businessmen and tendu leaves at 50 paise a bundle. The dadas have promised that they will soon get us an increased rate of Rs 10 a kilo for tamarind, and 70 paise a bundle for tendu.' There was hope in his voice.

That did not sound rich to me at all. I wondered if the Maoists would get rid of these people too, dubbing them 'class enemies'.

Gopinath said, 'The man who rode the other motorcycle lives in the city. He has a tractor and runs a business.' And then he added a juicy titbit: 'He used to be the sarpanch of this village until he was expelled for fraud.'

I wished Eknath had not gone away. I would have liked him to explain how the Maoists had no problem working with a sarpanch who had been expelled for fraud. But then, I knew that the Maoists had also worked closely with Mahendra Karma in the early years. In the beginning, when they are new to a place, the Maoists draw their sustenance from the upper class. But once they find their feet, the same upper class becomes the enemy and the fight becomes a class war.

In the house, a boy was getting ready for school. He said his name was Budhram and that his school was close to the place where the Tata plant was coming up. I asked him what he thought of the dadas.

'I have never been to their meetings. I live in the school

hostel, not in the village,' he explained, fingering his locket. I noticed the words 'Jai Sri Ram' inscribed on it.

'I am studying to get a job, but I don't think I will get one—because of corruption. Anyway, we are only allowed to be teachers or peons. In this village, just two boys have passed class twelve, and they managed to get temporary jobs for meagre pay.'

I asked him if he was excited about the Tata plant.

'No, I don't think I will get a job there either.'

He knew what he was talking about.

I was not surprised.

Educated and relatively well off young men, like Budhram, are not interested in the politics of the dadas, but I have often wondered if they will continue to remain indifferent in the face of personal disappointments. I asked Gopinath if he had any idea about Maoist recruitment since they had started visiting the area again. Gopinath thought about it, and came up with the figure of 'twenty-five full-time workers' in less than two years. 'At least five girls have also signed up.' He was sure that none of the members he could think of had studied beyond class eight.

The Party's strategy seemed to be the same: go to areas where people are being displaced or disturbed by 'development' projects; offer to help with their livelihood, and target the less educated youth.

The messenger arrived while we were talking. It was bad news: we would not be able to meet the other leader. Mustafa wanted to leave right away. Without the dadas, there was no opportunity to shoot pictures. I was not so sure. A non-conducted tour with direct access to people and no dadas hovering around seemed like a better idea. I felt that if people were free to talk, I would have a better chance to draw out honest responses.

But we headed back anyway.

It was indeed a failed trip, but I felt happy about one thing: maybe Vasu was alive. Maybe.

3

THE FOOT MARCH

I waited, but Anil was unable to get a second appointment because of 'heightened vigilance'. I, however, got another phone call—a long-awaited one.

I could just about make out that it was Vasu on the line. He said he had got the letter that I had left for him on the failed trip, and then his voice crackled out. We were disconnected. I must have sounded as eager as I felt when he called back, because I could hear the smile in his voice when he told me he was atop a hill. 'I had to climb a tree to talk to you. The signal is bad here.'

I was reluctant to ask too many questions on the phone, but Vasu was good at this cloak-and-dagger stuff. With minimal conversation, he conveyed a new plan. 'Same place, same time where you came last time,' he said, giving me a new date before the connection died.

Both Mustafa and I had waited out two failed appointments with Maoists at Chitrakoot. And yet, here we were at Chitrakoot again, at the appointed date and time—and we had been waiting for two hours. Carrying the bulky cameras, I felt conspicuous and vulnerable. Mustafa wondered if Chitrakoot would be unlucky the third time around as well. I called Gopinath, the sarpanch who had been our guide the last time. I managed to connect with him on his cell phone because, luckily, he was in town to seek permission for their next anti-displacement rally. Had he been in the village, his phone would have been unreachable. 'I will be with you as soon as I can,' he promised.

When Gopinath turned up, we were happy to see him, though he was not aware that Vasu had planned our visit.

'Maybe Raju dada told someone else to pick you up this time. But I will be meeting him tomorrow anyway to discuss the rally, so I can check with him about your programme.'

We could not go with Gopinath—he would need permission from the Party for that. It was difficult to decide whether to wait at the Falls and be noticed by every passer-by, or head home, only to find out later that someone had indeed turned up to take us into the forest.

Information in the Maoist world is like the private property of capitalism, passed on from father to son, and guarded jealously and fiercely. Only someone directly involved in the action to be taken would be informed, and even that person would know only the barest minimum of details. Even if the sarpanch did get permission, there was no way we could know whom we would find at the other end. My letter had reached Vasu, but who knew if this Raju dada was Vasu?

I weighed my options: we were conspicuous, and needed to move. The sarpanch said he would arrange for our safe

stay in one of the more remote villages, where we could wait
for him. Thankfully, he was able to connect with Raju dada
the next day.

The next morning, when, after an hour's walk in the
jungle, we spotted a woman with a rifle, I was relieved. As
we drew closer, I saw Vasu in green fatigues. He had gained
weight. He had a copious beard now and was wearing a cap.
He looked different, as I suppose I did too. His face was
lined—life had not been kind to him. I saw hardship there,
but his bearing was peaceful, as always, in contrast to the
AK-47 he was carrying.

He looked at home in that forest setting.

Up close, I was strangely happy to find him alive. We
slipped naturally into the comfortable relationship we had
always shared.

'Let's move,' Vasu said briefly. 'We will have to walk for
a couple of hours before lunch. Another team is waiting for
us there.'

As we began our walk, I noticed that Vasu needed a stick
to support himself. 'I had a bus accident some time ago and
fractured my knee,' he said, removing his cap. Most of his
thick mop of hair was gone.

'Did you not get my message postponing this trip?' he
asked. 'I had told someone to call and inform you.'

I explained that I had been travelling in the villages of
Orissa for the book. My phone had been switched off most
of the time.

Vasu stopped suddenly, and I nearly bumped into him.
'Wasn't Sabyasachi Panda arrested there last month?' he
asked.

'That is what I read in the papers,' I said. 'But that story was planted by the police, because I met him barely a week later.'

Vasu was relieved.

I could not help asking him: 'You are such a high-profile leader, and you do not know if your secretary in the neighbouring state has been arrested? The newspaper reports were published about a month ago. Couldn't you have got them verified?'

Vasu explained that it was not so easy. 'Getting news regularly is not possible. It calls for a lot of work and it is not possible to spare people to check every piece of news reaching us.'

I could now appreciate why the police might go to great lengths to plant stories in the media. It helps mislead the Maoists as well.

'My wife is in Raipur jail now,' Vasu continued, not sounding too perturbed. 'My daughter must be in engineering college. She lives with my younger brother. I have not called them in years because their phones might be tapped.'

Walking behind him, I remembered his wife. Many years ago, I had met her at Bilaspur railway station with Vasu.

My train of thought came to a halt when Vasu dropped a bombshell: 'We have not received any instructions from the Politburo about your book—there has been no communication from them in the last few months. And I cannot talk to you without authorization.'

Great, I thought to myself. Trying to be patient, I asked, 'Then why have you called us here, Vasu?'

'I will send you to my state secretary, Kosa, and maybe

he can talk to you—he is entitled to take these decisions.'

I felt a surge of hope. An opportunity to speak to Kosa was a big deal. All might yet be well.

'Your appointment is fixed for 8 June. Today is 29 May. You will be able to make it,' Vasu said, smiling at my excitement.

I sighed to myself. This was one story where nothing moved as planned.

I had an important CGNet meeting in Bilaspur on 6 and 7 June. 'Can I come back for the appointment on the 8th, then?' I asked him.

Vasu turned around and gave me a pitiful look. 'To reach Kosa, you need to walk for five days, because he lives deep in the forest.' Seeing the dismay on my face, he tried to reassure me. 'Be patient, let us think this through and work out what is possible.'

Vasu knew where Kosa could be reached that day and the next—a spot no less than eighty kilometres from where we were. I could meet him only if I were able to cover that distance in the next forty-eight hours. 'It is a two-day walk even for us, who are used to this terrain,' said Vasu. 'I don't think you can walk for more than four hours a day in this heat.'

In my eagerness to meet Kosa, I offered to walk at night.

'Our route is over several hills and through the jungle,' Vasu warned. 'It is not a level road. To cover a distance of eighty kilometres one needs to walk for about twenty hours. And if you walk at night, each hour stretches to one and a half hours. Which means that the same journey will take three days and you will miss him after all that effort.'

He presented an alternative. 'I can send Kosa a message on the 8th and get you a new appointment.'

'And when might that be?' I asked.

'That depends on him,' Vasu replied, stoic as always.

'But by 15 June, the monsoon may well arrive,' I pointed out, my frustration growing.

'Yes, and in the monsoon, each hour of walking stretches to two and a half hours.'

This was a tough call. I knew I needed to meet Kosa right then. Although I had met him earlier, it was important to spend some time with him for this book.

'No question, then, I will try and catch him tomorrow evening,' I told Vasu.

Mustafa, who had been listening to this exchange attentively, piped up, 'Will the secretary allow me to photograph him?'

'No,' said Vasu.

'Do I get any special pictures, in addition to what I can see around us now? Will there be a permanent camp?'

Vasu did not think so. 'He may have more people around him but visually the scene will not be very different.'

I was reluctant to encourage Mustafa to accompany me on this gruelling journey. I knew that his heavy equipment would delay us and we might even end up missing Kosa.

Vasu helped us decide. He pointed out that we would have to walk back the same way after the meeting as there was no other route. That ruled out the possibility of walking with camera and crew. Mustafa would spend time with Vasu and his team.

Vasu would give me a guide. He suggested we split up into two groups. 'I will give you five of my people because you will cross some areas that are enemy strongholds, and you should have enough cover to retreat in case of a sudden attack.'

I was familiar with this risk. On another occasion, when I was travelling with insurgents of the United Liberation Front of Assam (ULFA) in the North-East, we had been attacked by the Indian army. I escaped, minus my equipment, running barefoot, literally, and travelled on a bicycle for six hours to catch a flight to Delhi.

The less weight I carried, the easier my walk would be. So I left behind all my belongings, except my laptop. I hoped to transfer to my laptop whatever data I could pick up from Commander Kosa, now that I knew there were computers and generators in the forest. Suraj, the only Hindi speaker in the team of five, was appointed leader. His wife, Sudri, would also walk with us. Chandru, Bhime and Jitru would be my other companions on this journey.

We began our walk in a single file. I walked behind Suraj, the others following me. Suraj talked as he walked. 'I am from Takilod village, from the other side of the Indravati. Sudri, my wife, is from the nearby village of Pallewaya.'

I knew of Pallewaya from my research on the vigilante group, the Salwa Judum. 'Wasn't the first house burnt down by anti-Maoists in 2003 in Pallewaya?' I asked.

'Yes,' said Suraj, surprised that I knew. 'That was Sudri's house!'

'Why did they burn your house, Sudri?'

'I was the first to join the Party from that area in 2002, so they targeted my house first,' Sudri explained through Suraj.

If my memory served me well, the Danteshwari Samanvay Samiti, a precursor of the Salwa Judum, had torched the house in collusion with the police. 'Do you know the leader of the Danteshwari Samanvay Samiti, Chaituram Atami?' I asked Suraj, little expecting the response I got.

'He is my uncle, my father's younger brother.'

I stopped dead in my tracks. It was a small world indeed. I had been trying to get to the root of that story for years.

Suraj continued, 'My father moved to Takilod, in the interior, in search of land many years ago. My uncle, Chaituram, stayed in our ancestral village, Kasoli, near the town. He studied in Gummargunda, and had the opportunity to connect with the Shivanand Ashram. Later, he became a Hindu. With the help of the Ashram and some businessmen associated with the BJP, Chaituram started the Danteshwari Samanvay Samiti to fight the Maoists in 2003.'

Suraj's story confirmed my theory about the Salwa Judum. Though the state claims that the Salwa Judum is a spontaneous tribal uprising that reared its head in 2005, I have been writing that it is not the whole truth. In an interview in 2006, Chaituram himself had said to me that it was he who had started the anti-Maoist people's movement through the Danteshwari Samanvay Samiti in 2003. He also claimed that their movement had reached more than a hundred villages and was spreading steadily. But Mahendra Karma, with the support of the BJP, which in turn, was being pressurized by industrialists, had stepped on the accelerator and made it a superfast train. Chaituram had also predicted that this train would soon be derailed.

I told Suraj that I had met Chaituram at a Salwa Judum rally. While Mahendra Karma was busy mouthing his speeches, and the other leaders occupied themselves with threatening the villagers, I had quietly walked over to Chaituram.

'At the time, he was a simple man. I could tell that he wasn't trained to handle the media because he admitted those facts quite openly. He told me that he believed the only way to finish the Maoists was by razing the homes of their workers. The Danteshwari Samiti had set up Village Defence Cells in their stronghold villages to tackle Maoist retaliation, unlike the Salwa Judum, whose method is to shift villagers to roadside camps set up by the government,' I told Suraj and added, 'You are the perfect example of the kind of family I am looking for, where the uncle is a Salwa Judum leader and the nephew is a Maoist commander.'

'I'm sure,' he smiled, and continued, 'Both Sudri and I were part of the team that was sent to the Salwa Judum camp at Kasoli to kill my uncle. We were a team of forty, led by a man called Rajman. We attacked at midnight but there was too much light in the camp and Chaituram fled after the sentries began to retaliate. That attack was a failure.

'But I will kill him at the next opportunity,' Suraj said, his calm voice belying his intent. 'He has killed so many innocent people and destroyed so many villages and lives.'

I recognized the name Rajman: he was on my list of people to meet. I also noticed that Sudri had been affected by our mention of Chaituram. Although she did not know Hindi, she must have sensed the drift of the conversation. She is a warrior, after all. An exchange about the man who had burnt down her home must have triggered off traumatic memories.

'Both of us were part of the attack on Madhukar Rao as well,' she offered in Gondi, and Suraj translated.

Madhukar Rao was a schoolteacher, who, according to stories floated by the government, had inspired the people to defy the Maoists. 'I met Madhukar at Kutru camp,' I said.

'That was where we went to catch him,' Suraj warmed up. 'That night, he was not in the camp but was sleeping in his own house nearby. When we attacked the camp, he heard the gunshots and took to his heels. We did not know the exact location of his house, so he got away. Sudhakar had commanded that attack.'

He added enthusiastically, 'If we walk a little faster, we can meet Sudhakar's team on the way later today. He is returning from the Dhamtari attack with Devji. Their team recently killed thirteen policemen in Dhamtari near Raipur. We were also involved in the Telipenta and Chikka village attacks—one special police officer (SPO) was killed and five houses belonging to SPOs were razed.'

This admission was surprising. Senior Maoist leaders are cautious about what they say to journalists. I had never before heard a Maoist admit to burning homes. But then again, nor had I heard senior Salwa Judum leaders or government officials talk of lapses in executing a strategy. Perhaps that is the nature of conflict—what is a glorious battle for one side is an atrocity on the other.

I noticed that we had passed some broken-down buildings; one had definitely been a school and the other, I was told, was the panchayat office. A man on a motorcycle approached us with a picture of Danteshwari, the local deity, strapped to the handlebars. He stopped and introduced himself as the village schoolteacher. I asked him with a smile, 'Have the dadas broken down the schools so you teachers can have a long holiday?'

The teacher corrected me immediately. 'No, no, that is not true. The dadas do not want education to stop. They have broken down the school here because they do not want the police to stay in the building. In fact, they made sure that the villagers built a hut for the school, and that is where my classes are held.' He added in a sincere tone, 'Education continues full steam.'

I could not be sure if his words were intended to please the dadas who were with me, or were meant in earnest. There were many questions I wanted to ask, but this wasn't the time. He said he was only a para teacher, which implied that his salary would be less than Rs 4000 a month. He also said he lived in a town forty-five kilometres away. I wondered how he maintained his motorbike on such a small income. But we needed to move on.

'So, how many attacks have you been part of so far?' I asked Suraj.

'Oh, the biggest attack was in this very village. Sudri and one of our comrades had gone to the village market in plain clothes to conduct a meeting. But some informers recognized them and called the police. Thankfully, one of our informers in the police called to tell us that a police party had left for the market on motorbikes. We took our positions and ambushed them, killing nine cops.'

I wanted to know if they had laid a landmine on the road.

'Yes. But the landmine killed only one policeman. The rest were killed in the firing. We asked them repeatedly to surrender, but they refused. We arrested three of them, and released them later along with a letter stating that it was not the police we were against, it was the system.'

We stopped for lunch in Kamlapur, a village on the river bank. Sudri went off to collect utensils and food from the villagers, Bhime to look for firewood and Chandru to get water. Jitru was our cook. Resting under a tree, I was able to get a good look at Sudri as she bustled about.

She was a very attractive woman—tall and slim, with beautiful, wavy black hair. I could not help but think that she could not be more different from the image of a fierce Maoist fighter that I had in my head.

Sitting next to me, Suraj pulled out a copy of *Awam-e-Jung* from his backpack. It is a magazine published by their Central Military Commission and provides detailed analyses of all Party attacks, complete with maps. 'This issue has all the details of the attack in this village that I was just telling you about.' The magazine described it as 'a very successful ambush'. On a map accompanying the article, Suraj pointed out the exact locations where each of the constables was killed. It was not far from where we were sitting.

Jitru had turned on the radio for the newscast. The Maoists, I have noticed, switch on the radio like clockwork when it is time for news. Never for music or entertainment. The newsreader mentioned a cyclone over the Bay of Bengal. I hoped this meant some respite from the blazing sun.

Kamlapur was a typical tribal village—sparsely populated, with small settlements of a few families spaced some distance apart. Tribals do not huddle together as people in other rural areas do. They seek a sense of space and so, a few families get together and build shelters near each other. This works well for a people who depend on the forest as a hunting and gathering community. Their markets are mobile weekly haats. Even for necessities, like salt or oil, the villagers have to travel great distances. The conditions are far from conducive for setting up an infrastructure and governing the area smoothly. Teachers and health workers prefer to live in the nearest town and travel to the village every day, because of which their work suffers. With the escalation of conflict, schools, hospitals, subsidized food, and even people, are being used as weapons.

While this area in eastern Bastar has yet to see the full strength of the Salwa Judum, in other places, the state has deprived people of basic facilities as a strategy to push them out to roadside camps. City-dwellers are rarely seen here, and a journalist's arrival is nothing less than an event. So, I was not surprised when some villagers walked up to where we were resting. One of them introduced himself as Jeeturam Sori.

I posed my favourite opening question, 'Are there enough teachers here?' As expected, it set Jeeturam off on a tirade.

'The teacher lives in the town nearby and comes rarely, though we have built a hut for the school and the teacher to stay in.' He quickly moved on to the next issue on his mind: 'I am the former sarpanch of this village. I had a hundred acres of land, but was able to till only fifty. The rest was lying fallow. So the dadas requested me to give it away, and distributed it amongst ten families.'

'Did they threaten you?'

Jeeturam hastened to deny it, his words prompted by the presence of my companions, no doubt.

Suddenly, I heard the sound of an engine. Anxious, I asked him if it might be a police jeep.

Jeeturam reassured me with a smile. 'No, it is a tractor.'

'If you have a tractor, why couldn't you have farmed all hundred acres?'

Jeeturam responded with a cautious eye on Suraj, who was sitting next to me. 'Yes, but all of us should live amicably.' He sounded like a child who has learned a lesson by heart, and must now recite it before an audience. 'Another family in the village had fifty acres of land. They gave away ten acres.'

I felt the frustration of being an embedded journalist. It could well be that Vasu had instructed Suraj to introduce me to someone like Jeeturam, who would validate Vasu's claims that many landlords give away their unused land of their own volition. One is limited when one must depend on a single point of view.

'Who is your new sarpanch?' I asked Jeeturam.

'She lives in the town and has hired labourers to tend to her land. Her family refused to surrender their extra land, so they moved out of Kamlapur.'

Vasu too had spoken of such non-resident villagers.

Jeeturam went on, 'She embezzled government funds, and did nothing for the welfare of the village. She herself wallows in luxury now. Her family did not own even a bicycle, and now they have built their own house in the town. It must have cost Rs 3–4 lakh. Last year, they bought a tractor. Earlier, when the dadas were not here, government officials would pay us regular visits. But after last year's attack on the police, those visits have stopped. The ration shop too has moved to the city, twenty kilometres from here, close to the sarpanch's house.'

The list of complaints grew lengthier by the minute. There is no electricity in the village. Apparently, power poles had been put up ten years ago, and the village had enjoyed electricity for a year. Then the lights went out for good. Broken hand pumps have not been repaired, and now the village is solely dependent on the river.

Jeeturam shared his own political background. 'I used to work for the BJP. But when I started resisting the Bodhghat Dam, the police put me in jail for nine months. I have been jailed thrice so far, and while I was behind bars, the police beat up my father at home. Two people from this village have been in jail for the past six months. I got no help from Kedar Kashyap, our MLA, who is also a BJP minister. That's why I stopped visiting him. This time, he did not even come to us seeking votes. In the last election, only ten people voted from our village. The new sarpanch has done well; she has aligned herself with the BJP. Her husband, who is the panchayat secretary, is with the Congress.'

I asked him why he, a one-time BJP leader, did not take up the matter at the highest political level.

It was not easy for someone like him, Jeeturam contended. 'The only time I stepped out of Kamlapur is when I went with Kedar Kashyap to Ranchi by a bus that had been specially hired to ferry people to a BJP rally. I have never boarded a train!'

Prodding him further, I asked him about the rate for tendu leaf collection, the primary source of cash in his area. He was unhappy about that as well. 'The contractor gives us only Rs 60 for a hundred bundles. The dadas have started visiting us these last two years. Once they have a strong presence here, we will get a better rate for tendu—up to Rs 110. In places where they have been working for a long time, they have got villagers a rate which is higher than the one set by the government.'

I could see that the villagers communicate in their own style, and I needed to remain tuned in. Coming from the city, it is difficult to comprehend the limitations of the people of this area; here, even the Hindi-speaking ex-sarpanch has not been exposed to the outside world. These, indeed, are the fringe people. Jeeturam still speaks of the dadas as entities separate from himself. He may not have joined the Naxals yet, but he is already calculating the benefits of doing so. Who knows when the balance will tip? So far, only three people from Jeeturam's village, a boy and two girls, have joined the Party full-time.

What Jeeturam said matched Vasu's version of Maoist impact on and control of the area. The Maoists claim that they destroy school and panchayat buildings only when the residents understand their reasons for doing so, and support them completely. The first village we crossed this morning had its school building intact. However, their hold is better on this village. They have been able to persuade some villagers to donate what they consider excess landholding, but are not yet powerful enough to snatch away land from someone who does not want to give it up. All government buildings have been destroyed, but the village temple stands untouched. One needs to have a prolonged and close association with the residents of a place before their faith can be questioned, and the Maoists know this well.

By this time, the vegetables had arrived from the village—leafy greens called kholiari. Suraj helped with the cooking and we ate, resuming our walk soon after. Sudri had boiled some water from the river and filled it in bottles for us to carry. We were drinking hot, boiled water in midsummer! It was better than glugging contaminated water, I told myself.

Suraj walked very fast, enlightening me about whatever we saw. He was as enthusiastic about the snakes we spotted on the way as he was about the Party. Once, he darted into a clump of bushes pursuing a snake and listed its features, all for my benefit.

Sandwiched between Suraj and the others, I was barely able to drag myself forward in the heat. Whenever I slowed down, which was often, Suraj would rebuke me, 'If you walk like this, we won't be able to reach tomorrow evening and Kosa will be gone.'

The forest path was littered with ripe mangoes that had fallen off the branches heavy with fruit. All of it, I realized, would go to waste. There is no industry in Bastar that can process the fruit, and so, no one collects it.

'In south Bastar, where I come from, we dry and sell these mangoes,' Suraj explained. 'But here, people are too busy with their singing and dancing at this time of the year. They collect some mangoes for themselves, but do not preserve or sell them.'

I recalled that Vasu had spoken of the Party's plans to start small-scale industries to process mangoes and other forest produce, like tamarind. Seeing the profusion of mangoes growing naturally, it seemed like a better option than setting up an industry where only the educated middle class could expect to get jobs.

Walking through the dense forest, I was able to appreciate the dry statistics that had made little sense to me on paper. I remembered an interview with Mukesh Dholakia, an expert on minor forest produce, who said that 83 per cent of what the forest produces goes to waste. Even with only 17 per cent of it collected, forest produce accounts for business worth over Rs 1000 crore in Chhattisgarh alone. And production in these forests is annual, repetitive and self-sustaining. From this vantage point, it is difficult to understand the logic behind planning all development around iron ore reserves, which will, sooner or later, get exhausted.

My mind was swimming in the heat. I imagined us to be a marathon team with mango juice stalls on trees in place of water booths. I shook my head to clear my mind, and my eyes fell on Suraj's wrist—his watch had stopped at 7 o'clock. He said it had stopped ticking days ago.

'My friend needed my watch to keep his appointments in the city,' he explained.

His body seemed attuned to an inbuilt timer anyway, I thought. He gave me a five-minute break every hour. I checked my watch each time he stopped, and it was always within five minutes of the hour.

We crossed one settlement after another, not stopping once. A group passed us in the afternoon—it was the only time we saw people other than ourselves. The girls wore red and the boys bright green. They had elaborate ornaments woven in their hair, and carried drums. Suraj told me they were going to a jatra, a local cultural fair, in a nearby village.

Sudri, who had noticed a kholiari tree, asked one of the girls to pluck us a few leaves. That would take care of our dinner. The girl clambered up the tree, deft as a monkey, her sari no hindrance at all, and threw the leaves down to us.

I knew we had walked very deep into the forest when the women no longer cared to cover their breasts on seeing us. I noticed some wooden structures that I initially took to be Maoist monuments, but each had a trident mounted on the peak. There were no cement and brick temples in the forest, but I could understand why the BJP has been winning so many seats in tribal areas these days—they have penetrated very deep into tribal areas, not unlike the Maoists.

All the way, Sudri and Bhime effortlessly balanced heavy loads on their heads. Bhime might have been sixteen or seventeen, but she looked more child than woman. I was curious to know why she had joined the Party. She opened up just enough to say that she was from the Jagargunda area and had been captured by the Salwa Judum. She had joined the Party after being released from a Salwa Judum camp in 2007. She would not say more.

Gradually, the light faded. We had been walking for about eight hours. Suraj told me that we were on the border between Bastar and Narayanpur districts. We would stop at the next village, Bechcha, for food, and walk for another two hours.

At Bechcha, dinner was prepared the same way as lunch. Several villagers arranged for our food, so that no single family had to feed the entire visiting team. Though I wanted to determine if our hosts had contributed the rice willingly, or, in fact, secretly begrudged this enforced hospitality, it was too dark to see their faces.

I picked a Hindi-speaking villager as my dinner companion.

His village consisted of forty-one families, ten of whom had Below Poverty Line (BPL) cards. These cards enable one to get subsidized rations from the government's public distribution shops.

'My brother and I own six acres of land, so I am rich,' he said. 'I do not have a BPL card, though some of those ten families who have cards own more land than I do,' he laughed. 'The card is not worth much anyway, because the ration shop is thirty kilometres away, in the city. Now that shop has moved into the police station compound, making matters worse.'

It started to drizzle as we ate, and Suraj decided to call it a day. 'We have done only eight hours today. If we want to meet Kosa, we will have to walk for at least twelve hours tomorrow,' he said. 'We must start early.'

Sentry duties were assigned.

I drifted into a heavy sleep, listening half-consciously to the sound of drums and singing from somewhere close by. I would have liked to join the dancers but was too tired to move, and they would dance through the night.

It was Sudri's watch from 2 a.m.–4 a.m. She shook me awake at 4 a.m. sharp. I had slept fitfully while frogs and chicks hopped on and around me all night. I reached for my torch to check the time. Its light fell on a dead rat. I had been sleeping next to a decomposing rodent—a revolting thought, but under the circumstances, I was relieved it wasn't a snake.

We arose and began to walk without a word. It was as if there had been no break in this expedition of ours. Walking at night with neither roads to follow nor street lights to show the way is unsettling, to say the least. With nobody to seek

directions from and no maps to follow, a wrong turn would
simply not be noticed. It happened to us a couple of times.
Suraj spoke to the others in Gondi, and no one told me that
we were lost, but I could gather from the tone of the exchange
that we were not where we were supposed to be. We were
racing against time. The drizzle had made the ground slushy.
The wet mud stuck to my shoes, making it difficult to walk.
I was glad that I had not postponed my trip; this path would
be treacherous in the monsoons. In no time, I found myself
sweating like a football player after a gruelling match, and
it was not even morning.

I realized how different I was from the people who walked
alongside me. I could not, and indeed, would not, choose
to live like this my whole life. A life like this needs grit and
passion. And there is not much that money can buy here.

It was 7.30 a.m. and already as hot as noon, when I spotted
a team of four men coming from the opposite direction. Suraj
recognized them first. 'I told you we would meet Sudhakar
and his group,' he said, cheerfully. 'They must have camped
somewhere here.'

We could not stop to talk to them as we were already late,
but I saw that one of the boys had his right hand in a bandage.

'He lost a couple of fingers in an accident the other day,
when he packed more gunpowder into a bomb than he was
supposed to,' explained Suraj matter-of-factly.

Soon after, as we passed through a valley surrounded by
hills, Suraj told me that a helicopter had dropped off a group
of policemen there some time ago.

'Were they in black uniforms?'

'How did you know?' he asked me, amazed.

I was only putting two and two together. I had read reports that two planeloads of National Security Guards (NSG), popularly known as Black Cat commandos, had landed in Bastar. But the newspapers did not say why they had been sent there, or what had happened during their visit.

'They probably had information about arms and ammunition hidden in the forest,' Suraj guessed. He recalled that the commandos had headed straight for the house of the president of the Jantana Sarkar, which is a parallel government run under Maoist supervision, equivalent to the panchayat. Its president is the boy we had seen on the way—the one who had lost his fingers.

'The villagers fled into the forest fearing violence, but the commandos did not burn any homes. They simply dug up the ground beneath the president's house, looking for arms.'

I appreciated Suraj's honesty. He could have, if he had so wished, painted a dark picture of the commandos for effect. A journalist is indeed fortunate to have a guide who presents information as accurately as he can, especially when he is in a position of as much power as the Maoists are in their areas. There is no way to verify facts and one can only count on one's intuitive understanding and power of analysis.

Suraj's reference to the burning of homes reminded me of my visit last year to Jagargunda, Bhime's native place. I had heard that another batch of Black Cats had torched some villages there. Manish Kunjam, the leader of the CPI, had introduced me to eight girls from the area. They were amongst the many villagers who were picked up from their homes and lodged in roadside camps for months. All the girls had been gang-raped by the Salwa Judum.

Was that Bhime's story too?

During the next rest stop, I took out my diary and checked my notes. There, buried under all the facts I had jotted down while talking to Vasu, was the name 'Bhime'. Had he, then, sent the same Bhime with me?

As we climbed a steep hill under the blazing sun, my head was a tumble of thoughts. I had been able to get each of my companions to talk, but Bhime always walked away when I quizzed her. Was she shy? What about Suraj? He was so vocal about everything else, but would refrain from discussing Bhime. As the pieces of the puzzle fell into place, reality hit me hard. A sinking sensation grew in the pit of my stomach and I felt as if my legs would give way. Tears welled up in my eyes and streamed down my face.

I sat down.

I realized that at that moment, it was the enormity of the pain people here bore, which overwhelmed me. Suraj thought I was in physical pain, and assured me that we would soon go down the hill, and that in ten minutes, we would stop for lunch.

I was still thinking about Bhime. The need for scientific questioning and the hunt for facts had turned me into an insensitive beast that must forage for proof and feed on details. Bhime was hardly a woman yet. And there I was, goading her at every opportunity. In that moment of truth, I found it unforgivably cruel. Maybe it was just a mechanism to cope with the physical and mental exhaustion of the journey. Or maybe it was the catharsis I needed after bottling up my emotions during all those years of hunting for stories to convince the world of the magnitude of the horror in this region.

Suraj tried to get me to walk with the incentive of lunch. 'We will only have to walk for another seven or eight hours.'

I took out the packet of biscuits that Vasu had given me to nibble on during an emergency, and munched on a biscuit as I shuffled on resolutely. It was the most difficult half-hour of the journey.

Suraj had instinctively stopped goading me to walk faster: he must have concluded that I was a city-bred weakling. His 8-mm rifle was pointed directly at me as he walked in front. It was too close for comfort, and having heard his stories of firearms going off accidentally, embellished with details of injuries and deaths, I was acutely aware of the weapon.

'Is your rifle loaded?' I asked him.

'Of course,' he said in a reassuring tone. 'It is the best protection in an emergency.' He patted the magazine. 'This can fire five rounds. The others have 12-bore single-shot rifles.'

In this state of heightened sensitivity, it seemed prudent to keep a safe distance from everyone. I was grateful to just be allowed to walk silently. At our stop for lunch, I crashed under the nearest tree, while the others got to work to organize food. Sudri now got some chhind—a local variety of dates—from a nearby tree. She informed me that we were now in the first village of Abujhmad, the only un-surveyed area in the country. 'We are just ten or twelve kilometres away from Orchha.'

I could not help feeling good about myself—I had, after all, walked all the way to Orchha from Chitrakoot. Of course, we still had to meet Kosa, but this walk was an achievement in itself. As I reflected on this, I realized the chhind tasted really good on my tongue.

I think my breakdown helped Sudri and the others to open up to me. Sudri tried to describe a tribal home to me: 'One room is for pigs and one is for chickens and one is for cows and one is for humans.' Clearly, the concept of home and family includes man and his beasts. I got that. But the mistakes in her faltering Hindi had everyone in splits. With the help of the others, I could piece together the story of her home, which had been burned twice; the second time in 2005 by the Salwa Judum.

Vetti Gundiram was the sarpanch of her village, Pallewaya. Salwa Judum leader Mahendra Karma's daughter was married into Vetti's family. When the Judum was formed, Vetti left the village and went to live with Mahendra Karma. Behind his back, the Party distributed all his land to the poor. At that time, Sudri was the only Party member in her village. In 2006, the Salwa Judum attacked Pallewaya, and most of the villagers were shifted to roadside camps. Some escaped into the forest. Vendetta was directed at Sudri's family. Her brother, Veko Guddu, was convicted for life, but he escaped during the Dantewada jail break of 2007. Sudri last visited the village in 2008, to find that only two families, besides her own, were left there. The rest were living in the Judum camps. She had learned from a recent letter from home that eighteen families had returned from the camps and her village now had nearly two hundred residents.

The consideration that Suraj showed for me delayed us considerably. An old ligament injury in my knee had started acting up. I had torn a ligament when I came to see Kosa five years ago, and this walk must have aggravated it. I began to worry that we would miss Kosa. It certainly looked likely.

We would have to walk back eighty kilometres, and I didn't want to be carried on a stretcher. Suraj said it would take another two and a half hours to reach our destination, but at night, that could mean four hours of walking.

'I just cannot do it. I cannot walk any more. I will not blame you if we don't reach Kosa in time,' I told Suraj.

He just walked on.

It had rained somewhere, and thankfully, the heat was now bearable. We walked in the dark for what seemed like forever. I did not realize we were in a village till we walked into a cowshed, where I dropped off right away. When Sudri woke me up for dinner, it was probably past midnight.

After I had eaten, it struck me that I ought to be looking out for snakes: the cowshed had a thatched roof, and probably housed at least a couple of them. Suraj cheerfully acknowledged the validity of my concern: 'After the rains, the snakes are out.' We requested the villagers who had arranged for our food to give us a place to sleep. They did, and I tried to make the most of it. It can be unnerving to have someone switch on the torch periodically to check for snakes. But there is something to be said for exhaustion—I did fall asleep.

Suraj woke me up at 4 a.m. and I braced for the last leg of the journey.

Pain or no pain, one step after another, we shall make it, I chanted to myself. The transistor was tuned to the BBC. I seem to listen to news on the radio only when I am with the Maoists, I noted to myself, trying to divert my attention from my aching knee. Sushila Singh was reading the news. It was strange to think that we had worked together at one time, strange to think of anything except the here and now. The newscast updated me on Prime Minister Manmohan Singh's cabinet expansion and I learned that India had got its first Airborne Warning and Control System (AWACS) from Israel. The Pakistan army had attacked the Taliban.

We walked on, watching the sun come up over the horizon. Surely, we could not be too far from Kosa. But when Suraj declared that we had reached, all I noted was that there was no one on the lookout. Had Kosa left?

Suraj agreed that we would have been stopped by the sentry had Kosa been around. We waited while Suraj went ahead to check. In ten minutes, he was back to confirm my worst fear—Kosa was gone. But Suraj had found someone who knew of Kosa's next destination, and had already sent a messenger to ask for permission to approach. We would wait for the response. I needed to rest anyway.

4

AT THE EPICENTRE

Three young female comrades showed up after a few hours of our waiting and recuperating from the arduous journey. They would take me to Comrade Kosa and be my guides from this point on. I felt a twinge of sadness as I bid goodbye to the quintet with whom I had grown familiar these last few days.

One of them, Comrade Fagni, belonged to the same area as Suraj and Sudri, but she looked and sounded different. Her Hindi, for one, was fluent. 'I went to school and studied till class seven. But I did not get a job. My parents are poor, you see. The poor do not get any jobs after leaving school.'

'Maybe you should have studied some more,' I offered casually. I must have sounded patronizing, for she shot back, 'No, I left school because, with bourgeois education, one can never understand the problems of the poor.'

That was complex language all right, but I should have expected it. This was Maoist territory, after all. Much theoretical communist diction would be bandied about in the days to come.

In my last meeting with Kosa, I had asked him a simple question: What is the Party fighting for? In response, he spouted fifteen minutes of convoluted spiel, impossible for a layman to decode. It was all relevant, but somehow, coming from him, it sounded like another language altogether. At some point, he used the term Nav Janwadi Kranti (New Democratic Revolution) to explain their current struggle, and that was all I could take away from it.

Much to my relief, the final lap of the journey to Kosa's hideout was brief and we reached at sunset.

The camp was strategically located in an L-shaped clearing between two hills. A phalanx of fifty comrades greeted us with the Maoist salutation of 'Laal Salam' (Red Salute). I recognized Radha, Kosa's wife. Kosa's doctor, Anupama, was another familiar face. And then, I saw Kosa.

He was a changed man, physically so, at least.

The last time I saw Kosa, he was dressed for our TV cameras. Today, instead of military fatigues, he was in plain clothes. Older, mellowed and balding, he looked more like a retired headmaster than a revolutionary. He remembered having met me at the Bhumkal celebration in 2004.

'How did you manage to reach me so fast?' was his first question.

Kosa was expecting me. Suraj had sent him Vasu's letter, which bore the date of my arrival, well in time. 'Eighty kilometres in two days is very good speed,' he said, a smile spreading across his face. 'Now you are fit to join our PLGA (People's Liberation Guerrilla Army)!' Escorting me to his tent, he said, 'You walked the same path that Gundadhur, the leader of the Bhumkal rebellion, took. He started from a village called Nelnar, which is not very far from here. Gundadhur marched with his army to Jagdalpur and was able to capture the Bastar Raj for two weeks before the rebellion was crushed.' Bastar was one of the princely states that the British had allowed to function independently, having appointed officers who more or less ruled the state for them.

'You will have your own salfi tree to rest against, as our special guest,' said Radha, like any hostess waiting upon a visitor to her home.

'You have not lost any weight since I saw you last,' I teased her. I regretted the words as soon as I uttered them—I had been rather rude, I realized—and so, hastily added with a smile that putting on weight while leading a life as hard as this was unusual. Kosa rose to the occasion to defend his wife, 'I sent her to a naturopathy centre, but they too were surprised—she did not lose even half a kilo!'

I noticed that Kosa was wearing a pair of sturdy Bata floaters, while Radha apparently got on fine in her broken plastic shoes, Adivasi-style. Radha was the first Adivasi girl to have been recruited into the Maoist cadre, as far back as 1983. I discreetly refrained from discussing the subject of branded shoes, even as my attention shifted to the sound of a whistle.

'It is time for the evening class that I usually conduct,' said Kosa. 'But today, I will talk to you.'

Everyone except those in charge of preparing food headed for class.

About twenty temporary shelters—jhillis—had been rigged up in the clearing using blue plastic sheets. Kosa's jhilli was in the centre, and right next to it was the one allotted to me for the duration of my stay. Some things had clearly changed since my last visit—the camp was now lit up with LED lights.

'These LED lights have changed guerrilla evenings. When I first came here, we only had firewood from the forest. Those were difficult times indeed. Then we started using kerosene lamps and candles, but every strong gust of wind would leave us in the dark: it was a nuisance. Now all of us can read for a few hours every evening thanks to this new technology.' Kosa wanted to know if I had heard of a laptop that charges itself on sunlight.

I sheepishly admitted that I had not.

Displaying the prized gadget, Kosa said, 'I can charge my laptop regularly now. You see, there is a politics of science, too. Solar power can change the lives of the poor but there is no money to put into that kind of research. The poor can only afford a radio, whereas, what we do is the opium of hundreds of TV stations.' That metaphor was apt, I thought. Marx would have been proud of this follower.

Just then, Kosa's walkie-talkie, suspended from a tree, sputtered to life. He answered in Telugu, using what sounded like code words in Hindi and English. I could not make sense of the conversation. 'Up to what distance can you communicate using this walkie-talkie?' I asked after he had hung up. He could reach anyone within an eighty-kilometre radius. 'But the reach depends on the height. To catch a signal so far away, both users need to be on hilltops. I can talk up to south Bastar on this set,' he said.

Suddenly, the walkie-talkie intercepted an exchange between policemen. A voice seemed to be placing an order for rations: 'Two kilos of tomatoes and ten kilos of potatoes ...' Although I was familiar with the anxieties of the security forces about intercepted radio waves, I was a little shaken to see it happen right before my eyes.

Kosa looked pleased as he explained, 'We have a tracking system in this set, so it keeps picking up conversations between policemen.'

'Does someone here monitor it all the time?'

'Of course! Just like they monitor us. So we talk in code.'

That explained why the policemen had spoken of ration lists! Just then, I saw Sudhakar, the head of military for the Party in Dandakaranya, approaching us. We had missed him on our way. Kosa introduced us. Amused by my fascination with the walkie-talkie, Sudhakar smiled. 'It is getting difficult for us to track the police these days. They have installed a new machine in some stations that automatically garbles their talk. But mostly, they use mobile phones, which are out of our reach anyway. Where mobiles do not work, they use satellite phones.'

I was keen to talk to Sudhakar, but noticed that a group of young boys and girls had gathered in a circle for a cultural class—something I did not want to miss. So I excused myself and walked across, leaving Kosa and Sudhakar behind. The class was in Gondi. As the students, led by a teacher, broke into song, I could make out that the lyrics were about the Nayagarh attack in Orissa, where the Maoists had raided an armoury and looted a huge cache of arms in one of their biggest attacks. The next song was about Janki Didi. The teacher translated and explained for my benefit that Janki Didi was their comrade Anuradha Ghandy, wife of jailed

Maoist leader Kobad Ghandy. She had been the lone woman member in the Party's Central Committee, and had died of malaria in 2008.

Next came a quiz on the martyrs of Dandakaranya. There were thirty comrades in the class, and I was invited to interact with them. With the help of the teacher, who translated for me, I did a quick survey.

Only five of them had ever gone to school, and the most educated comrade in their midst had studied up to class seven.

'How many of you have seen a train?' I asked next, remembering that Jeeturam had never boarded one in his life. Six hands went up. None of them had ever travelled in one. Only thirteen had ever boarded a bus. Only one had watched a film at the cinema in a nearby town.

'How many of you do not understand Hindi?' was my last question. More than half of them did not.

Being around these men and women and trying to learn about their lives, I felt compelled to question every preconceived notion I had about them. I have visited Maoist areas several times for television features. Television crews travel fast; cameras roll whenever there are shots that will look good on screen. There is rarely any time to devote to the details of the lives we gloss over. This time, though, I was not in a hurry.

What did these people do when they were not wielding guns? After all, they only kill as often as police press releases say so. Clearly, there was more to their lives than what I had ever got the chance to know about. I walked back to Kosa, who was waiting on his jhilli with a cup of freshly brewed tea for me.

'Do you drink tea or sugar?' he asked. Seeing my baffled expression, he explained with a laugh, 'In Chhattisgarh and Maharashtra, people add so much sugar that one can hardly taste the tea. When I ask for less sugar, they immediately know I am from Andhra!'

'I will have mine with everything,' I said. I knew it was difficult for a tea purist to appreciate the need for additives. My boss at the *Guardian*, John Rettie, was a tea fanatic. He could never understand why I needed to add milk and sugar to my cuppa. Although I tried to explain to John that our objectives were different, he simply could not see what I meant until, one day, having gone without food for hours in a remote village, we stopped at a farmer's house. He served us a cup of chai each, Indian-style, generously laced with sugar and milk. John never questioned my sweet, milky tea again.

Kosa said he gave up sugar when Radha was diagnosed as diabetic. 'The Adivasis do not drink milk anyway; they believe that a cow's milk is for its calf. But don't worry, we have arranged for both milk and sugar for you,' he hastened to assure me.

It felt bizarre, sitting there, chatting with a Maoist leader over tea as if it were just another drawing-room conversation. 'Where is your son now? Was he not studying engineering when you came here last?' Kosa asked me.

'He has finished college and is now working in the United States.'

Inevitably, we spoke of the Party's role in creating work opportunities for the people in the region. Redistributing land amongst the poor in the thirty-odd years of their steadily growing dominance, the Party had ensured that people had land. Their main thrust now was to enhance agricultural production. 'Nobody dies of starvation any more but production in this area is appallingly low,' Kosa said. 'In Abujhmad, people mostly practise pedda, shifting cultivation. We are slowly trying to familiarize them with fixed farming, by teaching them the techniques of modern cultivation.'

'Where do you get teachers from?'

'We manage to do it ourselves. I spent most of today conducting a meeting of our agriculture committee. In the agriculture class, we discussed what we could do with these salfi trees,' he said, pointing to the tree against which I was leaning. 'Each tree can yield up to fifty litres of salfi a day. A tribal goes to a salfi tree thrice a day, getting so drunk on its juice that he is unable to work. We are considering making jaggery out of salfi. But the tribals are opposed to processing the juice, saying it will anger their god. Hopefully, over time, we will be able to convince them.'

I could not help but wonder how the tribals could dare to oppose this AK-47-toting man. His rifle, I noticed, was the same one that had been slung from his shoulder back in 2004. Its handle was painted green. I bantered with him: 'You have the same wife, the same doctor and the same AK-47!'

Kosa laughed, 'We got it for Rs 1.5 lakh—one of the first AKs we bought. Now they cost more than Rs 5 lakh each. We get AKs mainly from police raids. These are the best weapons. You can leave an AK underwater and use it after a month, and it will still be as good as new.' With that, he deftly went back to apprise me of the other changes that the Party is trying to bring about. 'Tomorrow, I will be meeting the health committee. I was not expecting you before the 8th, so I will not be free to talk before evening. In the meantime, you can speak to whomever you want.'

'Please do not worry about me,' I assured him. 'I plan to be here for some time if that is okay with you.'

He graciously replied, 'You are welcome to remain here as long as you want. See, nobody wants to even talk to us, and through you, we have got an opportunity to tell the world that we have the support of the people here. Their lives are not easy, and I know that outsiders only blame the tribal people for their lot. They say that tribals are lazy and do not work—even that they produce too many children. But the survival rate is so low here: of ten children born, only two or three may live. These are people who have never had access to doctors—it is only after our intervention that they have started to use medicines.'

It is difficult even to imagine that lives could be lived in so primitive a fashion in this day and age. 'How does the Party get all this know-how to the people?'

'We are trying to train at least one person as a health worker in each village. The method seems to be working, because now villagers call us whenever they need medical help, and mobile teams of doctors try to reach them as quickly as they can. Last year, we had a bona fide doctor with an MBBS degree attending to the villagers for three months. He trained many of our comrades. I myself spent three months training in a nursing home, and one of our comrades will soon join us here after having received medical training for a year and a half.' I wanted to know where they were being trained.

'Leave those questions out, please,' was the steely response.

I hastily switched tracks and asked him to tell me more about the Party's plans for change—a topic about which he was visibly passionate.

'Any change is difficult to bring about. But tradition needs to be re-evaluated in today's context. For example, in the olden days, after the harvest in November, the whole village would go hunting as a group. It was called Judum Peta, which, by the way, is where the Salwa Judum gets its name from, but let me not digress.

'The villagers would return after months on the hunt. Now, we are trying to persuade them to stay back in the village during these months and work collectively to dig ponds that can store water and boost agricultural production. In the past few years, hundreds of ponds have been dug under the leadership of the Jantana Sarkar.

'We have also decided to involve our PLGA in cultivation instead of treating it like a bourgeois army. They will participate in the sowing process from July to August as well as in the harvesting of the crop from November to December. Military work, though, will remain their priority.'

In the background, I could see people returning to their jhillis. The evening class was over.

Radha came over to where we were sitting. 'We are ready to watch the film,' she told Kosa. He stood up, laptop in hand. 'I was showing them *Mrityudand* on my laptop yesterday. Today, they will watch the second half.'

I had not seen it, but knew that it had a strong woman protagonist.

The choice of film had not been random. As Kosa explained, women form the backbone of the Maoist movement now. 'Today, 40–60 per cent of Party members are women. After land, women's issues are the biggest concern for the Party. When we came from Andhra, there were only men and their priorities. But women joined us in huge numbers and our women's wing, Krantikari Adivasi Mahila Sangh (KAMS), was formed in 1984. At that time, even Andhra did not have a women's wing.'

Sudhakar, perched atop a jhilli next to ours, chipped in, 'Even in our combat force, 40 per cent of the team comprises women. Companies are still led by men, but there are half a dozen women platoon commanders. Today, KAMS has over a lakh members.'

We walked across to our makeshift theatre—a small clearing with an upturned plastic drum placed on one side. Kosa set his laptop down on it, and all of us sat down to watch Madhuri Dixit play the proverbial woman of substance.

Kosa told me enthusiastically, 'I wanted them to know about the feudal world outside. I showed them another film, *Gangaajal*, a few days ago.'

The others did not like being disturbed by a pair of chatty viewers, so we stopped talking and concentrated on the film instead.

Some villagers had brought pork and fish for dinner. As a guest, I got to sample both. Kosa told me he would go to bed after listening to the BBC bulletin at half past ten. Three sentry teams of two comrades each would keep an eye out for any suspicious activity during the night. The sentry duty would change every two hours.

Chances of the police reaching this spot seemed remote, so deep had I walked into the forest. That was my last thought lying there on my jhilli, next to Kosa's.

I woke up at 5 a.m. as someone switched on the radio. An hour later, we heard the BBC newsreader announce that Binayak Sen had held a press conference in Kolkata. Had he been released while I was walking in the forest? Kosa confirmed that a couple of days ago, the Supreme Court had granted him bail. Sen was quoted as saying that the Maoists and the state were both using violence, and that in the crossfire, it was the villagers who were suffering.

I asked Kosa what he thought of the statement. 'Does he speak the same language when he is with you?'

Devji, a young military commander standing next to us, tried to speak his mind about 'these intellectuals who change their opinion according to their convenience' but Kosa cut him short. 'Binayak Sen always spoke that way about us. And all this talk about Binayak Sen having come into these jungles to train us is bogus. He is a human rights activist, and we have no connection with him.'

'But you sent him money for Narayan Sanyal's legal expenses, didn't you?'

'I have not checked the Central Committee's expense sheet that minutely,' he replied, sidestepping the question.

I recalled what K. Balagopal, a well-known human rights activist, had told me when I met him in Hyderabad a few months before his death. 'I tried to start a peace process in Chhattisgarh like in Andhra, but Binayak Sen opposed it. Our entire initiative was scuttled by his opposition,' Balagopal had said. I had cross-checked this with some members of Balagopal's peace initiative team. They had echoed Balagopal's views.

It appeared that the time spent in jail had helped Dr Sen revise his views on the subject of violence.

In the morning, I was given a set of house rules to follow. The women, I learned, would 'go' to one side of the camp and the men to the other. I was given a plastic bag—a collapsible bucket, if you will—to carry water. Everyone had to walk for four minutes to use the latrine. I wondered why the walk had to be for four minutes and not five, but held my tongue.

As his guest, I had the honour of walking with Kosa. On the way, he pointed to a bush called American Pudla in Gondi. 'This weed came into the country along with American wheat and has since spread all over the Bastar forest. It is so toxic, like American imperialism, that it does not allow any other shrub to grow near it!'

When we came back, I saw that one of the teams had already taken charge of the open-air kitchen. The comrades were out for their morning exercise; only the sick rested. Not trained to lead a disciplined life, I was free to do as I pleased, while Kosa did his yogabhyas near his tent. I noticed that he was the only one who had an inflatable pillow. Nearby, lay a book in Telugu, which looked like a collection of Mao's writings. Kosa must have been observing me, for he immediately explained, 'We are running a rectification campaign, so I need to read Mao's literature afresh.'

I wanted to know what a rectification campaign meant, but thought better of disturbing a man standing on his head.

Breakfast consisted of some leftover rice from the previous night, fried and served. Soon after, Kosa got busy with his health meeting and I was free to look for my next interviewee.

Walking around the camp, I found a temporary bathroom made of teak leaves and staves. 'Are there any bathroom rules?' I cheerfully asked a man as he stepped out of the makeshift booth. My joke fell flat as he gave his poker-faced response, 'Yes, the boys bathe till twelve, the girls after that.' I noticed that most of the girls had short hair. It reminded me of the women members of the militant organization, LTTE (Liberation Tigers of Tamil Eelam). Radha had walked over to keep me company, so I asked her about the availability of water. So many people living together would need a lot of it. 'We have a jhiri,' she said. 'It is a thin crack on the face of the mountain. It provides water all year round. This area has more than twenty such perennial water spots. In Abujhmad, especially, and in the whole of Bastar, water is not a big problem. The government, though, is busy installing hand pumps.' She sounded as if she disapproved.

'Is that not a good thing?' I asked, surprised.

'It is complicated. The other day, we caught a pump contractor collecting levies. He told us he gets Rs 1 lakh for installing each hand pump, and that though his expense is only Rs 15,000, he ends up paying bribes to the tune of Rs 75,000–80,000 for each pump. When we did not believe him, he showed us a list of names of the people he had paid off.' Cynicism was writ large on her face as she continued. 'That is the story of development. If these hand pumps are broken, no one comes to repair them and they become useless metal stumps. And anyway, people here do not want to drink water from hand pumps—they do not like the taste.'

I remembered a story I had heard from Dr B.D. Sharma,

the district collector of Bastar, in the late 1960s. He had got traditional huts built for tribal guests in the collector's compound so that his visitors could feel at home. 'But they would always complain about the water in Jagdalpur.'

As Radha opened up, I asked her why she had joined the Party. She was, after all, the first tribal girl to do so. 'There is not much to my story, really,' she laughed. I realized there was only so much she would talk to me about, and her past was not going to be part of it.

Looking up at the sky, she said, 'It is going to rain. I am in charge of the kitchen supplies and must protect them from the rain. Else, we will be stranded without a morsel to eat.'

'What will you do?' I asked her.

'Raise the food to a height so the rainwater cannot get to it. We cannot afford to waste anything.'

I noticed then that the kitchen supplies were indeed on the ground.

'How will you do that?'

'Watch us!' she said, calling out to the others. Almost immediately, a group of young men and women materialized around the 'store'. Sturdy stalks of bamboo had been chopped and stacked for just such a situation. Everyone knew what to do and got to work. Soon, a crude but strong platform had been rigged up; all the food was placed on it and covered with a plastic jhilli. As Radha had predicted, it did rain, but her stock of food was safe.

Radha is one of the doers of the world. She belongs here, gets work done, and has little to say. She did tell me how she met Kosa, though. He used to come to her village to conduct meetings. She belonged to a poor family that owned a single acre of land. There were two girls from Andhra in Kosa's team, who persuaded Radha to join the Party to fight injustice. And so she did.

I took shelter in the nearest tent, waiting for the rain to stop. Nirmala, the head of Kosa's eleven-member team of bodyguards—half of them are women—was there too. She is a thin and wiry woman in her early thirties.

'This life is very difficult, is it not?' I asked her.

'No,' she said vehemently. 'Life is difficult for girls even at home in the villages. We work all the time, grinding the paddy, taking the cows out to graze and doing all the odd jobs. And the men don't even allow us to marry someone of our own choice. They keep an eye on us when we go to the village fairs. Not a good situation to be in, don't you think?'

This was in sharp contrast to the books I read on Adivasi culture that said women were the ones wielding real power. I asked Nirmala how she had come to know about the Party.

'My sister was a member of the Party's cultural troupe, while two of my brothers worked for the Maoists from home. I attended some public meetings along with them and appreciated the role the Party was playing to resist the loot of Bastar and the cultural attack by Hindus.'

'What was the bigger draw? The admiration you had for Party politics or the repressive behaviour of the male elders in the village?'

'Both.'

Most of the women Maoists I have interviewed over the last decade cited similar reasons for joining the Party.

'Twenty people from my village, Dunga, are in the Party, and not one of them chose to become an SPO,' she said.

It was a significant detail, one that clearly indicated that the people of her village would rather trust the Party than the state.

The government has been recruiting tribal youth as SPOs, and the lure of a monthly salary and a firearm is hard to resist. The SPOs function as an extension of the security forces and work with the state police, the Central Reserve Police Force and deployed specialist forces like Naga soldiers.

To my mind, it is not an entirely desirable method. Handing firearms out to civilians who do not have the experience to make the kind of judgement that a law-enforcing arm of the government is expected to be capable of, has its consequences. No wonder that the Salwa Judum, along with the SPOs, has turned into a vigilante group, and is described in so many words in media reports and documents published by human rights groups.

The police department justifies the recruitment of SPOs saying that every Indian citizen has the right to protect himself or herself. But stories of SPOs stepping out of line and taking unauthorized action abound. Instances of journalists being harassed and personal scores being settled at gunpoint are a matter of public record.

Nirmala continued, 'We are five sisters. I am neither educated nor married. My younger sister, who has studied till class five, has also joined the Party full-time. Another passed class eight, and works as a peon in a school.'

'Haven't you ever wanted to go back home for good?' I asked her.

Nirmala considered the question for a moment. 'I don't think that is possible,' she said, finally. 'Here, I have a gun in my hands. If I go back, there will be no sentry to protect me. The police come to my village quite often and each time they do, the people run into the forest to save their lives. They cannot even go to the nearest market in Bhairamgarh— a four-hour walk away—for fear of getting caught by the Salwa Judum. They walk eighty kilometres to go to the market in Orchha instead.'

It started to rain again, which meant there was more work to be done. Nirmala excused herself, hurrying off to make sure that supplies, like oil, soap and toothpaste, of which she was in charge, were safely tucked under the waterproof tarpaulin.

Looking around her tent, I saw a book called *Padiora Itihaas*—'Our History', in Gondi—though the script was Devanagari.

A large chunk of the tribal population in Bastar speaks Gondi but in the sixty years since Independence, the state has produced few books in Gondi. The state-run All India Radio does not broadcast any news in Gondi. According to the census of 2001, there are twenty-seven lakh Gondi speakers in the country. The number of Sanskrit speakers, by contrast, is 14,000. Yet All India Radio broadcasts several Sanskrit news bulletins every day.

The book was meant for class three students, and had been published by the education wing of the Jantana Sarkar of Dandakaranya in 2007. It contained short biographies of tribal martyrs, like Gend Singh, Narayan Singh and Birsa Munda, followed by those of Bhagat Singh, Marx, Engels, Lenin, Stalin, Mao, Norman Bethune and Clara Zetkin.

It also had a list of tribal rebellions against the Marathas and the British. I counted three against the Marathas and six against the British, the last of them being the Bhumkal uprising of 1910 that Kosa had been talking about. The book said that the Santhal rebellion of 1854–56 culminated in the first war of Indian Independence in 1857, and that it had marked the start of the New Democratic Revolution in India.

I knew that the Naxals laid claim to Indian revolutionaries like Bhagat Singh as their predecessors and dated their revolution from the 1920s. But from these books, it was clear that in their minds, the revolution had started much further back in time. Clearly, history can be interpreted by its writers and the Maoists, too, would see the past the way they chose to.

A copy of *Dainik Bhaskar* dated 26 May—it had arrived five days late—was also lying around. It carried the news that Binayak Sen had been granted bail and that Nepalese Prime Minister Prachanda had resigned. Another report mentioned that more than a hundred students from Bhilai, Chhattisgarh's steel city, had made it to the Indian Institute of Technology, India's premier engineering college, that year.

Jawaharlal Nehru had called places like Bhilai the modern temples of India. These cities have given a lot to middle-class Indians like me—they have been veritable launching pads to prosperous lives. But how much have they given to tribals? I have yet to find a tribal from Chhattisgarh who has been admitted to any of the IITs in the undergraduate courses, though tribals have a 7 per cent reservation there.

Once, when I wanted to find out about the original residents of Bhilai, it proved to be a real struggle. The Bhilai Steel Plant does not even have a record of the ninety-five villages that were moved in the early fifties to make room for what is today the steel city of Bhilai.

Nirmala was back, and I pointed to a copy of a magazine called *Sangharshrat Mahila* or 'Struggling Woman'. Its lead article claimed that Adivasi girls take part in every stage of cultivation, from ploughing, making bunds (small dams) and harvesting to cleaning up storage spaces, but are not allowed to sow or carry the paddy home. They are also forbidden to enter the room where the paddy is stored.

'I was under the impression that Adivasi women enjoyed the same status as men do,' I said to her.

Nirmala's face darkened. 'Not at all,' she countered. 'One of my friends joined the Party because her parents were forcing her to marry someone she did not want to. Girls are struggling for equality. Even while hunting, everyone takes part in haanka—surrounding and trapping the animal—but the actual killing is done only by men.'

It is indeed a feminist war as well, I thought. Well, at least half of it.

We were interrupted by the trill of a bell: it was lunchtime. Kosa joined us. As we ate, he asked me if Fagni had told me how officers in the education department had harassed her sexually when she was studying in the government residential school. Fagni was the comrade who had escorted me to Kosa the previous day. She was standing across from us, and as I looked at her, recalling what she had said about joining the Party, she averted her eyes from mine.

I did not have the heart to tell Kosa that she had told me she left school because she realized that 'bourgeois education' would prevent her from understanding people's problems.

I did not even want to ask Fagni about her alleged sexual exploitation. She was training to be a doctor and would soon replace Anupama in Kosa's team of bodyguards. I thought I would rather talk to her about her training, though the chat would have to wait.

'Today we have indipudi curry, prepared in your honour,' Kosa informed me. 'Indipudi is an insect that nests in chhind trees.'

'I know chhind—I had those on the way,' I said knowledgably.

Kosa was watching me intently. 'It is a tribal delicacy. Indipudi is boiled, dried and stored to serve to guests or on special occasions.'

'It is new to me,' was all I could come up with.

'There is another insect that the tribals relish—it nests in bamboo groves. But it is disappearing now. So much is changing in our environment and we don't even know why. Look at Radha—she is eating kutki instead of rice because it is good for her diabetes. Earlier, eating kutki was a sign of backwardness and poverty. But now that research has proved its benefits, rich diabetics are switching to kutki. I fear that as the price of kutki goes up, tribals will sell it and buy cheap rice grown with the help of fertilizers. It will do them more harm than good.'

In an ominous tone, he added, 'This is your development. When a tribal wears a loincloth, he is considered backward. But most modern girls in your fashion shows on TV wear no more than a loincloth.'

I could not help but laugh at that one. He does sound like an old headmaster quite often. As we sat on the logs eating—a mixed group of men and women—I observed the way this group functions. A girl sat next to me and we ate together. This was unusual. Ordinarily, she would have been serving the food. That is the norm in most communities: the men dine first, and the women eat separately later.

She was a melancholy-looking Gond Adivasi called Champa. I began a casual conversation with her and learned that she too was training to be a doctor. Her father used to be a Maoist, and she lost him when she was very young. He was executed by the Party for a mistake that had cost it dear. 'I never tried to find out my father's story. I was staying in a hostel when he died, but soon after, I was arrested and sent to jail in Chandrapur for two years. After my release, I confided in my mother that I wanted to work for the Party. She felt that I was being irresponsible; I had two younger sisters to take care of. She told me that if I left, I should never return. But I went home last year and everyone, including my mother, was glad to see me. She understands what I do and why I do it. I am from the same area in Gadchiroli where sixteen policemen were killed last week.'

How could Champa bear to be with her father's executioners? Her face betrayed no emotion at all. Perhaps she had no choice.

Kosa could not remember why Champa's father had been killed. 'I will find out,' he said. 'But you should not look at it from your city perspective. This is not a feudal society where people try to protect only those dear to them. This is a tribal community. If an individual does something that harms the community, the family comes forward to have him or her punished. I know a woman from a neighbouring village, who

testified against her husband in a Jan Adalat (People's Court).
He was a police informer and she said she was sure that he
would never change. He was punished as he deserved. She
still comes to meet me. You should meet Gajendra, one of my
bodyguards—his uncle was killed by the Party.'

'How many informers have you killed?' I asked, expecting
to be diverted from the subject.

But Kosa thought for a moment and replied, 'We have
killed more than 200 informers after the Salwa Judum was
formed. We may have killed around 900 informers since the
start of the movement in Dandakaranya.'

Was that pause a sign of regret, I wondered. But he
went on, relentlessly driving his point home. 'There is no
other way. We have to kill informers if we want to keep the
movement alive. We do not have a jail where we can lodge
them and stop them from thwarting our efforts.'

The casualties on their own side have been far greater,
Kosa claimed. He said that more than 12,000 comrades and
supporters have martyred themselves since the movement
took off in 1967 in Naxalbari in Bengal. 'More than 2000
class enemies have been killed so far by the Party, 1200 after
the start of the Salwa Judum,' he said. Class enemies, for
Maoists, are policemen and informers. The figures he gave
me are difficult if not impossible to cross-check as there are
very few accurate police records, and numerous claims and
counterclaims on the killings.

Kosa spoke almost innocently of the killings perpetrated
by the Party. I was unable to decide on an appropriate
response to his words. Perhaps I should have been better
prepared, because I remember he had never been apologetic

about the killings. When we met in 2004, he had mentioned that they had killed two people to ensure the safety of the Bhumkal rally. He had looked me in the eye as he said it, and his face had been as stoic as it was now. While I wanted to appreciate his point of view, my inability to do so might have reflected on my face.

Kosa's bodyguard Gajendra, whose uncle had been killed by the Party, tried to explain. 'All of us tried to reason with my uncle and make him understand that what he was doing was wrong but he would not listen. His sons also work for the Party.'

I could only argue from my own context. 'How can any rally be more important than a human life?'

A strapping young man standing next to Gajendra with an AK-47 in his hands had been listening to the exchange. He spoke up. 'When I lost my parents within the same month to a brief illness, I realized that people do not die of disease. They die because of the politics that does not send doctors to rural areas. I understood this all the more clearly after having attended Party meetings.'

I could tell that he really wanted me to see his point of view, for he went on, 'My mother tongue is Gondi. It is much closer to Telugu than it is to Hindi. Yet schools in Chhattisgarh teach in Hindi. Don't you see that it is all political? That is what I want to change.'

Two more Party workers joined in. Both of them had studied in a nearby school under the Ramakrishna Mission. One of them, Suklal, said, 'They teach us well, but want to make us Hindus.' Lachhu piped up, 'At least in the Ramakrishna Mission schools, some education is being imparted. In government schools, teachers don't even turn up. Our Party has not killed a single teacher or health worker but that does not stop them from using the Party as an excuse for not showing up for work. Recently, I met a government schoolteacher who wanted to take some students to write the fifth-grade board exams. I told him he was free to do so if any of those children could read the numbers from 1 to 10, and, would you believe it, not a single child could. The teacher remarked that it was impossible to teach tribals. "What were you doing all these years? Why did you accept your salary, then?" I asked him. I think teachers get some money when children pass the fifth grade, so they take these students to the exam hall and help them pass by cheating.'

I needed to think about the allegations I had just heard. I asked for some of their Party literature so that I could sit by myself and read for a while. I had already read some of the books and pamphlets that they keep sending me—books with bright red titles on their white covers. They read like propaganda material: never subtle, rarely artistic, mostly literature I found difficult to relate to. But in that moment, I could not help but feel one with the 'oppressed'. These people are not just mouthing a philosophy; they believe in it because of the way their lives are. Young people are risking their lives for the very people who killed their loved ones. The dream of equality, of an existence where everyone eats the same food together, of participation in decision-making, of having some semblance of control over their own lives— this is what drives them. And they are making it work in the limited area they control. It is hard to deny that.

Down the years, they have been handed out judgements

by gram panchayats where only a powerful few take decisions. No one has ever asked them what they want. Bureaucrats in cities have created schemes that are not relevant to their reality, and the implementers have siphoned off most of the funds. They have seen the Jantana Sarkar cut the rich and influential down to size. Through the influence of the Party, and on the strength of their guns, they have been able to wield power in a way they never imagined possible.

I spent the afternoon reading booklet No. 1/09. It is for Party members' eyes only, but no one seemed to mind my reading it. It explained the rectification campaign that had started on 23 March, the day commemorating Bhagat Singh's martyrdom, and would continue for the whole year. It acknowledged some faults and failures. Here's what it said:

Some members have developed a tendency to over-spend, and we must be careful about growing bureaucratic, paternalistic, anarchist, dogmatic and anti-people attitudes in the Party. The enemy had been preparing for the start of the Salwa Judum for more than a year, but we could not anticipate it. That was a major mistake. We failed to study the changing situation. Today's Dandakaranya is different; it is more literate; people have more links with market forces and the market has more influence on their lives. The land situation has also changed, but our thought process has not. In some places, punishments have been cruel and despicable. No revolutionary should even think of such methods. It is for these reasons that we have an attrition rate of 35–40 per cent amongst our comrades. This is a very serious situation and must be checked.

I remembered Kranti, who had been my bodyguard the last time I came to meet Kosa. I am told he married a didi (that is how the comrades address a female Party worker), who was keen to go back to a regular life. Both left the Party and set up their home in the village, where Kranti took up farming. It was clear from the booklet that he was among the 35–40 per cent who leave.

Along with the booklet was a leaflet dated 28 April 2009. In it, the Party apologized for the killing of five people deployed at polling booths in Kamkasur village of Rajnandgaon during the election. They had been mistaken for policemen. It also said that the Party took responsibility for the killing of Chhannu Karma, brother of Mahendra Karma, in April 2009.

That day, I observed Kosa from a distance. He spoke at the group meeting all day on the subject of health. I asked Radha if he usually talked this much.

'Oh, he used to talk much more earlier. People did not understand what he was saying because our philosophy was alien to them, and they needed to be told the same thing again and again. When we first came here, people used to call us Kosku, which means government servant. At that time, our Party was not strong, so we had to return to the jungle after every meeting. It has been hard work for us these last few years; a lot of talking, and a lot of walking. Now, there are many people who have formed long associations with the Party.' She pointed to a young girl. 'She is Fulo, a second-generation revolutionary. Her uncle, Unga, was the first recruit in the party in Abujhmad. He is a commander in the Indravati region now. You will always find her cheerful.' She pointed to another girl. 'Indira there, is the daughter of the head of the Jantana Sarkar in Takilod, Suraj's village. He spends most of his time in the Party while her mother spends most of her time in bed owing to her fragile health. So her grandparents wanted to marry her off. When Kosa visited that area, he realized that she was being pressurized into marriage, and suggested to her father that she be sent to us instead. She has never gone back.'

'Do you ever think of going back home?' I asked Radha.

'No, no!' she laughed. 'Now I have reached the age of going to God's home, why should I think of going back home?'

'How many times have you faced the police?'

'In 1994, we were attacked four times, thrice in the same month. That was when Maharashtra started a special operation with a Commando 60 force, like the recent Special Police Operations with the Salwa Judum here.' Radha sounded nostalgic, like someone recounting a difficulty overcome in youth. She and Kosa have been living in a safe den in Abujhmad for fifteen years, taking in their stride the ups and downs in the fortunes of the Party. But 1994 was a difficult year that saw the Party deplete in strength as one comrade after another fell to police bullets.

Kosa, who had joined us in the meantime, interjected to explain how methodically they had handled the situation. 'We did our own survey and found that the police took around four hours to reach us after they got our location from an informer. So we restricted our stay at any village to three hours. Then we killed a few informers, while the rest of them moved to the safety of police stations, and the attacks were over.'

So this was management, Maoist style, I thought.

I wanted to know what the situation was like in Gadchiroli district, and how it compared with Bastar. Though Gadchiroli is in Maharashtra, it is a stronghold of the Party in what it calls the Dandakaranya 'state' and is under Kosa's administration.

Kosa explained. 'In Bastar, the king was neutralized by the state. Tribal chieftains, like Mahendra Karma's father, were running the show with the help of the corrupt administration and the business community, which consisted entirely of outsiders. We were a threat to this nexus because we were organizing under our wing, the very people whom they were oppressing. It was tough to find shelter in the forests of Bastar at that time because the guards were mostly outsiders and did not cooperate with us at all.

'The maharaja of Gadchiroli, by contrast, was progressive. He was against the Congress and led an agitation for a separate state, Vidarbha. He even donned a black cap as a sign of protest. His stand helped us, and initially, we were able to make good headway in the area. The forest guards were local Adivasis, and once they understood our politics, they were very cooperative. In fact, the forest guards' association in Gadchiroli used to buy more than a hundred copies of the Party magazine. Some time in 1988, a policeman tried to molest a forest guard's wife. The guards immediately took out a procession and shouted slogans threatening to become Naxals. But later on, when the maharaja grasped our philosophy he turned against us and the scales were no longer tipped in our favour.'

As I began to form a picture in my mind of the Party's initial days in Dandakaranya, I told Kosa that I would like to discuss its history in detail. Kosa responded enthusiastically. 'No one has compiled such a history, even within the Party. As you have seen, there is no single comprehensive source of information on the subject. What you have suggested is a great idea, and I would like to involve other Party workers, who can add their bits. But it will take time,' he warned.

I assured him that I would stay for as long as it took, and that I was willing to travel to other locations if required.

The more Kosa thought about the idea, the more he warmed to it. Dandakaranya, after all, had been his home from the time it first appeared on the Party map. 'See, I was part of the original team sent by Kondapalli Sitaramaiyyah. Seven batches of seven people each were sent off to Dandakaranya in 1980 to develop it as a back-up area which could be used when the Party faced rough weather at the headquarters, then located in Andhra Pradesh. Of those forty-nine men, I am the only one left on the ground. Some have died, some are in jail, and many have surrendered. But let me think about it tonight. We will talk tomorrow,' he promised.

I could not think of anyone better suited than Kosa to reminiscing about three decades of the Maoist movement in these forests. He has been witness to so much of the Party's history.

5

THE FIRST YEAR

I walked over to the bamboo clump where I had seen a class being held the previous day. Today, though, I was the only student, and Kosa my teacher.

'My grandfather was an illiterate farmer,' Kosa began. 'My father became a teacher. I wanted to be a farmer like my grandfather, but my father insisted that I go to college. I took a year off and worked with my grandfather in the fields in the hope that my father would be convinced, but he was adamant. He wanted me to join the Industrial Training Institute (ITI) at Peddapalli in Karimnagar district, Andhra Pradesh. It is the same place your former prime minister, P.V. Narasimha Rao, hailed from. The Raos were a prominent land-owning family; the Party redistributed much of their land amongst the people.'

Interrupting him, I voiced a question I have often pondered: Why is the beginning of left wing extremism in India considered to be Naxalbari and not Telangana? 'The Telangana communist rebellion started in the same area before Independence, didn't it?'

Kosa explained that it was Naxalbari that gave the communists a clear line and policy. Before Naxalbari, land had been the main issue, but the land-based movements were not coherent. There were random efforts and each attempt had its impact, but there was neither vision nor direction. Land reforms were announced after both the Telangana and the Naxalbari uprisings, but the landless got less than 10 per cent of what they were entitled to by law. Only a third of the land snatched from landlords in Andhra in movements following Naxalbari could be retained by the new allottees, and much of it is still lying vacant.

'I was drawn to this land-based struggle and joined the students' wing of the Party in the ITI,' Kosa said, returning to his own story. 'There, I heard a lot about Ramji, whom you have met. As a young boy, I thought of the Naxals as supermen. I was very disappointed to see Ramji when he was released from jail after the Emergency,' Kosa laughed. 'As you know, he is a thin, puny man. I had a larger-than-life picture of him in my mind. But Ramji became my guru.'

'Why did he choose the very religious name of Ramji?' I could not help asking. 'Was it not a use—misuse, rather—of religion, although you proclaim yourselves to be against it? And now he goes by the name Kishenji!'

'Ramji's name has nothing to do with the mythological character of Ram,' Kosa clarified. 'He named himself after Ramji Gond, the tribal rebel from Adilabad who fought the British in the 1920s. It was Party tradition to assume such names. One of our Central Committee members assumed the name of Jampanna, after the chief of the tribal army that rebelled against the Kakatiya kings in

Warangal in the fifteenth century. Ramji's real name is M. Koteshwar Rao.'

After the Naxalite debacle, and the death of Charu Mazumdar, the architect of the Naxalbari uprising, in 1972, the first serious effort to get all factions of communists together was made at a meeting in Nagpur in 1976. A decision was taken to concentrate on the districts of Adilabad and Karimnagar in Andhra Pradesh. These were the poorest districts of the state and had enough forest cover for the Party workers to camp in.

'The Party sent Tushar Kanti Bhattacharya, a Bengali from Hyderabad, to form the first squad in the Mahadevpuram area of Karimnagar. That is where the borders of Andhra Pradesh, Maharashtra and Madhya Pradesh meet. The year was 1977. Tushar was established as a Registered Medical Practitioner (RMP) in Mahadevpuram. Under that ruse, he built the first armed squad for the Party, which was arrested in 1978 even though its members did not have enough weapons to justify being called an 'armed squad' or dalam. Tushar used to visit me in my hostel room at ITI. But it was only after his arrest that I found out he was a dalam commander.' Just like Vasu used to visit me, I thought to myself.

'In 1977, the Party started a "Go to the Village" campaign, and college students in Telangana joined the anti-landlord struggle in hordes. Within a year, the movement gained strength in Karimnagar. Even though it was an overground non-violent struggle, the pracharaks or Party organizers were provided with bombs.

'My room-mate, Kumarswami, was the first accidental martyr of the Party which had just been formed. He died in an accident while working on a bomb. He was a great friend . . . I still miss him.'

In 1979, Kosa joined the Party formally as a part-time member. At the time, he was working as an apprentice in the Birla cement factory near Peddapalli, and had become a member of the trade union. A year later, he was arrested for the murder of Hasnuddin, the head of the trade union in the factory. 'That was the first and last time I went to jail,' he recalled with satisfaction. 'But after my arrest, my family came to know about my political commitments.'

After his release from jail, Kosa gave up his job and joined the Party full-time. Ramji's younger brother, Sonu, was also in the Party as a pracharak. 'I have already sent Sonu a message. I want you to meet him,' Kosa said.

He grew nostalgic as the memories streamed back. 'Those were heady days. In January 1980, in Kokalagudur village, eight kilometres from the Birla factory, we conducted a Jan Adalat—a people's trial. The landlord was found guilty and roughed up. In retaliation, a police case was slapped against me and I went underground.

'In May, that same year, we killed Hasnuddin. He was a regular worker just like us, but when he became the head of the trade union, he started working for the company as a broker and formed an alliance with the Congress. We attacked him in his house. That was the first time the police landed up at my door.'

Carrying out cold-blooded executions seems to be an intrinsic part of Kosa's persona. I was not convinced that it was the only way his objectives could have been achieved. However, I discreetly refrained from voicing that sentiment.

Unaware of the turn my thoughts had taken, Kosa continued. 'By 1979, the Party had prepared a document called the Guerrilla Zone Perspective. It spoke of developing "rear areas" for the Party—places to which the cadre could retreat in emergencies. These could also be developed as guerrilla zones in the future. The idea was Sitaramaiyyah's and he chose Dandakaranya for the purpose. It was a 1,00,000 square kilometre sprawl of trees, hills and treacherous paths, and spanned across Madhya Pradesh (now Chhattisgarh as well), Maharashtra, Andhra Pradesh and Orissa.

'One day, sometime in 1980, Ramji told me that seven teams were to be sent to develop Dandakaranya as planned. He asked me if I would like to join one. I had no idea where Dandakaranya was, but agreed to go anyway. At that time, the Party was known as the Communist Party of India (Marxist-Leninist) Kranti after a magazine that it used to publish. But soon, KS gave it a new name—the People's War—and got elected as its first secretary. I don't know how we came to be known as People's War Group—the word "group" was never part of the name. The media always calls us PWG.

'All of us bound for Dandakaranya got a fifteen-day training session with KS. That is where I first met Gopanna. Both of us shared the same name—Satyanarayana Reddy. Amongst those forty-nine comrades dispatched to Dandakaranya in 1980, I am the only one still in action.' (Kosa may not be the only one any more, though. Sayanna, or Malla Raj Reddy, who had led Kosa's team, was released from jail some months after this interview and immediately 'disappeared'. He must be back in action.)

'Gopanna was the last one to be arrested.' Kosa looked at me. 'You have met him, haven't you?'

'Yes, he was in charge of north Bastar then.'

Kosa continued, 'Fifteen days before we were supposed to leave for Dandakaranya, I went home. My mother shed some tears, but my father and brother did not oppose my plan. By then, my brother had become a teacher. Back in the field, Sayanna was appointed our team leader, while Veeranna, Ramanna and Sudhakar became my teammates. Each team needed a courier to carry reports to and from the Party, and Chandranna was picked for the job. He had company—Kumaranna, Sayanna's nephew. Kumaranna was stuck in an unhappy marriage and wanted to get out of it. He pleaded to be taken along and so, he too was appointed a courier. It made ours the only team with two couriers, but it was useful to have him with us: he belonged to the area through which we were to walk into Dandakaranya, and had relatives in those villages.'

I thought I had a good understanding of the revolutionary. I have met some who wanted to bring about a revolution, others who wanted to avenge police repression, and still others who wanted to teach landlords a lesson. I have seen many girls who joined the Party because their parents wanted to marry them off against their wishes. And so, this story of marital unhappiness pushing a man into joining the revolution was just another example, albeit surprising, I must admit. More often than not, though, politics becomes a part of the revolutionary's life only after maturity of experience and insight.

Kosa was back to his story. 'I don't remember the exact

date when we set off. But it was the day we had the first rain of the season, so it must have been late June or July. All seven of us were supposed to assemble at Sastulapalli, Sayanna's village. We changed into dhotis and shirts, and Sayanna's wife, Nirmala, gave us food in a plastic packet to stave off hunger for at least some part of the journey. She too joined the Party later, as our first woman comrade. She was martyred in Bastar in 1997. But that day, when she saw us off, Nirmala was just a worried wife with a fuzzy understanding of her husband's mission. It was late afternoon when we started walking. That was thirty years ago,' Kosa laughed, 'and I am still walking.'

That walk has changed thousands of lives in Dandakaranya for many years to come. Whether it has been for the better— or not—only time will tell. With that thought in my head, we broke for tea.

Rejuvenated by the strong tea, Kosa picked up the thread of his narrative. 'We set off with just one double-barrel gun, two pistols and ten bullets. Each of us had plastic sheets, an extra dhoti, a bedsheet, some utensils, medicines, a few books, and some money, may be Rs 2000–3000. We were from poor or middle-class farmer families. I was the most educated one in the team. Sayanna had studied till class twelve, Sudhakar and Veeranna till class ten, and Ramanna till class eight. Kumaranna had never been to school.'

My understanding, however, was that there were quite a few highly educated people in the Party at that time, and Kosa confirmed this. There were many students from the Regional Engineering College (REC) at Warangal in the cadre. An REC graduate, Shivaji, headed Gopanna's team, which went to Bastar. He later joined the police and now works for the intelligence branch in Hyderabad.

'The complete plan for Dandakaranya was not known to anyone except the top brass: ensuring safety was paramount. What nobody knew could not be revealed even if some comrades were arrested. All we knew was that three teams had started from Warangal, two from Karimnagar and two from Adilabad.

'Ramji had given me a map and explained the route we would have to take. On the first night, we stopped at a village from where we would have to cross the Maneru, a tributary of the Godavari. But it had been raining incessantly and the river was so swollen that we could not cross it for the next five days.

'Sayanna, who had led the anti-landlord struggle in the area, knew the terrain well. The villagers respected him and allowed us to stay there while we waited for the rain to abate. It did not, and Sayanna decided to try another route. We had to walk to the bridge and cross over, but lost our way and spent the night in the forest. The next day, we walked for nearly five hours before we found a village. There, we bought rice and lentils and cooked for ourselves. We were already a week behind schedule, and walking would not get us far. So Sayanna decided to take a bus from there, a prudent move, since the village was only minutes from the main road. But once we boarded it, most of the people on it, including the driver and the conductor, recognized Sayanna. Our gun was a dead giveaway.

'We got off the bus just before we reached the town, and resumed walking. After a couple of days on foot, we crossed the Godavari at Chandur, Bhadrakali, by boat—my first boat ride! Once we reached Bhopalpatnam in Madhya Pradesh (now Chhattisgarh), we were back on our original route.

'Our first task in Bhopalpatnam was to survey the area. We chose Reggudem as our first political destination in Dandakaranya because the people there had been very cooperative with communists from 1945–51, during the Telangana movement. Wary thereafter, the administration had built a police station near the village at Bhadrakali in the 1950s. We steered clear of the police station as we crossed the river.

'Speaking to the villagers at Reggudem, we learned that a group of five or six people from Andhra had left from there that very morning. They sounded like our people. After the meeting, we walked to a nullah just outside the village, looking for water to cook our food. The team we had just heard about was there too. They were at a height and their sentry spotted us first. They mistook us for forest department personnel and trained their guns on reflex. We did the same. They were about to fire, when Gopanna—who had trained with me in KS's camp—recognized me. What a blunder it would have been had we fired on each other!'

Sir Wilfrid Grigson, in his book *The Maria Gonds of Bastar*, writes that a British captain called Blunt tried in 1795 to enter Bastar across the Indravati, and through the Bhopalpatnam zamindari area. Some miles upstream from the confluence of the Indravati and the Godavari, Blunt was fiercely attacked by the Bastar Gonds, and though their bows, arrows and axes were no match for his firearms, he abandoned his plan to enter Bastar. He later learned from the Maratha chief of Deolmari that he had retreated just in time: word had spread from zamindar to zamindar and they were planning to combine forces to plunder his party.

The British had approached Bastar from the very spot that the Naxals did. The Gonds had been vigilant when the British came, but slackening when the Naxals arrived was to cost them dear. Reading Grigson's passage, I wondered if the Gonds might have been the first Indian freedom fighters against the British.

Kosa's anecdote about the averted shootout reminded me of a similar experience. Featuring in life-threatening accidents seems to be standard practice for Gopanna. When I had gone to meet him last, Gopanna had sent a jeep to pick us up from the appointed place. I was sitting next to the driver, while two colleagues from the BBC were in the back seat. We had been driving for hours through the forest at night, and I had dozed off. Suddenly, the driver slammed on the brakes and the jolt shook me awake. In the headlights, I saw people moving into position with guns—and we were the targets! Before we could react, there was a frantic blowing of whistles: the gunmen lowered their weapons and assembled on one side.

Gopanna, with his many commitments, had forgotten to inform the comrades about our arrival. When the sentries saw the headlights of our jeep, they thought we were the police. By sheer luck someone remembered we were expected and blew the whistle in the nick of time. Kosa found the story amusing and, having survived the event, I was able to appreciate his sense of humour.

Kosa went on, 'There, at the nullah, Gopanna told us that they had just been to Bhopalpatnam, and that the police knew about our arrival. That location, therefore, was best avoided. They would proceed deeper into the forest and make their way to Tarlaguda in Bijapur.

'Sayanna did not heed Gopanna's advice. Although the risk of getting caught was high, he had not been able to send any news to our leaders for the past two weeks as we had taken an obscure route all along. Now, he planned that the couriers should catch a bus from Bhopalpatnam back to our base.

'The next day, we got off about five kilometres short, at Chintawagu nullah. Three of us stopped there, while Chandranna, Kumaranna, Sudhakar and Ramanna walked to a tea stall for a quick round of chai before catching the bus.

'Bhopalpatnam was a very small place, though not really a village. Our dhotis were meant to help us blend into the rural milieu, but instead, they drew unwanted attention. The chai-wallah overheard the boys talking amongst themselves, and gathered that despite their dhotis, they were hardly the country bumpkins they appeared to be. He grew suspicious and informed the police, who arrived immediately and arrested them. Ramanna managed to flee and came to us. The rest were taken to Jagdalpur and thrown into jail.'

In the course of my research, I had found news reports stating that three Naxals had been arrested on 30 August 1980, while one had managed to escape. Though the place of arrest mentioned in the paper was Tarlaguda and not Bhopalpatnam, I concluded that this was Kosa's team. There was mention of another group of five Naxalites seen in a village called Pujari Kanker near Bhopalpatnam; they had evaded the police. That must have been Gopanna's team, I thought.

Kosa continued, 'This was the first arrest for the Party in Dandakaranya and a big setback for our team, which had hardly got going. It was important to give the news to the leadership in Andhra. In those days, phones were not as ubiquitous as they are now. Besides, the Party sympathizers were poor people, and did not have phones at home. We could not use post office phones either. There was no option but to go personally, and Sayanna decided to be a courier himself. He asked me to lead the team and travel in the area while he was away.

'Bhopalpatnam would not be safe, so Sayanna decided to take a circuitous route. He would go to Sironcha in Maharashtra. From there, he would go to Chandrapur, Ramagundem, and then to Karimnagar. I was told to explore the region and return to Karimnagar after fifteen days. But Ramanna feared for his life and said he wanted to go home. He was missing his mother. So Sayanna took Ramanna along and I was left with Veeranna.'

I could not help laughing at the picture of the revolutionary that Kosa drew this time.

'We have all types of people. Sometimes they miss their family and need to go back,' said Kosa. 'And, like I said earlier, revolutionaries are not supermen.'

As Kosa and Veeranna surveyed the area, they would meet people, talk to them and try and understand their problems. 'Gradually, people began to understand that we meant well. News of our presence must have travelled by word of mouth, because even villagers working in the fields would inform us of police movement.

'Once, we were talking to villagers in Reggudem, when

some policemen spotted us. We did not know that they were the police till they shouted out to us in Hindi, asking who we were. Immediately, we ran towards the forest—the densest I have ever seen. They followed us, but as we ran deeper and deeper into the forest, we realized that they had stopped chasing us. The chase must have drained them or maybe they thought they had lost us. We spent the night under a tree, and decided to hide the double-barrel gun in the forest—it was no longer safe to carry it around. I kept a pistol with me; Sayanna had taken the second one.

'The next day, we went back to Reggudem village, and a villager, who was also called Chandranna, gave us food and helped us cross the Indravati to enter Maharashtra. Chandranna later became a Party member and we are still in touch. We spent the next night in the forest. Asreli was the first village on the Maharashtra side, but the residents told us that buses would not ply from there because of the rains. They suggested that we go to Ankisa instead, where we could get a bus.'

I was surprised by the level of detail in Kosa's narrative. I don't think I can remember the names of all the places I have visited as a journalist. But then, my life has never been at stake as often or as intensely as Kosa's has been. All the places where I faced grave danger, I too remember vividly.

'Wiser after the Bhopalpatnam fiasco, in Maharashtra, we decided to split up and go to two different tea stalls. It turned out to be a sensible precaution—all that people were talking about over their thick, sweet tea, was the arrest of Naxalites in Bhopalpatnam. They were also speaking of more batches of Naxals coming in. In Maharashtra, young people did not wear dhotis, and there I was in one. Naturally, people noticed me and started asking questions. But this time, I was prepared. Sayanna had told me the names of his relatives who lived in the bordering villages of Andhra.

'Villagers may look simple, but they are far from gullible. When I told them the name of a family member, they wanted to know the name of his father. I almost got caught! But I had not been garrulous, and had not stated the exact nature of the relationship. So, I could get away with saying that those people were relatives of a friend. But I learned to talk carefully, and speak as little as possible.

'The survey was no cakewalk. We were often misled by people who did not have information but would try and help anyway. This usually meant walking much more than was necessary. But that was to be expected—without maps or phones, especially in villages, one could not hope for more. We finally met Sayanna after two weeks.

'Our team grew as new members joined us, and soon we were seven again. In Maharashtra, we found that the police had already cautioned people that some dacoits from Andhra were in the area, posing a danger to property and womenfolk. People were warned not to give food to strangers. Even shopkeepers were instructed not to sell their wares to unknown people. The rumours were so strong that people would run from us, literally. But we had our task clearly cut out and persisted in our effort to approach people individually and tell them about our politics.

'By then, we were spending the nights only in the forest, in line with Party directives. We were ordered to get to know the forest well enough to be able to move around there at night. During the day, we were to go to the villages in civilian clothing and explain our politics to the people. The circular said that once people had enough confidence in us, we should start a movement centring on any one of their problems.

'We landed in trouble off and on. One day, we sent a new member, Suranna, to Moibinpeta to buy food. The rest of us were in the forest. When the villagers asked him who he was, he said he was a trader. But people disbelieved him, called him a thief and chased him. The police too gave chase. Suranna fled and came running straight to our makeshift kitchen. We had no choice but to drop everything and run into the hills to save our lives.

'Another team from Adilabad was also in the same region. Some of its members went to Moibinpeta to buy food, and roused suspicion. This time, the police opened fire and Peddi Shankar, one of the members of that squad, was killed. He was the first martyr from the Party in Dandakaranya. We heard about it on the radio when we tuned in to the Telugu news that evening, but could not make out which village it was in as we knew Moibinpeta simply as Peta.

'The next day, Suranna and another comrade went to a nearby village called Amraju to buy rice. There was an influential landlord there called Rajpantalu. He became suspicious of Suranna and caught him. But when Suranna threatened him with his pistol, he let him go.

'After that incident, no one would give us food. The shopkeepers feared police retaliation if they indulged us. We had to go hungry for four or five days, and then, we decided to move to Mahadevpuram in Andhra Pradesh. But that was a long way off.

'I decided to give it one last shot and walked to a village called Somanpalli. I went from door to door till I reached the last house—I still remember the owner's face. He gave me rice and fish and went to the market to buy food for us. When I came back late at night with rice, the others could finally eat after having gone without food for days. His daughter is a full-time worker in the Party now. She is a member of the combat team that passed through here yesterday.

'Thereafter, we decided to work only in the border villages—a decision that made it easier to protect ourselves from the state police. Just by crossing the border we could shake off the team that was after us.' The strategy is still being used by the Party.

'In 1981, the Party organized its first military camp in Mahadevpuram, where all the squads assembled. It was a ten-day camp with only thirty-five of us attending from five dalams. In our second camp in Bastar, a former army officer trained us. One comrade each from the Maoist Communist Centre (MCC), the CPI (ML) Party Unity in Bihar and our Tamil Nadu committee, also participated in that training session. Gangaram, a comrade from the Adilabad dalam, died while making a bomb during that camp. He too was a graduate of REC Warangal. He had been active in the Party since 1977 and had done a lot to organize the Singereni coal miners.

'In April 1981, we decided to start our first struggle for tendu leaf rates. In Andhra, the tendu movement had started in 1975–76. The Pulla Reddy group (one of the many Naxal groups) took the lead in these struggles, which the CPI and the CPM followed up. We had seen the rate in Andhra double. But traders used to pay a ridiculously low rate for collecting tendu leaves in other areas. We formed committees in many villages in Dandakaranya, demanding that the rate paid for tendu leaves be doubled. The headmen did not mind our movement because it did not hurt them the way land issues had done in Andhra. And it gave us breathing space.'

A clever move that did not annoy the local aristocracy, I thought.

'The contractors were all from Andhra. Traditionally, they would come with a coconut, agarbatti (incense sticks) and a token amount of Re 1, give it to the headman and start collecting tendu leaves. But this changed in 1981, thanks to our efforts. This time, the headmen demanded that the rate be fixed before work started. We organized rallies on the issue, and the contractors agreed to hike the rates. The new rate for 1981 was fixed at Re 1 for eight hundred leaves, which would be packed into sixteen bundles of fifty leaves each (seven paise per bundle instead of five). This was our first victory. Word spread like wildfire that the dadas were not thieves; they were there to help. The first year was the most difficult, so we used the tendu victory to extend our area of operation.

'In 1982, I was made commander of the dalam.'

6

FROM 1981 TO 2005

I realized quite early in my exchange with Kosa that it was important to speak to as many people as possible, because of the way information is shared in the Party. Driven by their need for secrecy and the limitations of the means of communication available in their kind of terrain and work, no one knows everything. Kosa had agreed to let me talk to people attending a significant meeting in south Bastar. This meant travelling long distances, which I was happy to do.

I had been in the jungle for a while now, meeting people at different locations. I had begun to feel feverish and wondered whether the preventive malaria pills were doing their job. The meeting had been going on for two days. I was impatient to talk to the members, but they had their own priorities. Kosa had also invited Sonu, who had been documenting the history of the movement as fiction. I knew the meeting would give me a chance to meet some of the best brains in the Party—leaders who had worked in different parts of Dandakaranya, taking care of various functions of the Party.

That evening, Kosa gave me a tablet for malaria, to be taken with 'special food'—freshly fried puffed rice—while the others ate leftover rice. One man came to me, patted me solicitously on the back, and said, 'So you too are suffering from men's menstruation?' I was taken aback. He looked old enough to be one of the senior members, and this was rather tasteless as jokes go. 'What do you mean?'

'Malaria is called men's menstruation in our Party. All of us get malaria here every twenty-five days. Boys keep count of the days and if one of them has not contracted malaria in three weeks, everyone gets anxious. It is not considered natural!' When he had stopped laughing, he continued. 'Jokes apart, malaria is a big problem here. It means each of us loses three or four days every month. The women are dealing with other consequences; some have reported two menstruations, and we think it is because of the malaria pills. We have lost three Central Committee members to malaria so far, so be careful and take rest. I hope the comrades are taking good care of you.'

I was wondering how seriously to take this man, who seemed to have interesting stories to tell, when he introduced himself as Comrade Sonu.

'Were you not called Bhupathy when you headed the Dandakaranya "state" for the Party earlier?' I asked him, feeling a sudden rush of energy.

He nodded. 'Yes, I am the Central Committee representative for Dandakaranya now. I have also been deputed to talk to you about the history of the Party in

Dandakaranya. But for now, please take rest. I will come back to you once our meeting is over.'

Sonu walked off to the meeting—a huddle of people under a mango tree, talking, talking, talking. The comrades talk a lot, was my last thought as I dozed off.

As promised, Sonu returned and invited me to join him where he was staying with his bodyguards. 'Would you like some coffee?'

Coffee would be very welcome, I told him. It would be my first cup in weeks.

One of his bodyguards, a young, tall, non-tribal girl from Garhwa in Jharkhand, prepared 'special coffee' for us. So, besides the ailing, leaders too could get special treatment, like an occasional coffee, I mused, not very charitably.

'You should keep drinking as much fluid as you can when you are down with malaria,' Sonu cautioned.

I thought he looked like Charu Mazumdar and told him so. He had heard that often. 'Charu Mazumdar, who started the Naxalite movement, believed that the annihilation of the class enemy would generate an atmosphere for revolution and preclude the need for mass organizations. But under the leadership of Kondapalli Sitaramaiyyah, the Party focused on building supportive mass organizations with peasants and students. I started working as an organizer there in the struggle against zamindars, like P.V. Narasimha Rao,' Sonu said. 'But the most significant decision KS took was to develop Dandakaranya as a base area.

'Dandakaranya is huge. The undivided Bastar district alone was larger than the state of Kerala. The railway line connecting Delhi to Hyderabad borders Dandakaranya on the west, while the sea, near Visakhapatnam, flanks it on the east. The railway line connecting Kolkata and Mumbai near Rajnandgaon in Chhattisgarh marks out its border in the north.'

'So, would you say that Dandakaranya is the heart of India?'

Sonu was pleased with the metaphor. 'You could say that,' he replied, thoughtfully. 'The forest here is very important to the nation. It produces oxygen of more than one kind: the political experiment in Dandakaranya could well be a life source. But I want you to understand that our goal in coming here was not to dominate territory like the LTTE. We are fighting a guerrilla war and sometimes need to retreat to the rear areas when the going gets tough.

'When we entered from Andhra, we forged initial ties with the Telugu-speaking Dorla tribe. They used to be in the majority until the 1940s, when their population dwindled after an epidemic. At that time, several Gondi-speaking tribes from the north of Bastar had shifted south. The Koyas were one of those tribes. They now form 60 per cent of the population of south Bastar. We learned Gondi very quickly, as they formed a significant part of the population when we entered Dandakaranya.'

'These Koya tribals from the north are your main contacts now, aren't they? Haven't many Dorlas joined the Salwa Judum? Is that not the strategy of the system—to divide the residents along tribal lines? It seems to have worked well in favour of the Salwa Judum and the government,' I said.

'The state did try to exploit the difference and create a Rwanda-like situation during the time of the Salwa Judum. But fortunately, it failed. It is true that more than 80 per cent of our supporters today are Koyas, but it would be wrong to say that the Party does not have supporters amongst the Dorlas.

'You must understand that all tribals, whether they are Koyas or Dorlas, see government employees and people living in cities as outsiders and exploiters. Even we used to be called "paikas" (outsiders) at first, and the tribals would run away on seeing a dalam. Nonetheless, all village headmen gave us food—that was the Bastar tradition. It is not as though outsiders have not found acceptance in earlier times. You know how the tribals revered the king although he was from Warangal because they realized that he was less oppressive than the Marathas and the British. I think the people chose us because we worked on issues that were important to their lives.'

'Are you now developing an association with the new king, Kamal, because the tribals accept him? Is having him on your side a strategy?'

'Let us say we want to form a united front with anyone who stands by the people,' was Sonu's diplomatic response. 'We picked tendu rates as the first concern of the people, but you have spoken to Kosa about that.'

At this point we were joined by a small, dark man who was visibly partial to bright colours. His printed cotton shirt and pyjamas stood out in the earthy colours of the surroundings. His AK-47 looked old, his ammunition pouch ancient. They were worn out from overuse. Sonu introduced us. 'Ramanna is the right person to speak to for our second area of concern—the atrocities of the forest department. He is the head of south Bastar for the Party.'

I know that this deceptively ordinary-looking man has wreaked havoc. He has led almost all the major attacks by the Maoists.

Sonu returned to the story, 'In the 1980s, there were very few revenue villages—villages governed by the civil administration—in south Bastar. Most settlements in these forests were villages that people from the north had occupied after cutting down trees. The forest guards used to harass these settlers when they tried to go into the forest to procure what they needed for their daily use. The guards were mostly non-tribals or tribals from north Bastar. They would demand bribes, and if they were not paid, they would file Primary Objection Reports (PORs) on flimsy excuses. Then the accused would have to run from pillar to post in cities, and the police and the lawyers would exploit them. Many tribals were even put behind bars.

'And these roads that you see were built only to transport timber from here to the factories. No vehicles plied on these roads to ferry people. All the roads in this region have been built by the forest department using begar or free labour. This system was started by the British and continued till the 1990s. Later, they started paying the labourers, though it was only a meagre amount. I recalled reading the diary of Bastar's first Indian collector, R.C.V.P. Noronha, where he had mentioned that begar labour was prevalent in the 1950s, but I did not realize it had continued into the 1990s. The tribals were cheated more often than not. And they got no help from the CPI, though Mahendra Karma had become an MLA from that Party by that time.'

'I have a list of tribals who were incarcerated for anything between a week and a year or more,' said Ramanna. 'In 1980, in Velamgonda village in south Bastar, a tribal called Selvam Lachchhanna was beaten to death by a forest guard. His son, Ganesh, is a full-timer in the Party today. The village in which we are sitting now was burnt down thrice between 1980 and 1983. Hundreds of villages have been torched by the forest department.'

The place where we sat talking about the atrocities perpetrated on tribals would be the very spot where Maoists, under Ramanna's leadership, would kill seventy-six policemen in an audacious attack in April 2010.

Sonu went on, 'In 1982, we held our first Jan Adalat, or people's court, in Dharmaram. A forest officer named Gopinathan was charged with capturing more than fifty head of cattle from the tribals and forcing them to tend to the animals. That was the first time we took a forest official to task and the move placed us on a firm footing.'

Ramanna added, 'That same year, a forest officer was thrashed—a first for us. The forest ranger, named Srivastava, was beaten up in a Jan Adalat in Kistaram. Sunnam Rama, the headman of Kistaram, was chosen to do the honours.'

I met Srivastava, living a retired life in Jagdalpur, much later. He flatly denied the incident. I tried to look for Sunnam Rama next. He was long dead, but his son, a postman in Maraigudem camp, confirmed the story of his father having beaten up Srivastava. He had witnessed it himself.

Ramanna also recalled having cordial relations with certain forest officials. 'Lata Usendi's father, who was a forest ranger, used to publish our literature in Narayanpur.' Lata Usendi is a minister in Chhattisgarh, and her father is the president of Abujhmad Development Agency, a government body.

He went on, 'I have been to the home of Vikram Usendi, the current minister for forest, to have lunch with his ex-headmaster father several times. He had participated in our rally in favour of the Sixth Schedule in Narayanpur before he became a minister, and had even delivered a speech. (The Sixth Schedule of the Indian Constitution gives exclusive rights to Adivasis but is not applicable in Bastar.) But people do not acknowledge their earlier interaction with us once they come to power. After Usendi became an MLA, I asked him to meet me. He came in his car, but left without meeting me.'

I gathered that this was just a name-dropping exercise because Ramanna was back on track in no time.

'The year 1982 was significant in our struggle against the excesses of the forest department. It was the first time we exchanged fire with the department staffers. It happened in Gangler village, when a forest officer fired at us. We fired back, but there were no casualties.

'One day, during a meeting in Singaram, I noticed a woman trying desperately to say something and garner the support of her listeners. Her complaint was that a forest officer had arrested some tribals for felling trees. We rushed to the forest office, and indeed, found an officer, Sadhuram, and his staff, whipping seven tribals with their belts. Seeing us, however, Sadhuram's aggression melted away. He feared for his life and meekly accepted our punishment—holding his ears and squatting on his haunches like a schoolboy—and also gave a written declaration that he would never again lay a finger on a tribal.

'Sadhuram pleaded that he was only a lower-level officer and was responsible for the protection of the forest. He was grateful to the Party for sparing his life and from that day on, he would send messages offering to do whatever he could for the Party, and kept in touch till he died.

'Although these were small interventions on behalf of the people, they had an impact. They helped the people acquire a sense of power, and the forest department learned that the tribals were not alone any more. As far as forest laws went, nothing changed. But with the entry of the Party and some beatings here and there, the tribal had reclaimed his forest, which had first been taken away from him by the British.

'You must understand that a tribal depends on the forest for more than two-thirds of his income. These days, an average family in Bastar earns around Rs 10,000 a year from the forest. Of that income, Rs 3000–5000 comes from tendu.

'Till 1990, forest officials used to connive and bribe their way to a Bastar posting. Now, they pay to get out of it. Over the years, the Party has been moving in and acquiring a position of strength, and the government has been moving out slowly but surely.'

'Have you ever killed a forest official?'

Sonu was dismissive. 'A couple of forest officers were killed in Gondia in Maharashtra. But we reviewed those killings, and decided that they were unnecessary.' He continued sagely, 'The Singaram forest office is an example of how the Party is moving in, while the government is inching out.'

'Is Singaram the village where the police killed "nineteen villagers" in an "encounter" in January 2009?'

Sonu nodded. 'In 1990, the forest office moved from Singaram to Golapalli, a nearby town, and then in 1995, it shifted to Konta, the block headquarters. The Party tore down the forest office in Singaram in 2006 to stop the police from using it.'

Ramanna picked up the thread. 'When they declared the area a National Park, the government gave us another readymade issue around which to rally the people: fifty-two villages were ordered to relocate to make way for Indravati National Park and fifty more for the Pamed Wildlife Sanctuary.'

I could not help adding that the same story was now being repeated in Dhamtari, next to Raipur, where villagers were told to relocate after the state announced two tiger reserves in 2009. I recalled meeting Sudhakar on his way back from Dhamtari, the blood of thirteen policemen on his hands.

'That is the reason for the meteoric rise of the Party there last year,' Ramanna responded. 'Gopanna was developing the Party in Dhamtari—he was arrested there. The state never learns. They did exactly the same thing in Abujhmad in the late 1980s when we started working there. There were no landlords or moneylenders there. Government officers did not tour the area; even forest department officials stayed away. But then, an industrialist close to Chief Minister Motilal Vora wanted to cut down the forest to set up a factory. The bureaucrats relocated villages from the hills to the plains, uprooting the people and forcing them to adjust to a new way of life. Naturally, they grew resentful of the government, making it easy for us to enter Abujhmad. It is a simple story that is being repeated in one place after another, in the name of a steel plant or a dam or a national park.'

Ramanna's words echoed what a friend working for an NGO near Dhamtari had said. The people with whom he had worked for years, who had participated in peaceful rallies, were beginning to question non-violent methods of dissent. The government simply did not respond to them. He said that he was beginning to see why people wanted to switch to the side of the Maoists.

'Around the time that the Dhamtari project was announced, the government declared that a similar reserve would be set up in Achanakmar near Bilaspur. There are no Maoists in Achanakmar to take up the cause of the tribals. Despite opposition from NGOs and activists, the relocation process has started there. But in Sitanadi, near Dhamtari, forest department officers have been too afraid even to enter the jungles since the Maoists started making their presence felt a year ago. What message does that give? Why should a journalist like you be surprised that Maoists are able to kill thirteen policemen at one go in Sitanadi? Have you considered that perhaps it is only because of the Maoists that the people of Sitanadi will never be kicked out of their homes? After all, the Maoists have helped people remain where they belong—none of the villages in Indravati National Park or Pamed has been relocated in thirty years, thanks to the Maoists,' Sonu said.

When I met the director of Indravati National Park in his office in Jagdalpur, he confirmed this. 'I can't even enter the park, let alone get any work done there.'

I did not ask what happens to the crores of rupees that are ostensibly spent on the park each year.

Having taken on the role of key narrator, Sonu continued.

'By 1983, the first batch sent off to Bastar had grown large enough to be split into two squads. The second squad was created in the Konta area of Bastar, with Chalapati as its commander. Ramanna was a member. The third squad was formed in 1984 in Basaguda, and Gopanna was named its commander.

'Although detractors mock the work of the Party in Chhattisgarh as being led by outsiders from Andhra, we have examples of members like Kamalakka—Gopanna's wife—who was an anganwadi worker from the Raipur area, posted in Bastar. She gave up her government job to join the Party. She was the first tribal woman martyr.'

The mention of Gopanna distracted me. I remembered meeting him a few years earlier. He had a very low opinion of MCC comrades from Jharkhand, because, he said, they were 'not disciplined'. I asked Sonu, 'You have fought bloody battles with the MCC in the past, but now, after the merger of 2004, you are part of the same Party. Is it difficult to work with colleagues of whom you have such a low opinion?'

Sonu was unfazed by my question. 'That is Gopanna's opinion and not the Party's. Individually, we may hold any opinion, but once the Party takes a decision, we follow it. That is what discipline means.'

His point established, he resumed my history lesson. 'Unlike Gadchiroli, the movement in Bastar was quite weak until 1984 because the first leader of the Bastar dalam, Shivaji, could not identify the class contradiction there. He contended that there was no animosity between the rich tribal landowners and the masses, and decided that the Party was not needed there. Some of the leaders from his dalam left the Party and we did not have the benefit of their combined vision and understanding. Kosa's team had moved to Maharashtra by that time.'

Shivaji was the same REC Warangal alumnus whom I had mentioned during my chat with Kosa. His rise in the Party was meteoric, as was his fall: he left the Party and joined the police.

Sonu continued, 'Shivaji's judgement was inaccurate; he did not understand the mentality of the villagers. They thought the Party would be a temporary phenomenon, made up as it was by people from outside, who would eventually depart, leaving the villagers to their own devices under traditional leaders, like Mahendra Karma's family.

'So they told us about the atrocities of the outsiders but did not reveal the economic and cultural repression they faced from their traditional leaders. The visionaries did not have a complete understanding of the class dynamics, which is why, until 1985, we had four squads in Bastar, each made up of three to five members from Andhra, with almost no local representation.

'In the meantime, in 1985, the Central Reserve Police Force (CRPF) was deployed in Andhra for the first time, and they started staging encounter killings. Till 1987, we concentrated only on reining in the landlords, but when the false encounter killings became a regular occurrence, the Party decided to target the state too. That was when it began to consider strengthening its military prowess. It was around this time that some communists in the LTTE, who were fed up of their leader Prabhakaran's authoritarian attitude, contacted our Tamil Nadu unit. One of them,

Suresh, conducted our first full-fledged military training in Bastar. That was in 1987. Forty of our leaders, including Ganapathy and Ramji, participated. That was the first time we came across the two most powerful weapons in the guerrilla arsenal—ambushes and landmines.'

I could not help comparing this to the interventions made by the USA in other parts of the world, as in Afghanistan, where it had first armed the Islamic militants to fight the Russians. Closer home, the same thing had happened in Punjab with Bhindranwale, a close ally of the Congress, who had been groomed to fight the Akalis. The Indian army had trained Suresh at the Indian Military Academy in Dehradun while he was in the LTTE. Now, it was his turn to teach the Maoists to fight the Indian security forces. What goes around comes around.

'Suresh conducted the second training session in 1989, and I was chosen to be the first military instructor for the Party,' Sonu said.

Ramanna switched back to the Party's agenda. 'The sexual exploitation of women by outsiders was rampant in Bastar, and the Party took it up next. We had heard tales of the forest camps; tales we did not believe initially.'

'What are forest camps?'

'Those were camps where the personnel of the forest department would take tribals who had been given contracts for manual work, away from their village homes. But the officials were exploiting them in other ways. One story went that the women would be asked to sleep in a row at night, so that any staffer of the department could pick a girl of his choice by torchlight.

'We verified this and were shocked to find that it was actually happening. I witnessed it myself, hiding behind trees under cover of darkness. This was in 1985, in Kannaiguda village. The next morning, we summoned a forest ranger, Kushwaha, and a forest guard, Yadav. We bound them to a tree and invited all the people from nearby villages to witness what would happen next. A Jan Adalat was held and the same exploited women were asked to beat them up. That was the end of the forest camps. It was all quite easy, actually. Under our pressure, the forest department decided not to hold any more forest camps and people started looking for work near their villages.'

'Is that the same village between Konta and Golapalli, where ten Mizo jawans were killed in 2008?' I asked Ramanna. He confirmed this and recalled another incident. 'One night, we saw a woman running through the forest as though her life depended on it. She said she was fleeing from the tahsildar of Narayanpur. We went straight to the village and locked him inside a room, but the local patwari helped him escape.'

The exploitation of tribal girls in exchange for small gifts has been well recorded. The tribal attitude to sex is not easy to appreciate in the middle-class context, so I was not surprised by what Ramanna said next. After all, revolutionaries too have their own vantage points dictated by their individual backgrounds and conditioning. Perhaps the comrades have streaks of Hindu morality, which they are as likely as anyone else to thrust upon the tribal.

Ramanna said, 'It is not as if we do not know that immorality of girls was growing in tribal society. The elders admit it, and thank the Party for timely intervention. You must have noticed fair-skinned children even in this remote tribal area. It was common for a state officer to have a wife at home and several in the villages. Now nobody can do it openly.

'With these small steps that the Party took to improve the situation of women, our following expanded. We took on the patwaris or revenue officials from 1984 onwards. They were a terror in the villages. Whenever a patwari visited, he was carried into the village on a charpoy because it facilitated his perverse intention—to be massaged by beautiful girls. The headman worked in connivance with the patwari, and together, they would demand a land tax that was higher than the official rate so that they could make money on the side. Things changed quite fast, after a few thrashings here and there. Where the Party acquired strength, people found that their complaints were readily addressed.'

Sonu intervened to give his perspective on the situation. 'It is interesting that the administration stepped in only when we began to hurt the interests of the big traders. But then, in Andhra too, the state woke up only to protect the big landlords. Traditionally, right from the seventeenth century, traders from Andhra would come to Bastar. But by the 1950s, the Thakurs from Uttar Pradesh and Bihar also began to arrive. Exploitation by these traders was an inevitable outcome. The dalam members picked this issue around 1984, preparing small skits and songs to spread awareness amongst the people.'

Ramanna spoke about the barter rates. 'In 1984, traders would give a kilogram of rice in return for two kilos of tora or mahua seeds. We demanded that this rate be doubled. In retaliation, the traders stopped buying tora altogether, but they soon fell in line. We did not even have to use force. Now tribals can get two or three kilos of rice in exchange for a kilo of tora, while a kilo of gum collected from trees can earn five to seven kilos of rice. A kilo of amla can get a tribal three kilos of rice. This is much better than what they managed to get on their own.

'Then we realized that the traders would agree to raise the rates in our presence, but as soon as we moved to new areas, they reverted to their tricks. The lesson for us was that stronger punishment than public beatings was required. We planned an attack on Errabore market on 30 September 1985,' said Ramanna. His mind works with the precision of a computer when it comes to dates. 'We looted material worth Rs 5 lakh from traders and let the people take it all away. More than 2000 people from forty villages participated in the attack, and over a hundred of them were sent to jail. Tammaiah, the sarpanch of Nendra village, was in jail for more than a year and a half.'

I have been to Nendra several times in connection with a Human Shield Experiment. The Salwa Judum had repeatedly torched Nendra, compelling the villagers who survived to migrate to Andhra. The Human Shield Experiment brought the people back from Andhra, and Gandhian peace activists began to stay with them to stop the attacks. I have met Tammaiah and spent much time with him while covering this. But he had neither told me about his past association with the Maoists, nor mentioned being jailed for supporting them. By sheer chance, I remembered seeing a Maoist document outlining an important meeting in Nendra on one of my visits there, and knew that Ramanna was telling the truth. The more I thought about Tammaiah, the more I appreciated the acuity of the tribal, who has learned to share the right information at the right time with outsiders—including seasoned journalists and activists.

There is really no conclusion to be drawn about who is on which side in the local dynamics. People take the side they have to, and their loyalties cannot be counted upon.

Sonu pointed out that the CPI did not intervene in local matters. 'At that time, Mahendra Karma was the MLA from the CPI. A comrade called Ganesh was working overground in Jagdalpur and used to meet all the CPI leaders. All of them said that we were on the side of the same people.'

Now that Sonu spoke of it, I recalled reading news reports in which Mahendra Karma had praised the Naxals. A CPI member had recounted the story of the then superintendent of police warning Mahendra Karma not to cosy up to the Naxals.

'But when we found that the CPI was collecting money from tendu contractors, telling them we were one and the same, we brought out a leaflet in 1984, declaring that we were a separate entity.'

I wanted to know how things were between the Naxals and the CPI: it seemed to be a love-hate relationship.

'The CPI likes the fact that we are a force against the Congress and the BJP,' Sonu said. 'We salute them for opposing fake encounters. They were the first to oppose the Salwa Judum. But they do not like it when their members start joining us. In 1988, the CPI brought out a leaflet questioning our refusal to contest elections. Then, they started giving the police information about us, so we first killed Gopal Rao, their leader, in Konta and then, in 1989, Nageshwar Rao in Bijapur.

'In Dandakaranya, there was no plan to attack the state; not until 1991. In Andhra, this decision had already been taken in 1987, so the Chhattisgarh state police must have been preparing for such an eventuality in their state as well. They came up with new ideas all the time,' said Sonu. 'In 1984, there were only fifteen police camps. Between 1984 and 1988, when we started attacking businessmen, forty more camps were set up. But they only patrolled the roads and did not enter the forests—we clearly intimidated them. They did try to use horses from the Chambal to make their way into the jungles. We did the same, but the plan fell through because of the weather conditions here. Now there are 105 police stations (including camps) in south Bastar—police presence has grown seven-fold in twenty-five years.

'Gradually, the police formed a nexus with outsiders from the business community and powerful tribal leaders. Thirty families of Thakurs from Uttar Pradesh had made Chintalnar in south Bastar their home. In 1987, twenty Thakurs and ten policemen attacked our dalam under Guddu Singh of Dornapal—he is a Salwa Judum leader now. In August the next year, thirty of us from the Party and over 500 people from the nearby villages attacked the Thakurs in Chintalnar. We looted goods worth Rs 6–7 lakh and got hold of fifteen 12-bore rifles and two 8mm pistols from the homes of the Thakurs. Fifty-five people were arrested and put in jail after the incident, but the message had been driven home. After that, we simply had to attack individual traders sporadically whenever they disregarded the rates we fixed.'

Sonu said it was only around 1987 that the struggle in Bastar began to reveal itself as a class war. I too had always thought that tribals did not have class differentiations, and was curious to know how the Party decided otherwise.

Sonu gave me some examples. 'Some families had become very powerful. Kalma Deva, a relative of Mahendra Karma's, came from the north and captured more than 300 acres of land. He was a terror in the neighbouring villages. But in our interactions with the villagers, they would not speak of the wrongs perpetrated by their traditional leaders. We were still outsiders: why would they admit their internal problems to us? Initially, we were looking for Kalma because he had helped the police arrest our commander. We could tell that he was a powerful man, someone from the upper class. You may even have heard that he was a great speaker, much better than Mahendra Karma.'

Ramanna said, 'We attacked Kalma for the first time on 31 March 1987, but he was with his armed guards and we had to retreat. We finally caught him on our next attempt on 3 June and after a Jan Adalat in Ittampara, we shot him.'

Sonu took over again. 'That was also the beginning of our direct conflict with Mahendra Karma and upper-class tribals. Word got around, and people started telling us about the split within the tribal community. But it was 1991 by the time the change became visible. On 16 July 1989, three of our leaders, arrested in 1986 because of Kalma Deva, escaped from jail by sneaking out from the roof after removing the tiles. This was our first jailbreak. It was widely reported in the media.'

After a brief pause, Sonu continued, 'There were other influences that complicated the situation for us. Hindus, like Bihari Das, were not the only problem. The news of our success in resolving the problems faced by the tribals living in the forest reached north Chhattisgarh. They realized that the south was better off because of our work. Many people belonging to the Oraon tribe started shifting to Bastar from north Chhattisgarh. With the Oraons came Christianity and many of our workers became pastors. The explanation for conversion they offered to us would often be as unreasonable as "Jesus saved my ailing son".

'Our clash with Christian missionaries was mild. We did not have a problem with their religion, but we told them not to proselytize. It was a mistake to burn churches; we realized it soon enough and our fight with the church was over by 2003–04. But our tussle with Hindu proselytizers, like Bihari Das and his followers, who attacked tribal villages and burnt down the ghotuls (the traditional village clubs where unmarried tribal boys and girls spent their nights before marriage), was bitter and long. Bihari Das made Hindus of tribals by giving them sacred threads. He and his followers would call the non-Hinduized tribals 'katwa' or untouchable, thus creating a division amongst them. The current tribal MP from Bastar is named Kashyap, a name of Hindu origin. Mahendra Karma's original name was Kalma Masa. We countered all these Hinduization efforts.

'Government-funded Hindu proselytizers, like the Ramakrishna Mission, are slow poisons. We do not oppose their work in education and health, but then, you have to consider that their work has extended to the Salwa Judum camps now.'

It is no secret that some of the schools of the Ramakrishna Mission are funded by the state, and I have seen followers of Sri Sri Ravishankar holding regular classes in the Salwa Judum camps. 'But you too burnt ghotuls, didn't you?' I asked.

'Oh no, you cannot compare the two,' Sonu replied. 'Bihari Das burnt the ghotuls by force, whereas we educated the tribal girls and they led processions and burnt the ghotuls themselves.' He did admit that some tribals who were against the closure of ghotuls were beaten up by Party supporters. 'It was not the right thing to do, and we did send a circular explaining to the comrades that people cannot be expected to change overnight; they have to be educated.

'Though we did not have orders to attack the police, police attacks on our comrades continued. I remember one fearless police officer, former DIG Ayodhya Nath Pathak, who held office in the early nineties. He forced us to be on our toes for as long as he was here. There has been no one like him since.'

I was not surprised that the Maoists remembered DIG Pathak after so many years, and knew that the respect was mutual. 'Maoists are honest and dedicated people. They do not kill innocent people,' said the retired DIG, reclining on the sofa in his Bhopal home, chewing one paan after another when I had met him some months back. 'I was looking for their Achilles' heel, but I can say with certainty that they do not succumb to the usual weaknesses for money and women—the easiest frailties to manipulate. If you want to fight them, you will have to live like them and think like them.' During his tenure, Pathak had shifted his office to undisclosed remote areas, far from the city. He emphasized that it would take a team of trained and devoted police officers and talks at the highest level to solve the Naxal problem, not hollow statements and fake encounters.

'You are telling me that you did not attack the state before 1991 but if I recall correctly, sometime in 1989, newspapers reported that you tried to blow up a police jeep with a landmine in Karkeli, the same village where the Salwa Judum was supposedly started,' I said to Sonu and Ramanna.

'There was no landmine,' countered Ramanna immediately. 'I was part of the team. You are right, the first police casualty occurred in that incident. But he died in the firing, and in self-defence. We used a landmine for the first time on 21 May 1991 in Kanker. That was the day former Prime Minister Rajiv Gandhi was assassinated, so no newspapers reported the landmine attack.'

Sonu recalled the Jan Jagran of 1991—a counter-propaganda campaign by the police—as the turning point. Until then, the Party had consisted mostly of people from Andhra who were working on awareness and recruitment. 'The decision to attack the state was taken under the leadership of Ganapathy, our new general secretary after KS, in March 1991. It was his first meeting for the Dandakaranya region, and it was called the Bastar Plenum.'

I remembered that I had heard the phrase Jan Jagran for the first time way back in 1982.

Sonu agreed. 'Jan Jagran was started by Vishwaranjan, the then SP of Bastar, in 1982. Vishwaranjan later became the police chief of the state and helmed another version of the Jan Jagran, which was named Salwa Judum.'

I also remembered that the media had not had much

to say in favour of the Jan Jagran programme. Banshilal Sharma, reporter for *Deshbandhu*, wrote, 'To check Naxal influence, the police chief of Bastar has started an innovative programme called Jan Jagran Abhiyan. Under the Abhiyan, he sends policemen to villages to perform songs and street plays to make people aware of possible ill-effects of helping Naxals. But the Abhiyan was a failure. Instead of performing . . . the policemen misbehaved with the villagers.'

The Jan Jagran, in its first avatar, could not win the confidence of the public and ended abruptly. 'What was the background of the second Jan Jagran in 1991?' I asked Sonu.

'The Rashtriya Swayamsevak Sangh (RSS) was working in Bastar with its sants and Ekal Vidyalayas (single-teacher schools) even before 1980, but we could not foresee their growing influence. In 1990, the BJP came to power. That was when Mahendra Karma was named in the Malik Makbooja case. Even though he was no longer an MLA, Karma enjoyed the support of the business community. Karma is a fighter: he has never compromised. One must give him credit for that. People like Karma became the enemy once we began to articulate the war in terms of a class struggle around 1987. We killed a relative of Karma's to illustrate that the equation between classes was beginning to change. A friend of Karma's, Bandi, was the leader of a village called Majji Mendri. Bandi's brother, Masa, was a rifle-wielding thug. They terrorized thirty-odd villages near Bedre, a middle-class cluster on the banks of the Indravati. They even levied fines on those who disobeyed their orders. Though many villagers from the area used to work in the police force, Bandi and Masa continued to persecute them.

'The Party, meanwhile, was gaining strength in that area. We held many rallies against the forest department. A team of Party supporters, accompanied by the local Congress MLA, Drigpal Shah, also went to Delhi and Bhopal, taking up the issue of injustice meted out by forest department staffers. Victims of Bandi's excesses slowly started to join our ranks, as did lower-class tribals, and that is how the class war started to take shape. In 1990, we executed Bandi. Naturally, Karma was furious.

'Karma and his cronies were losing support, and began to look for an ally—someone like Masa—who nursed anger and hatred towards the Party. With the support of the police, Masa began to attack villages that supported the Party, and torched Majji Mendri. Karma needed the BJP to save his skin in the Malik Makbooja case, while the traders wanted to fortify their position with some local muscle. With the BJP coming to power, it became easy for them to unite against the Party.'

However, some time ago, I had met Lachchhanna, the former Party chief of Dandakaranya. Lachchhanna has since surrendered and now lives in Warangal. He had told me that Mahendra Karma had sent the Party a note suggesting a compromise.

'Why did the Party not respond?' I asked Sonu.

Sonu sidestepped the question, claiming he was not aware of any such letter, and moved on. 'With the BJP in power, we knew that state repression would increase, but expected no more than strong police action—the way it had played out in Andhra. We did not anticipate anything like the Jan Jagran of 1991. We were busy holding political classes and were alerted to the campaign against us only after a month, in October. In the meantime, Masa held meetings in Bedre, inciting the people against us. Party supporters were beaten up; they were forced to take oaths with rice and blood in their hands that they would not help the Party in future, or else the curse of the goddess, Maa Danteshwari, would be upon them. A rumour went around that if a village did not join the Jan Jagran, it would bear the brunt of police attacks. Jan Jagran supporters also looted houses and raped women.'

I remembered meeting a woman who had been gang-raped by Masa's men at that time, for which a police case had been filed. A daring policeman posted in Kutru police station at that time had filed the case, defying the orders of his higher officials.

'When the CPI joined the Jan Jagran, a meeting of all our commanders was called in December. There, we planned our retaliation. Though it took us a few months to react, we killed some key leaders of the Jan Jagran and put an end to the campaign.'

'Some claim that you killed hundreds after Jan Jagran in 1991.'

'The number of people killed was not even in double digits,' Sonu insisted.

I had been doing my own research on the subject. DIG Pathak had been critical of police participation in Jan Jagran, which had started before he reached Bastar. When he found that his officers were giving speeches at Jan Jagran rallies, he immediately ordered them to stop. 'Jan Jagran is a bad strategy,' he said. 'If people are unhappy with the Naxals they are likely to give us intelligence. We need to protect them by keeping them undercover. We make them easy targets by bringing them to rallies or shifting them to camps as is being done now.'

To find out where the Jan Jagran of 1991 had actually been planned, I had met Arvind Netam, a tribal leader from the Congress party in Bastar who rose to the level of a Union minister. Now all but retired from politics, he runs a petrol pump in Jagdalpur, which is where I met him. Talking to retired people has its own rewards—they give great interviews and sometimes, you actually get at the truth. Somewhere in the middle of a long-winded interview, I asked Netam how he had been part of the planning for Jan Jagran. He revealed that the plan had been drafted in Bhopal by BJP and Congress leaders, in meetings of which he had not been a part.

To understand why the CPI had joined the Jan Jagran in 1991, I met its former MLA Nanda Sodi, who had been kidnapped by the Naxals for interrogation during the Abhiyan. Sodi said, 'In hindsight, I realize that through the Jan Jagran, the BJP had planned to finish off the CPI. It was clever of them—a political master stroke, I would say. After the Bhopal meeting where the second Jan Jagran was planned, there was a second meeting in Dantewada, which we attended. The BJP knew that it was the CPI that could draw crowds to Jan Jagran rallies. They also knew that after the rallies, the Naxals would attack the CPI members who attended the meetings.

'Sudhir Mukherjee was our leader at that time. He accepted the invitation to attend Jan Jagran rallies. As expected, the Naxals attacked the people who attended. It alienated our supporters. Many of our village leaders had to move to the cities to escape the violence. Jan Jagran in 1991 was the beginning of the end of the CPI in Bastar.'

It was the beginning of the rise of the Naxals, though, and the BJP as well. Left and Right, both extremes gained from that plan.

Sonu confirmed this. 'Until 1990, a few local villagers would join the Party every year, but most of them would drop out. In 1991, we had five squads of twenty-five to thirty people. But things changed after the Jan Jagran. Forty Adivasis joined us as full-timers in 1991 alone. The lower-class tribals realized that they would have to join the Party to fight the tribal upper class, which was exploiting them through the police, the administration and the business community.'

Forty-nine men had come to Dandakaranya in 1980; that number had gone down to twenty-five in 1991, but it was as if the government had made arrangements for more people to join the Maoists! Similarly, the BJP, or its earlier avatars, had never won any seats in Bastar before 1991. Now, they have made a habit of winning almost all the seats.

'After 1991, every divisional committee meeting would see twenty to thirty full-timers signing up. These were people who had been village sangham members for a few years and had the sanction of the Area and the Divisional Committees. Now there are ten divisions in Dandakaranya. As many as three meetings of the Divisional Committee are held annually. Many Area Committees constitute one Divisional Committee. The Party's Central Guerrilla Platoon consisting of three sections of eight comrades each was also formed in 1991. From the next year on, Party Area Committees had local representation at the top. By 1995, the Party began to deliberate on an alternative development policy for the kind of government we wanted to see in the areas under our influence. That is how the idea of the people's government or Jantana Sarkars came up,' Sonu said.

It was news to me that their 'development policy' was the result of careful consideration. I wanted to know how the Jantana Sarkar differed from Gandhi's Gram Swaraj or village self-rule.

'We are not Gandhians. What we are saying is that there is a need to neutralize the top 5 per cent of every society that consists of lumpen elements who control everything.'

'You mean with guns?' I interrupted.

'If you want to put it that way, yes. But that is reality. When this crooked lot is silenced, democracy works, because only then are the people able to decide what is good for them. That is the main difference between Gandhi's Gram Swaraj and our Jantana Sarkar.'

'So how do you decide which 5 per cent needs to be neutralized and who are the leaders?'

'The people decide,' countered Sonu.

I thought it was a remarkably naive notion. I am not sure how people decide 'freely' under the shadow of the gun, or indeed, under any kind of pressure. But in the real world, I also know that poverty and deprivation are as oppressive as physical violence is.

Sonu went on. 'The process of forming these Jantana Sarkars or local governments at the village level started from 1996. They are still at a nascent stage and have been implemented in around fifty villages so far.

'In 1996, Mahendra Karma started yet another Jan Jagran with some of his landlord friends near his home in Dantewada. But this time, Karma did not get any support from the Congress. Digvijay Singh was the chief minister of the state at the time. The Party got to its feet immediately and killed a couple of key leaders, nipping the third Jan Jagran in the bud.

'In Dantewada, the Party had taken on a number of powerful landlords who crossed over to Mahendra Karma's side. We understood their intentions and planned public attacks. One of them was on the house of Karma's brother, Podia, in Takilod.'

Researching the genesis of the Salwa Judum, I had taken note of Podia Karma's killing in 1998 as a significant point in the Party's trajectory. 'I would like to hear about him in detail,' I said. Sonu suggested that I speak to Rajman, who had been part of the team that killed Podia and had recently been promoted to the post of Party secretary in Abujhmad.

'By the year 2000, there were 800 full-timers in Dandakaranya, 650 of whom were local residents. We had grown tenfold since 1991, the Party was on a roll,' Sonu said.

So the decision to attack the state and the subsequent rebuttal, the theory of class war and the Jan Jagran: all or some of them had coalesced to boost Naxal strength, I thought to myself.

'The Party held its first congress in 2001, where it was decided that Local Guerrilla Squads of nine to eleven people each would be set up for military activities. We also created Local Organization Squads of seven to nine people each for administrative duties. This way, those with military training would not "waste" their time on other chores. Both kinds of squads were to remain under Area Committees. Special Guerrilla Squads were also constituted for special operations.'

Sonu's descriptions reminded me of what Lachchhanna had told me—that he had left the Party because he believed it was wrong to divert the best people into military operations. Administrative work was left to the weak and the ineffective. People grew resentful of the quality of work that this group did, and their bitterness was exploited by Mahendra Karma to organize the Salwa Judum.

Sonu said, 'It is Lachchhanna's view. Why did he not raise these issues while he was the head of Dandakaranya?'

Sonu told me that the first company (of three platoons) was formed in 2004, the year that the People's War Group and the MCC merged to become the Communist Party of India (Maoist).

I wondered if it would be right to say that at the time of the merger, the MCC was militarily a stronger force than the PWG was because it had already formed its company back in 2000. I did, and Sonu agreed, adding, 'We are a guerrilla army that can only execute hit-and-run operations. We aim to convert that ability into a mobile war, where we can attack with larger formations and engage with the enemy for longer periods to push them back if required. The Nayagarh armoury attack, where we charged ahead with 192 guerrillas, was our first experiment in mobile warfare. That attack by our Central Military Commission took months to plan and guerrillas from several states took part in it. After the attack, fifty guerrillas from Chhattisgarh walked back for three months undetected, carrying two AK-47s each from the armoury.

'For us, Dandakaranya is a guerrilla zone at the moment; we want to convert it into a liberated zone. At our ninth congress held in February 2007, we were given the task of developing Dandakaranya and Jharkhand into stable bases and of evolving the People's Liberation Guerrilla Army into a People's Liberation Army. Displacement and Adivasi pride are two issues that can potentially be harnessed to build a mass organization in Dandakaranya.'

Every Jan Jagran ended up giving the Party fresh loyalists. Was there a lesson for the state in this, I wondered. After the latest Jan Jagran—the Salwa Judum—Naxal strength went up by a factor of at least three, if not more. I wanted to know what else had boosted recruitment.

'The cultural wing we formed in 2004 has been a runaway success, especially in drawing the youth. Today, we have almost 7000 cultural activists in Dandakaranya. But you should talk to Leng about it; he heads it,' said Sonu, turning to the man who had just joined us.

Leng looked familiar.

'Did you come to Dalli Rajhara along with Gadar in 1983 to perform in a programme organized by Shankar Guha Niyogi?' I asked him. Gadar is an overground Maoist supporter and a cultural activist.

'Your memory is very sharp; you are a dangerous man!' Leng smiled, absolving his words of any offence. 'Yes, it was my first trip to Chhattisgarh. I used to work in Andhra then. I moved to Dandakaranya five years ago.'

Sitting down next to Sonu, he said, 'The Party started cultural activism in Andhra in the 1970s, and in all those years, we only had half a dozen writers. But here in

Dandakaranya, it is as if Mao's dream of mass culture has found form. In just a few years, we have put together a pool of more than 350 poems and songs, most of them written by the people. Hundreds of them turn up with their drums at any competition that we organize. We just divide them into two groups—immediately, a poetic debate begins, and songs spring from it spontaneously.'

I see this as a function of the community-oriented nature of Adivasi culture. Professor Hiralal Shukla, a Gondi scholar who has written several books about Bastar, had similar stories to share. He mentioned one particular group of Adivasis who penned the Ramayana in Gondi based on episodes they had heard from him. But when he went back to Bastar after twenty years to look for them, they had disappeared. He felt that they were the cream of Bastar tribal society and feared that most of them had become Naxals.

Sonu knew of Professor Shukla but did not share his enthusiasm about the Gondi Ramayana. It had been distributed amongst the tribals by the state on the fiftieth anniversary of India's independence in 1997—a move that Sonu viewed as an attempt to Hinduize the tribal community. 'We burnt it,' he said. 'NGO workers and PhD students are now the two categories of people we see as potentially harmful in Bastar, second only to religious groups. We know that organizations, like the Médecins Sans Frontiéres (Doctors Without Borders) pass intelligence on to the FBI, and it travels to the home ministry. We allow them to work only because people here are in dire need of health care. We know that many of them are actually funded by organizations like the CIA. Maybe your book project too is funded by them!'

Sonu was quite impartial in his distrust of the world at large. He went on. 'Brahminical expansion is no different from the way the Europeans went to Africa—with a sword in one hand and the Bible in the other. The state does the same. It has two policies: suppression and reforms. Policies like the Forest Rights Act are reforms that only hoodwink the people. We will not allow NGOs, like the Vanvasi Chetna Ashram, to bring the government and the police back into the villages under the pretext of rehabilitating the people.'

I probed. 'But you do not seem to mind a link with the king, or the fact that the Vanvasi Chetna Ashram takes cases of police atrocities to court?'

'Yes, we will stand by anyone who raises issues that concern the people—even a king,' he said magnanimously. 'But our future depends on how we develop in cities, where capitalism is in deep trouble. When Jeet and Mukti Guha Niyogi left the Party, it was a big jolt to our efforts to make legitimate platforms of expression outside these forests.'

I was glad that Sonu had spoken of Jeet and Mukti. I had heard that they had links with the Party, and it was nice to have got confirmation without digging for it.

Sonu went on, 'Theoretically, when the enemy attacks in the forest, our people in the cities should attack the enemy from behind. The ruling class is creating favourable conditions for us but the future will depend on how we are able to use this opportunity. On the ground, we have just finished training twenty-five young boys and girls who will be dispatched to work in the cities.'

There was no point in probing for the details of those young trainees, I realized.

So I asked instead, 'What about the state security forces? They are making headway too.'

'Neither Jungle Warfare Colleges nor Brigadier Ponwar can turn a mercenary into a revolutionary,' Sonu replied.

The Counter Terrorism and Jungle Warfare College, Kanker, has been set up by the Chhattisgarh government with the help of the army to train its police forces under the directorship of retired Brigadier Basant Ponwar. I had written about the college, and it had not escaped Sonu. My story said that the college was built on illegal forest land, and ran under the headline, 'Break the law and fight a guerrilla', mocking the motto of Brigadier Ponwar's College: 'Fight a guerrilla, like a guerrilla'. Sonu asked me what had become of the land acquisition row. I had checked with a high-ranking officer who agonized over the lapse, observing sagely that people in power ought to show respect for the law.

Sonu went on in a condescending tone, 'The poor policemen are fighting for their existence. One day, they will understand who the real enemy is. There will be a crisis in the Indian police soon. They fear for their lives: we heard last year that ten CRPF jawans died of heart attacks in Bastar, and no officer wants to come here.'

There were other questions that I would have liked to ask, but Kosa had joined us, and I decided to cut to the chase. 'What is your budget these days?'

'Our budget crossed the Rs 1-crore mark in 2002,' said Kosa. 'Now it is Rs 10–12 crore. We earn Rs 5–7 crore from tendu these days. Our expenditure in Dandakaranya is Rs 2–3 crore. Last year, the people contributed about Rs 40 lakh.'

But Sabyasachi Panda had mentioned a far more inflated budget when I met him in Orissa—Rs 50 crore. He said that in Orissa, funds were raised from the mining industry.

Some time ago, I had also met Balkrishna, the secretary for what the Party calls the 'Andhra-Orissa Border State'. I had information from an off-the-record conversation with the police chief of Chhattisgarh that Essar was paying Maoists, and I confronted Balkrishna with the details he had provided. He admitted to having made the 'mistake' of accepting money from Essar Steel. As the Maoists claim to be fighting against steel majors in tribal areas, I posed the same question to Sonu and Kosa. 'Didn't you take Rs 1 crore from Essar?'

Kosa immediately refuted that claim. 'There are also rumours that our budget is hundreds of crores! Does that mean it is really so?' But almost simultaneously, Sonu began to explain that taking the money from Essar had been a mistake.

I felt Sonu had sensed that I had information about the money having changed hands and therefore readily accepted something that Kosa would rather deny. At that point, I would have liked to ask Sonu why Balkrishna was not punished for his 'mistake', but he quickly distracted us by announcing that coffee had been served.

Balkrishna had told me that after the 'mistake', they had not accepted any more instalments. All the while that the instalments were being paid and accepted, the Essar pipeline that carries iron ore from Bastar to Visakhapatnam on the coast was never attacked, though it passed right under the noses of the Maoists. During the same time, however, the government-owned mining company, National Mineral Development Corporation (NMDC), was attacked repeatedly.

When I met Ganesh Uike, the Party head in the areas near Bailadila mines, I asked him the same question. 'We did try to blow up the Essar pipeline, but the explosives got wet,' he claimed. It sounded rather lame. It may have been a coincidence but soon after my exchange with Balkrishna, the Maoists blew up the Essar pipeline and work was stalled for a couple of years. However, it has started again, fanning the suspicion that another deal has been struck.

Sipping his coffee, Sonu deftly changed course for comfortable waters. 'More than three lakh acres of land have been created and distributed in Dandakaranya—no one is landless any more. People here feed us and face the brutality of the police. I salute them. Although they have not had the benefit of an education, they are eager to learn. Their crops, their diet, everything is changing because of the Party. Instead of jowar and kosra, they grow rice and even an oilseed crop.'

Big achievements all, if the claim is accurate, but there is no way I can verify the actual impact. And then, there is the matter of method. I have questioned the lack of a space for non-violent dissent in the Indian democracy, but is it possible even in the Jantana Sarkar? Is not distributing land by violent means an invitation to more violence, sooner or later? Once the Party is gone, will the tribals be able to hold on to the land the Party has handed to them, especially if the opposition resorts to the same violence the Maoists used to get it? Will there not be an equal, if not more violent, state response in the future to set things right as it deems fit?

'Do you see any hope for your Party?' I asked instead.

'It is the biggest challenge to Manmohan Singh,' said Sonu proudly. 'Dandakaranya is only the start. People need to understand that the Maoists are not a problem. If there is no problem, there will be no Maoists,' he elaborated with a beguiling smile, entirely leader-like. And with that, I had to be satisfied, for Rajman's bodyguard had arrived to take me to him.

She was from Garhwa in Jharkhand. On the way I tried to get her to open up by talking of my tribal activist friend from the same area—a particularly well-educated tribal boy from one of the best colleges in Ranchi. He could have landed a good job easily, but instead, chose to go back to his village to serve his own people. The Maoists speak up for the tribals and work for them so that they get to have a say in issues that govern their lives, but they did not like his independent approach and he had to return to the city to save his life. The girl refused to bite my bait and discuss the Party's reaction to dissent. But perhaps that is exactly what helped her to become the formidable bodyguard she is—the ability to hold her tongue.

I found Rajman wearing his trademark green cap, bang in the thick of things. He was quite the big man now, despite his youth. The other leaders I met at the camp were all older. I had met Rajman's wife, Phulbati, on one of my earlier trips. Her light skin had convinced me that she was Nepalese. She denied it, though, and I took it to be a strategic response. As a journalist, one wants to explore the most complex angle and, for a while, I believed the theory that the Nepalese-Maoist connection had reached Bastar. I was almost disappointed when a friend confirmed discreetly from her village sarpanch that Phulbati was indeed from Bastar. She sang beautifully, and we had used one of her songs as the background music for a documentary on Maoists. There are rumours that she has left Rajman and married again. His bodyguard informed me that Phulbati left Rajman because of her 'anarchic behaviour', a phrase that sounded absurd in this scenario. What could be anarchic for anarchists! Despite the murmurs, no one would tell me where she lives with her new husband.

Rajman was busy, and I offered to return later. 'There is only the here and now for a comrade! Why don't you take a look at our quarterly magazine, *Bhumkal*? We can talk while I put the finishing touches,' said Rajman as he worked on the magazine, which was in Gondi. He appeared to be a multitasker. 'Maybe you could give me some suggestions too?' he asked, without sounding too welcoming. He did not even look up from his work.

When I finally had his attention, I told him, 'Though your Party documents say the Salwa Judum started in June 2005, my research shows that it started in 2003, on the other side of the Indravati in your area of operation.'

Rajman was surprised I had noted this. 'Yes, you are absolutely right. The Party too is coming to the same conclusion.' He handed me a booklet. 'Take a look at our latest Rectification Campaign booklet. It says that preparations for the Salwa Judum started years ago; we just did not see it coming. Their attack was so potent that it put us in a defensive mode, and recovering from it took some time.'

I wanted to hear the story of Takilod, home to Suraj, and also to Podia Karma, Mahendra Karma's cousin. Takilod, I thought, was central to the history of the Salwa Judum. Once he had finished his work, Rajman began. 'For many years, we used to pass through the Indravati area only to travel between north and south Bastar. Farmers would approach us for help against the atrocities of Podia, who was a terror in Takilod. He had seized hundreds of acres of land and must have killed at least half a dozen people. His word was law in that area. If you did not do as he wished, you would pay the price for it. He was also an elected leader for the Congress, so there was large-scale misappropriation of government funds.'

Suraj had told me the same thing during our walk in the forest, but I did not want to interrupt Rajman.

'Strategically, we chose not to intervene because that passage was critical for us to get to the south from Abujhmad. The area is quite close to the main road, which made it fraught with danger for us. We knew that Podia was informing the police about our movements. On one occasion, I was followed for quite a few kilometres, but managed to give the police the slip. We wanted to avoid police attention. But Podia played a big role in the Jan Jagran of 1996, and that was when we decided to take action. Also, we had realized that unless we cut him down to size, we would not be able to organize ourselves there. The people were too afraid of him. We decided to get him out of the way.'

I remembered similar stories justifying the killing of CPM leaders by the Party in Lalgarh in West Bengal.

'Podia lived in a sprawling house in Bhairamgarh, a nearby town. We formed a team of seven with four Party members and three farmers. On the night of 16 June 1998, we made our move. It was summer, and Podia was asleep on the terrace. When we caught hold of him, he tried to escape by pretending to be someone else, but the trio of farmers identified him and we made short work of him right there.

'Then, we called a meeting of eighteen villages in Takilod. Podia's sons were also summoned. They apologized to the people for the atrocities committed by their father. They returned Rs 72,000, which Podia had collected as penalty, and promised to refund another Rs 50,000. They also gave the people three quintals of rice, three pigs and two goats as token compensation for the damage their father had caused. They pleaded with the people not to take away all their land and agreed to release the land they held in the villages of Ekul and Got, requesting that they be allowed to farm on the rest of it. The people agreed. However, once we left the area, the sons gradually stepped into their father's shoes and started terrorizing the villagers. We called another meeting in 2001 and it was decided that the Podia family would have to give up the land they held in Bedma village as well.

'The Party was gaining in strength, even as Podia's sons tried to wield their waning power. Matters came to a head in 2003, when the sons tried to kill Bhimal, the vice-president of the Jantana Sarkar in the area. We called a meeting of twelve villages, and decided that the Podia family would be expelled from Takilod. After the meeting, the angry residents attacked Podia's house. The crowd looted 300 quintals of rice, forty cows and fifteen goats, and we distributed 230 acres amongst 122 families. We kept twenty acres for the Party which the villagers now farm for us.

'But there are plenty more characters in this story. Chaituram Atami (Suraj's uncle) was trying to build a temple in Satwa in the same area with the help of Nandu Swami aka Nandram Lekam, a tribal member of the Shivanand Ashram in Gummargunda. Nandu Swami had a friend called Budhram, who hailed from Alur, which is adjacent to Mahendra Karma's village, Faraspal.

'Campaigning for the temple, they used to go around the villages singing bhajans and asking people to turn vegetarian. We told Chaituram we had no problem with any religion as long as it was practised inside the home. But we would not allow campaigning in the name of religion, and no Hindu temple would be built in Satwa. Adivasis have their own god and their deity does not need a temple. Nearly 80 per cent of the people in Satwa were with us but the remaining 20 per cent, who had been Hinduized, sided with them. We started a counter-campaign of eating meat.

'Chaituram was secretly running a money-lending business using the cash collected for the temple. He had grabbed thirty-five acres of land from people who could not repay their loans. Podia's sons joined Chaituram and his group and we heard that they were planning to attack us. We were surprised by their audacity but found out that they had the support of some influential people. We thought it better to attack first, and killed Budhram in 2002. But his family apologized and was allowed to stay in the village.

'In 2003, Chaituram formed the Danteshwari Samanvay Samiti with the help of the Shivanand Ashram and a few businessmen. The RSS backed them. The BJP was just back in power in Chhattisgarh. Combining forces, they started attacking the houses of our supporters with the help of the police.'

'I have seen some old Salwa Judum identity cards that also had Danteshwari Samanvay Samiti written on them,' I told Rajman.

'Yes, I know. Anyway, the nexus soon developed cracks, and Nandu Swami was found murdered inside the Shivanand Ashram. We did not kill him.'

The police, though, had blamed the Maoists for the killing.

'The Danteshwari Samanvay Samiti formed village protection committees in certain villages. The house of Sudri, Suraj's wife, was the first to be attacked in Pallewaya village that same year. They burnt it down.'

Sudri had told me about the incident herself. Newspaper reports from that time quoted the then governor of Chhattisgarh, General K.M. Seth, as saying during a visit to the Ramakrishna Ashram that 'Jan Jagran was the only way to be safe from Maoists.' General Seth vehemently denied any connection to the Abhiyan when I asked him later about the timing of his statement. He said he had used the phrase generically for an awakening of public consciousness. But later, it became known that it was he who had conceived of the Jungle Warfare College and handpicked Brigadier Basant Ponwar to execute his plan of training Chhattisgarh's security forces in guerrilla warfare. I remembered meeting General Seth in Kupwara in Kashmir, where he had tried similar experiments before he retired.

Rajman continued, 'When police reinforcements arrived for the Lok Sabha elections in 2004, they razed many houses with the help of the CRPF. They also raped three girls, Pali, Sanni and Budhri, and killed Budhri in Dharma village.

People surrounded Bhairamgarh police station to protest, but the police claimed she was a Naxal. In Pali and Sanni's village, Jili, the house of one Prakash Oyam was also burnt. Prakash was studying in Bijapur at that time and complained to the SP against the Samanvay Samiti, but his complaint fell on deaf ears.

'In August 2004, we attacked Budhram's house again. The family apologized yet again. But just two months later, they killed one of our members, Shivram, when he was returning from the market. We felt we had to retaliate, and after Shivram's cremation, we organized a procession from his village to Satwa. The attackers had already fled. We ordered the women and children of their families to leave the village peacefully; they shifted to Chintalanka, next to Mahendra Karma's village. Their property was distributed amongst the people.'

From these very families came the key members of the Salwa Judum in 2005. When Raman Singh, the Chief Minister of Chhattisgarh, asked Mahendra Karma to restart the Jan Jagran, they became the natural choice. The leaders of the Salwa Judum wanted to lend some credibility to the story of spontaneous revolt and started to look for specific places where villagers had grievances against the Party. Secret meetings were held in Shivanand Ashram and in Geedam, a town in Dantewada. Finally, the arrest of some innocent locals after an incident of Naxal violence in Karkeli became the trigger to set off the Jan Jagran Abhiyan, which was later called the Salwa Judum.

7

'PEACE MARCH'

The year 2005 was a watershed. It was the year when conflict matured in Chhattisgarh. The year when companies like Tata and Essar signed their MoUs (memorandums of understanding) with the state. The year the Salwa Judum started.

The Salwa Judum, the sequel to the Jan Jagrans, started on 5 June, coinciding with the arrival of the Tatas in Chhattisgarh. Mainstream newspapers were awash with reports of a 'spontaneous people's uprising', in which a human stream poured into roadside Salwa Judum camps to escape the 'Naxal threat'.

The Naxals had been in the state for more than twenty-five years. Why, then, were people leaving their homes en masse now? I had been travelling in Chhattisgarh for some years, asking questions. The answers did not come to me in any clear sequence. Piecing together the voices around me, I began to see a picture not only of the lives of the people there, but also of the Salwa Judum.

I had often pondered over the creation of the state of Chhattisgarh, and spoken of it to the people who ought to have known how and why it happened. The carving out of the new state, to my mind, was the first chapter in the story of the Salwa Judum.

Chhattisgarh was granted statehood in 2000. India had changed and matured as an economic power since the opening up of the economy in 1991. The formation of the state of Chhattisgarh underlined that change, since it was home to nearly 15 per cent of the country's mineral deposits, the main fuel for this growth.

There had never been a strong demand for statehood in Chhattisgarh as there is for Telangana, Gorkhaland and Bodoland. The locals joke that there weren't even thirty-six people on the roads, referring to the name of the state— Chhattisgarh or thirty-six forts. Why, then, was Chhattisgarh created?

The cynical answer to that question is that it's easier to manage forty-six MLAs than 146 of them. Not many people realized this initially, because the equation between the state and the Centre did not work out quite as expected. The BJP was in power at the Centre when Chhattisgarh came into being, but the state went to the Congress. And when the BJP came to power in Chhattisgarh in 2003, the Congress soon took control of the Centre. This lack of synchronicity may have slowed things down, but money-backed plans are not usually abandoned. The creation of Chhattisgarh was an economic necessity.

One of the first laws that the BJP regime tried to change in the state was to enable the industrial takeover of tribal lands. But this was challenged in court, and the law has not been passed yet. The second change was the privatization of the tendu trade. I wondered why a state intent on wiping out Naxal presence would ease their road to economic strength. On the one hand, the state launched the biggest offensive against the Naxals and, on the other, it willingly submitted to their demand for privatization of the tendu trade, which is their biggest source of income! I wondered if this was an attempt to create a monster to justify the state's aims and ends.

The official story of the rebellion was that the tribals were fed up of the Naxals because of the ban they had imposed on plucking tendu. It was implied that the Naxals had made a demand for better wages. Not only was this demand quashed, but the Naxals also banned the people from plucking tendu, which meant a loss of income also for the tribals, and so they had rebelled.

A little investigation, however, revealed much.

The contract for plucking tendu leaves is negotiated by an auction a year in advance. I found that in exactly those locations where the Salwa Judum started in June 2005, no one had applied in 2004 for the upcoming tendu season!

I got in touch with the businessmen who had won contracts that year, and they revealed that in the summer of 2004 they were asked by forest department officials not to apply for certain locations for the next year. These were the places where the Salwa Judum 'started' in 2005. None of those contractors wanted to be quoted, for obvious reasons.

From this, I deduced that planning for the Salwa Judum had started at least a year in advance, if not earlier. Then,

I looked at the auction process in 2005 for the following year. Again, no one had applied for those areas that the Salwa Judum would occupy in 2006. However, applications poured in for the areas that had been left free for the Salwa Judum in 2005, so business returned to normal in those pockets in 2006.

What seemed like a contradictory action was, in effect, a well-thought-out strategy.

The Maoists' long-standing demand for privatization of the tendu trade does not show them in a good light, either. Why should a Party that opposes all privatization change its tune when it comes to tendu?

Going through old newspapers, I found that only two local dailies—*Navbharat* and *Hindsatt* of Jagdalpur—had reported the start of 'a spontaneous uprising' of tribals in villages near Karkeli. I got in touch with the reporters of both newspapers in Kutru, which was closest to Karkeli. Both denied having written the report. So I rang the editor of *Hindsatt*. He told me that his reporter from Kutru had sent the report. When I challenged that claim, he promised to check and call me back. I never heard from him.

The bureau chief of *Navbharat* in Jagdalpur claimed he had got an anonymous call. I wanted to know how he had confirmed the news before publishing it. He said he had checked with a police officer in Sukma. This was hard to digest. Why would the editor of *Navbharat* not call his own reporter based just hours from the scene, and instead, ask a police officer stationed miles away? In those days, there was no mobile connectivity in the area and it was very unlikely that someone in Sukma would have a clue about what was happening in Karkeli.

I was also sceptical of blindly accepting the Naxal version of the story of the Salwa Judum; after all, they have a vested interest in maligning the movement. But the Naxals are thorough with their details and sharp in their speculations, and I was able to get valuable pointers from them. The facts in their version coincided with the official story, though they often analysed the situation differently.

The official story came to me through hours of off-the-record conversations over years of meeting people in the right places. Jan Jagran or Salwa Judum was a plan prepared by the central government, drawn up when L.K. Advani of the BJP was the Union home minister. Much later, when I had enough data and appropriate questions, the head of the Naxal cell in the home ministry would confirm to me, off the record, that there was truth in the story that the Salwa Judum had been planned in Delhi.

It was also true that twelve villagers had been arrested from Karkeli in the first week of June for the theft of police rations from a tractor that had, in fact, been looted by Naxals. They were roughed up in the police lock-up and the village elders were told that they would be released only if, in exchange, they brought in Raju, an Area Committee member of the Party. An urgent meeting of village elders was called, and Raju was asked to attend it. When the unsuspecting Raju went to Karkeli with five Party members on 5 June, the villagers beat them up and handed them over to the police. One of Raju's team members escaped and told the Maoists what had happened.

This was a rebellion indeed. But the role that Dunga Seth of Kutru played in this sequence of events has not been publicized. Dunga was close to Mahendra Karma and the group that had spearheaded the earlier Jan Jagrans. In May, Karma had invited Dunga Seth and a supporter, Gannu Patel, to Jagdalpur to plan another Jan Jagran. The Karkeli incident gave them just the opportunity they wanted.

On 9 June, around 200 people assembled near Karkeli, and on 18 June in Tarmendri, to discuss problems created by the Naxals. But because there was no police protection, the Naxals managed to disperse the crowd quite easily.

On 19 June, in a similar public meeting in Matwara, the police and some politicians joined in too. Among them was MLA Mahesh Gagda of the BJP. The assembly began to acquire the garb of the earlier Jan Jagrans and a rally marched to Kotrapal, which was known as a Maoist stronghold.

Before the rally reached Kotrapal, however, the villagers got wind of an impending attack and fled, leaving only the Party members behind. The procession started torching houses and immediately faced the wrath of the Party as arrows rained on them. Three of them were killed, while eight were captured by the Maoists. The retaliation proved too much for them and they retreated. The next day, members of the Party's State Committee reached Kotrapal. They kidnapped and interrogated four local leaders who had participated in the attack, and learned about the meetings of Dunga Seth and Mahendra Karma.

The Naxals do not shy away from admitting that they attacked meetings and were the first to kill. But they are also clear in their understanding that the Salwa Judum was planned; it was not peaceful, and certainly not Gandhian. They also point out that all the Jan Jagran campaigns were launched conveniently in a sixty-kilometre stretch along the Indravati where Naxal presence was not strong.

It is just as true that the villagers harboured a great deal of anger against the Naxals, and the initial anti-Naxal meetings held in June had been spontaneous. But parties with vested interests, who had long been preparing a counter-offensive against the Maoists, swiftly hijacked the people's rebellion. What followed the Kotrapal fiasco is on record as the mainstream press had started reporting the events. A crucial meeting was announced in Bijapur on 25 June, which was attended by the collector and the SP of Dantewada, the SP of Bijapur, deputy inspector general Longkumer and BJP minister Kedar Kashyap. The meeting also saw the first public appearance of Mahendra Karma, who named the movement Salwa Judum or Peace March. From the podium, he issued an ultimatum to the villagers of Kotrapal to surrender by 1 July.

After the Bijapur meeting, mainstream newspapers began calling it a 'spontaneous tribal revolt'. I remember having contacted a journalist in Bijapur to confirm the story of the 'people's uprising' against the Naxals. He advised me not to base my conclusions on media reports, and said that the meeting, which had the full support of the police, was a government-sponsored programme, just as the earlier Jan Jagrans had been. Indeed, one of the men he had seen on a propaganda jeep announcing the meeting was inspector Majji, later spotted in uniform in the Bijapur police station. His name tag left no room for doubt. Majji's wife was a sarpanch in the same area where the Salwa Judum started.

On 1 July, a Salwa Judum procession, led by Mahendra Karma under the baton of the Bijapur superintendent of police, D.L. Manhar, with more than a hundred policemen, staged a second attack on Kotrapal. The village was deserted but for Uike Sannu and Vanjam Mangu, two aged residents, who were too feeble to flee. They died in the fire as the Salwa Judum set the abandoned homes ablaze. An old woman was shot at; she still bears the bullet in her stomach.

On their part, the Naxals tried unsuccessfully to get their side of the story out in the public domain. They held a press conference in the jungle in July 2005, where they declared that the Salwa Judum was the latest state-sponsored version of the previous Jan Jagrans. Only a couple of local TV channels carried the news in brief. The Naxals also circulated a recording of a walkie-talkie exchange between Manhar and his subordinate. Manhar was heard ordering the subordinate to tell the people that each of their villages would receive Rs 2.5 lakh if they joined the Jan Jagran. 'Tell them once, tell them twice; if they don't listen, burn the village and yes, if you see any journalists around, just kill them.' A copy of that CD came to me too, and I ran it on CGNet but not many journalists wrote about it.

Some human rights activists questioned the state government on the basis of what Manhar had been heard saying. But the official stand was that the recording was 'fake' and, soon after, Manhar was transferred to the state human rights commission. That was the end of that story. The national media was silent. But the international press picked up the stories from CGNet—reporters from the BBC, the *Guardian* and the *New York Times* later trickled into Kotrapal.

After Kotrapal, the Salwa Judum resorted to the same

tactics in other villages to establish its power. In village after village, they held meetings, forcing the residents to participate. The Naxals tried to attack these meetings but failed to curb the rising tide of the rebellion. The people had nowhere to go when they were forced to abandon the villages, so the state set up camps for them by the roadside. The first camps came up in Kutru and Bhairamgarh in August. The theory was that if there were no villagers, the Naxals would not be able to survive. I wrote about this 'strategic hamleting' policy of the government that had been adopted earlier in the North-East. It was difficult to buy into the government's story of a spontaneous uprising, a story the mainstream media parroted ad nauseam. There were pictures of truckloads of villagers moving out into the camps. Someone, surely, was paying for it.

All the roads leading to the villages burnt by the Salwa Judum were closely guarded by security forces. I got in touch with some young tribals from these villages who were studying away from home, living in hostels. I travelled with them, taking circuitous routes through the forest to visit the destroyed villages and shoot them for a documentary.

I made repeated trips to the camps to get the people to talk to me freely. Once I got a chance to talk to some tribals without the security forces listening in, they began to confide in me. 'We have been brought here like cattle by the security forces,' one of them said.

I also met a constable of the Chhattisgarh police force, who was visibly disturbed by the turn of events. 'We go into villages with the Salwa Judum members, and the tribals literally run away from us. We catch them and try to bring them to the camps. If someone tries to escape, we shoot them. We are killing these tribals like chickens, dogs and pigs; it is not right. Please tell DGP sahib that it is not right. I know that after you write about this, I will be summoned for an inquiry. But I will be happy to face that. This madness must stop,' he said, distraught. I wrote this in my weekly column and offered to give the name of the constable to the DGP for further investigation. There was no response.

Some villagers also said they were frightened to return home because they had been made to take part in the Salwa Judum processions that burnt villages and killed people. 'If we go back, the people will not spare us,' one of them said.

The second phase of the Salwa Judum began with the arrival of the India Reserve Battalion from Nagaland in July 2005. Operation Green Hunt kicked off with Naga forces in the first week of August 2005, on the other side of the Bailadila hills—a place where colonies and roads were yet to spring out of the rugged earth. (The same name was adopted in 2009 for a much larger police operation against the Naxals, spanning several states.) The offensive continued for a week.

It was a week of bloodshed and terror. In Iril, a villager called Karam Pandu was beheaded and his body strung up for everyone to see. In the villages of Vechapal, Hurepal and Harial, ten tribals were rounded up, made to stand in a row, and shot at point-blank range. Eight of the dead bodies were beheaded and six heads were carried off as trophies. Two were found dumped some distance away. This was the prelude to a bloody operation that would last for many months. I had heard these stories from villagers, but was never allowed to reach those villages to verify the accounts.

I would have written it off as an exaggeration by the Naxals, had not a top police officer in Chhattisgarh confirmed on condition of anonymity that 'the Nagas took the heads to Nagaland'. During the first Jan Jagran, a rumour was circulated that if someone did not join the movement, the curse of Danteshwari would split his head into two. After the beheadings, the rumours turned more vicious—there were whispers that the Nagas were cannibals who would eat the tribals if they did not move into the camps. Later, I met many Adivasis who said they had gone to the camps driven by this very fear.

The Naxals retaliated by planting landmines in Padeda school where the CRPF was camping. Two jawans were killed. It was the first attack on security forces after the start of the Salwa Judum.

In the second week of August, Manish Kunjam, a former MLA of the CPI, issued a press release saying that the Salwa Judum was not a spontaneous movement. But the media let it go.

On 23 August, the Party blew up an anti-landmine vehicle of the CRPF near Ponjer, killing twenty-three jawans to avenge Operation Green Hunt. This was the first anti-landmine vehicle attack, and the Naxals claim it was led by Deve, a tribal girl. So far, the Party had only tried to convince people not to join the Salwa Judum; they had not attacked any civilians associated with it. The Ponjer attack led to a brief lull: the second round of Operation Green Hunt began the very next month, with the Naga battalion once again.

I wondered why the state attacks were concentrated on this area. The answer lay in its location. These villages are only a few kilometres from the Bailadila mines numbered 1 and 3, leased to Tata and Essar by the NMDC. A team of revenue officials had visited these villages with Mahendra Karma to ask for land to make roads, ponds, an airport and railway lines which would facilitate mining, but the villagers had driven them away. Many of these villages are not even mentioned in the government revenue records and so, they are unlikely to be compensated for any land they give up.

People here are witness to decades of neglect. Even the NMDC's presence in the vicinity for the last fifty years and the resultant 'planned development' has not ensured that they have roads, electricity and ration shops. They have a single school—run by a Christian missionary—to send their children to. The river that sustains them has been choked with iron ore dust discharged by the NMDC. Good health is a rarity, and life expectancy is low. And only a few weeks of private industrial interest had led to the launch of Operation Green Hunt!

The unrest did not, however, deter the Tatas from applying on 3 September 2007 and 19 September 2008 for a licence to look for iron ore in the 100 square kilometre stretch on which these villages stand. Other companies followed suit. Concerned citizens and activists began to voice their surprise at the way the signing of MoUs with the Tatas and Essar coincided with the start of the Salwa Judum. The work plan of the collector of Dantewada, K.R. Pisda, even mentioned that Essar had funded some of the camps, lending credibility to the hypothesis that the entry of industries into the area and the rise of the Salwa Judum were connected.

Soon after activists pointed out that the Tatas had signed their MoU on the very day that the Salwa Judum was launched—5 June—the Chhattisgarh State Industrial Development Corporation changed the dates on its website. As of now, the date of the MoU with the Tatas is 6 April, while the one with Essar has been changed to 7 May. The Tatas also issued a press release claiming that the MoU had been signed before the start of the Salwa Judum. If it were a simple coincidence, why did the dates need to be changed?

I discovered other procedural lapses. Every village that decides to give away tribal land must hold a Gram Sabha meeting to get the consent of the residents and hammer out the details. I met a tribal near Jagdalpur, who told me that official records show him as having presided over the Gram Sabha where it was decided to give away land to the Tatas. The day the meeting was shown to be held, however, he was in Maharani Hospital for a medical check-up.

The state was ostensibly helping the industrial houses. But I also witnessed Mahendra Karma and other Salwa Judum leaders forcing tribals to give their consent to the upcoming Essar steel plant. I was almost beaten up when the angry tribals mistook me for an Essar official during one of the public hearings.

The local media ignored these blatant irregularities. Some spread outright lies.

In September, the state started to appoint some Salwa Judum members as special police officers or SPOs. That was the trigger for the Naxals to begin targeting the Judum camps. The Kutru camp of which Suraj and Sudri had spoken, was the first.

State propaganda on the Salwa Judum named a certain Sodi Deva as a mythical leader carrying the movement on his shoulders. Salwa Judum press releases in his name carried a fax number—it was of the local police station. The idea of a mythical leader was ludicrous, but a senior police officer told me with a straight face, 'Sodi Deva will appear at the right time. If he is exposed now, the Naxals will attack him.' The Naxals, though, were looking for Madhukar Rao in Kutru camp—he was the real Sodi Deva—but failed to find him there.

A couple of months after the Karkeli incident, Kamlesh Painkra, a local tribal journalist working with *Hindsatt*, reported the Salwa Judum atrocities. This was the first report in the local press of any human rights violation by the Salwa Judum. He had written about the burning of homes in Mankeli village, a Party stronghold. Maoists claimed that twelve people had been killed there. The local police chief, D.L. Manhar, called Kamlesh and 'advised' him to retract his report. Kamlesh refused, and lost his job at *Hindsatt*. His brother, a schoolteacher, was accused of being a Naxal supporter and put behind bars.

Kamlesh's home happened to be on the compound of the CRPF camp in Bijapur. An officer vouched for Kamlesh's brother, and said that he could not possibly be a Maoist supporter as he lived literally in the CRPF's backyard. The officer was transferred and the CRPF later bulldozed Kamlesh's house to make room for a volleyball court.

The CPI visited Mankeli after reading Kamlesh's report and even wrote to the prime minister in November. Newspapers did not consider it worth reporting. Kamlesh learned from his sources that he could become the victim of an 'encounter' soon and decided to leave the area. He now works as a translator for an NGO.

Over the next six months, the Naxals issued six press releases reporting the deaths of more than a hundred innocent people at the hands of the Salwa Judum. Only one newspaper, *Deshbandhu*, published them.

Two groups of human rights activists also visited the affected areas around this time. With one of them came Dr Binayak Sen, who was later arrested for his alleged links with the Maoists. By this time, Chhattisgarh Chief Minister Raman Singh was calling the Salwa Judum a Gandhian movement. As if on cue, Prime Minister Manmohan Singh realized that the Maoists are the biggest internal security threat to the nation.

In January, the Salwa Judum shifted its attention to Dantewada district. The then police chief, O.P. Rathor, identified villagers who could be appointed leaders of the Salwa Judum. At a meeting held in Raipur—arranged by a local journalist—these villagers were told that they could think about the offer and join the Judum, or face the consequences. They decided to join. I heard about that meeting from Soyam Erra, who later became the head of the Dornapal Salwa Judum camp.

The other arms of the government machinery were also being mobilized methodically. I met some local Adivasi schoolteachers and health workers who claimed they were beaten up by the police when they tried to enter the villages to carry out their duties. There were others, though, who drew salaries without even having to show up for work.

One such government employee was Madhukar Rao—the mythical Sodi Deva—who pocketed his salary as a teacher during the years that he led the Salwa Judum, without having taken a single class. In Dantewada, the chosen leader was Soyam Muka, a schoolteacher, who, like Madhukar, regularly received his pay without working for it. His father, Jogiah, was a Congress MLA. Muka belonged to the Adivasi upper class: his family owned hundreds of acres of land in Gaganpalli. He led the first Salwa Judum rally in Dantewada in January 2006.

Education, health and subsidized rations—everything was being used as a weapon against the Maoists. The public distribution system told its own story. Dantewada and Bijapur districts have 7,00,000 residents between them. At any point, the Judum camps in these districts, the state claimed, had a maximum of 57,000 inmates—less than 10 per cent of the population. Yet, more than 90 per cent of subsidized food was diverted to the camps.

I considered the figures for Konta block. A report of the collector of Dantewada said that of the 340 villages in Konta, 140 had joined the Salwa Judum. It was less than half the total number, and not all residents of those 140 villages had shifted to the camps. Nevertheless, as food officer Netam told me, the administration closed down forty-eight of the fifty-five ration shops there. The seven shops which remained open were spared as they were located close to the main roads. I also learned that of 5100 quintals of sanctioned grains, 4500 quintals—nearly 90 per cent of the entire amount—were diverted to the camps. Netam also revealed that all the ration shops on the 'other side' of the Indravati, still a Maoist stronghold, had been closed down.

The local MLA, Kawasi Lakhma, later alleged in the Assembly that 338 schools had shut down in Konta block since the start of the Salwa Judum. Once the schools closed down, health services were no longer available and ration shops moved to the camps, people would have no choice but to move—this was the undeclared strategy.

The Party decided to answer with brute force. After the second phase of Operation Green Hunt, the Naxals attacked a Salwa Judum camp in Gangalur on 29 January 2006, killing nine people, three of whom were SPOs. Barely a week later, on 6 February, they killed ten members of the Naga forces in an ambush in Kottacheru.

Konta had its first Salwa Judum meeting, attended by Mahendra Karma, on 26 February. After the meeting, the attendees marched through the villages of Mukuttong, Gorka, Sunnamguda and Ategatta, burning down homes.

The Party had already decided to attack these rallies, but needed more explosives to make a dent in the swelling ranks of Judum supporters. On 9 February, they raided the NMDC iron ore mines, looting twenty tons of gelatin. It was enough to last them a few months. On 28 February, as a truckload of Salwa Judum supporters returned after a rally, a landmine planted under their vehicle went off near Darbhaguda, killing thirty-five of them.

In March, the Salwa Judum moved to Basaguda, a new territory for them. They held a meeting on 4 March, after which they herded the villagers into the camp. Three days later, the Naxals struck there, killing three people. The police did not fight back. Basaguda was a town of rich traders; the attack prompted more than three-quarters of the inmates to move to the safety of towns and cities. Only the poor stayed behind in the camps. In the second week of March, the Naxals attacked a camp at Injeram.

The war was getting bloodier.

The violence with which the Naxals reacted caught the state by surprise. K.P.S. Gill—the man who is credited with quelling terrorism in Punjab—was sought out and appointed adviser to the government of Chhattisgarh on 16 April 2006. That very day, the Naxals mounted a daring attack—it was their 'welcome message' for Gill. Early on the morning of 16 April, sixty comrades boarded a bus for Murkinar, which hosted the Chhattisgarh Armed Forces. There, they attacked the police station in broad daylight, killing nine policemen and capturing fifty-four weapons. Those injured in the attack received no medical aid till evening. It was a huge blow to the morale of the Chhattisgarh police. The Naxals filmed the entire attack and circulated the video to the media.

Gill's arrival was significant for the Salwa Judum as well. Mahendra Karma had a week-long programme scheduled in the Dornapal area, starting the same day that Gill arrived. Perhaps he too wanted to show Gill what his boys could do. While the Party was firing on the police at Murkinar, Karma was on his way to Arlampalli with an entourage of eighty motorbikes and ten four-wheelers carrying 200 Salwa Judum members. Another Salwa Judum leader, Rambhuvan Kushwaha, and the chief of Dornapal police station were with him in a jeep.

On reaching Arlampalli, Karma stepped out of the jeep and proceeded to perform the bhoomi pooja ceremony. In a flash, one of the villagers tried to shoot him, but his pistol—a locally made weapon—did not fire. Karma beat him till he tired of raining blows on the man, but did not kill him. One could almost call Karma magnanimous, and I speak from personal experience when I say this. I have written much about him that has often foiled his plans, yet he has always treated me with the utmost restraint.

The Salwa Judum looted and torched the entire village. By this time, news of the Murkinar attack reached Karma and he cancelled his elaborate plans.

Two Salwa Judum groups of fifty members each had already left from the Errabore camp that day with menace on their minds. The first group went to Gaganpalli and the second to Nendra. They burnt down both villages, killing three people in each attack. They also captured seven people and dragged them off to the camp, killing five of them over the next few days.

The Murkinar bloodbath could not go unavenged— three Salwa Judum teams started from the Injeram, Konta and Errabore camps on 22 April. They burnt down village after village—Gorka, Ategatta, Darbhaguda, Kottacheru, Gerapad, Mukuttong, Neelamadagu, Bande, Kannaiguda, Bateru, Bhandarpadar, Palakitte, Sunnamguda, Atekal, Uskevaya, Ramnagar, Regadgatta and Onderpara—over the next three days. Only those who managed to flee into the forest escaped. In Neelamadagu, the Salwa Judum found no one but a twelve-year-old boy, Madvi Rama. His body was later found chopped into pieces. In Gerapad, an old man was hacked mercilessly. In Kottacheru, they killed Madkam Hadma, the sixty-year-old father of Madkam Hunga, the former block president of Konta who had been killed by the Naxals in 2004.

As many as 40,000 people had been shifted to the roadside camps by this time; they would be taken to Salwa Judum rallies by trucks as far as the roads went, covering the rest of the distance on foot. I attended some of Karma's meetings. Though there was no violence, at least in my presence, they were frightening. Karma's deputies carried lists of alleged pro-Maoists: the villagers were ordered to produce them or face the consequences.

People were being sucked into the violence, forced to side with whichever group presented itself as stronger. The newspapers were silent about the attacks by the Salwa Judum, choosing to report acts of violence only by the Party. The local media and my fellow journalists resented my determination to expose the atrocities of the Salwa Judum. Journalists too faced security threats. The Naxals did not harm them, but the Salwa Judum had the immunity of police protection. When *Hindsatt* reporter Afzal Khan wrote unflatteringly about them, he was beaten up and had to go underground for months.

The Party did not take the attacks by the enemy lying down. Fifty Party members, along with 300 villagers whose houses had been burnt a week earlier, attacked Injeram camp on 28 April at 3 a.m. and killed six SPOs. The Naga forces did not engage in the fight and the SPOs, having given up their arms for the day in accordance with the camp rules, had no way of defending themselves.

The same week, forty people from Dornapal camp, who had returned home to collect their belongings, were caught in Manikonta village by the Naxals. That strike left nine SPOs and two villagers dead. The remaining people were released. The Naxals said the SPOs were given a chance to defend themselves in a public hearing, where they admitted to having slit the throat of Madkam Podia of Tongguda and then beheading him. They also confessed to taking part in the burning of Arlampalli, Medvaya, Gorgunda, Tetraya, Badikunta and Gaganpalli.

The press carried stories that the captive people were forced to drink urine in this attack. The Naxals claim that the stories were false, agreeing to apologize publicly if the charge were ever proved. After the horrific attacks by the Salwa Judum, they needed to act just as strongly to build the confidence of their supporters, they reasoned.

Slowly but steadily, the tribals mustered the courage to oppose the Salwa Judum. In June 2006, a Judum rally was driven out of Madded town. Mahendra Karma, who had been helming it, hid at the police station in Madded until the coast was clear for his escape. After this attack, plans to take the Salwa Judum to Bhopalpatnam were hastily dropped. But the local media chose not to report this.

Emboldened by their previous attacks, the Naxals mounted their biggest strike on the Judum on 16 July. A mob of 110 comrades and more than 500 villagers broke loose on Errabore camp. The Naxals had done their homework— they had surveyed the site for a week and gathered from the inmates that the camp had 120 CRPF and forty District Force personnel. The Party set the camp ablaze, but only after instructing the inmates to evacuate. The attack started at 11 p.m. and continued till the attackers retreated at 1.20 a.m.

A woman inmate and her child died in the fire—the Naxals acknowledge it as a lapse on their part—but no one knows why she went back into the camp. The security team swung into action in the safety of anti-landmine vehicles only after the attackers left. Thirty-six SPOs were killed in the raid. Ten people, including four SPOs whom the Naxals later killed, were captured. The six remaining hostages were released.

During the Errabore attack, many tribals who had been forced to stay in the camp made their getaway. I later met two women who ran away to Andhra. They were among the seven people picked up from Nendra. The five men kidnapped along with them had been killed and buried near the Errabore camp by the Salwa Judum.

Five days later, on 21 July, the state called in helicopters to airdrop security forces in the area. At 1 p.m. villagers of Ragadgatta watched two helicopters whirring overhead. One carried personnel from the Naga battalion and the other, the CRPF. As the people dashed helter-skelter for cover, the forces opened fire. Three villagers were killed and one injured. Two villagers were captured and taken by the forces. One of them was thrown off the helicopter, but survived the fall. Another helicopter reached Gondum village the next day and security forces picked up three people. They were beaten up and thrown into the river Shabri. One swam to safety, to a village called Kurti in Orissa, and returned home after a week.

On 27 July, a helicopter carrying a team of forty CRPF men and SPOs landed at Gellur. They torched the village of Thummal and caught an old man, Koram Nanda, whom they threw into a burning house. They had planned to walk to Jagargunda but decided not to, when, in Surpanguda village, a farmer attacked a CRPF jawan with an axe for burning his house. The helicopters were recalled after this, and the operation was abandoned. The same day, another helicopter had gone to Bandarpalli village near Awapalli. There, security forces arrested Kanniah, the father of a Divisional Committee member of the Party.

Kanniah had returned to the village after being released from the Salwa Judum camp after nine months. I use the word 'release' with good reason. Although the camps may not have been like prisons structurally, inmates have spoken repeatedly of the difficulty of returning home from there. Whether it was on account of Naxal reprisals or the pressure of the Salwa Judum, the fact remained that people were not free to make their own choices.

As the weeks passed, the police made it increasingly difficult to visit villages which had been the scenes of violence. I could not confirm many of these incidents that I heard of, but noted them down in the belief that they are factual accounts that can be cross-checked at a later date.

There was a false sense of peace after this bloodbath. In reality, the plunder simply shifted to smaller villages, carried out by smaller groups of attackers.

There were so many villages and so many attacks: the names of the dead came to me in an endless stream. To begin with, I noted it all down thinking it would substantiate what I would write. Finally though, I was not sure that the names of pillaged villages and their dead would really convince anyone. Still, I wanted to write about at least one representative village that would evoke the horror that villagers have gone through since the start of the Salwa Judum.

I first heard about Takilod from Suraj. Takilod has not seen the most bloodshed, nor have its residents needed to flee to other states as thousands from other villages have had to. But it survived as many as nine attacks.

When the Salwa Judum started, monsoon was round the corner. The rains came, and a swollen Indravati made it impossible to cross over to the other side, where Takilod was located. In November, came the first attack. Two villagers, Dunga and Bedma, narrowly escaped with their lives, while two others, Budru and Dukaru, were killed. About a hundred homes were burnt.

In the following months, Mahendra Karma drummed up a frenzy about the murder of his brother, Podia, by the Party seven years earlier. He announced that Home Minister Ramvichar Netam would visit Takilod and hold a meeting on 8 January 2006. Takilod perhaps held a personal significance for Karma.

The Party, at this time, was in bad shape; its energy devoted entirely to saving the property of the people. The comrades even hid food supplies in the forest so that the Salwa Judum couldn't destroy them.

On the day of the meeting, 500 policemen and 1500 Salwa Judum members—including the police chiefs of Dantewada and Bijapur, and the collector of Dantewada—split up into groups and crossed the river at seven different points. They killed Chhannu, a villager, in Palli and burnt the hamlet down. On their way, they set fire to the villages of Bodga, Ponad, Belnar and Dharma.

The Naxals had laid booby traps that injured more than twenty members of the Judum. When the helicopter carrying

Mahendra Karma and the home minister was about to land in Takilod, another booby trap blew a CRPF jawan's leg off. The Salwa Judum crowd dispersed and the meeting was cancelled. Karma, however, did not leave until some more homes were torched. The Salwa Judum did not return for a whole year.

On 8 February 2007, ten policemen died in a landmine explosion on a road that ran parallel to the Indravati. The next day, a team of 300, consisting of policemen from the CRPF, soldiers from the Naga battalion and SPOs, crossed the river. In this third attack, they caught eighteen women who were picking vegetables near the hills just outside Takilod. They took away four young girls and released the rest. All four were raped and killed and their bodies were taken away. On their way back, the team killed three men, Budhram, Mundru and Buse, and burnt houses. A team of twenty comrades was in the area at that time. They tried to fire on the police team but were outnumbered, and lost Comrade Pandu in the crossfire. The next day, the police dressed the dead bodies of two of the dead girls, Aite and Silok, in military fatigues and fed the press a story of 'a successful encounter'. The bodies of the other girls, Adme and Somli, were found in the river.

On 21 February, the police attacked Takilod for the fourth time and killed five unsuspecting villagers as they sat under a tree drinking salfi. They left one of the men, Pandu, for dead. But he lived to tell the tale.

In March, the then police chief, Vishwaranjan, came to Orchha by helicopter and planned a fifth attack—between 15 April and 20 April—to take over Takilod. The resilient village was clearly hurting their ego. According to the plan, three teams under a trio of police chiefs from Narayanpur, Dantewada and Bijapur would attack Takilod from three sides. The Maoists attacked the Narayanpur team, injuring five jawans. They had to be airlifted to safety, which must have broken their morale as all the teams turned tail and went back on 16 April. The police caught two people, who are in Jagdalpur jail now. The elaborate operation was a flop.

In their sixth attack on 8 December, they killed a villager named Maniram and injured a young girl, Munni.

After the slew of attacks, a village team was set up to keep an eye on the riverbank from where the police had arrived. On 23 January 2009, when the team made its way to the riverbank, the police caught them by surprise and killed five of them.

Ninety policemen and seventy SPOs took part in the eighth attack on 3 May 2009. As they marched on, they raped two girls, Moti and Sona, in the villages of Bogda and Utla, respectively.

I wondered if the accounts of the killings that I had recorded in such detail would have any real impact. The stories numbed me, and I found myself unable to put down the facts blow by blow. Besides, there was no way I could verify all the stories.

In the last attack on 3 February 2010, a team of policemen and SPOs arrested fourteen tribals, killing seven of them.

That is a head count of twenty-nine dead. In one village.

But not one of these killings was ever reported as they happened.

***

Towards the end of 2006, the Salwa Judum slowed down in the areas where it had first got a foothold, and extended its reach to Golapalli, where Jagargunda camp was set up. This was the area for which the Tatas applied for a prospective licence to look for iron ore reserves in November 2008.

Here too, just like Mahendra Karma and Soyam Muka, another upper-class representative was chosen. Sunnam Nagesh was one of the richest men in Golapalli, and had tried aligning himself with the Party for a while, before finally joining the Salwa Judum. This was a choice he would later regret. The state strategy has been to leverage the support of upper-class members, like Sunnam, amongst the tribals, and use force on the masses.

I had travelled in the Salwa Judum camps and also spent considerable time with the Naxals for a documentary for the British broadcaster, Channel 4, in 2006. It was a trip from which I returned with many stories, not all of which I could put down on paper. I tried to share the information I had with other journalists, but it was received with deep suspicion. It was implied more than once that I was sympathetic to the Maoists. Even journalists who knew me well could not relate to what I was saying.

By this time, a Public Interest Litigation (PIL) had been filed in the Supreme Court accusing the Salwa Judum of killing 548 people and raping 99 women. The Supreme Court ordered an inquiry by the National Human Rights Commission (NHRC), which concluded that there were some killings that needed further investigation, but no rapes could be confirmed.

The PIL mentioned a village called Pusbaka, where

twenty women had allegedly been raped—the highest number in any village. The area was difficult to approach and, without Naxal permission, it would be impossible to travel safely. But I felt compelled to make an independent inquiry.

Pusbaka lay on the other side of the river Talperu and could be accessed by a bridge that was closely guarded by a contingent of security forces. I was warned that it was not safe to cross the border, that beyond the river lay 'Pakistan', enemy territory. I first heard this term from a police officer, who explained that the river Indravati and its tributaries are like a boundary for the area occupied by the Maoists. Beyond it, lies 'Pakistan', which has only grown over the years. Police officers now say on record that the state controls only 40 per cent of the area; 40 per cent is under the control of the Maoists in Bastar, and the remaining land is still being fought over. Maoist areas differ from territory occupied by the LTTE—there are no check posts demarcating the areas of control. It is possible to slip in, though hardly easy. One is likely to be detected in no time and captured for at least an interrogation.

I was told that I could reach the police chief in Raipur on my phone to seek his help if I climbed a rooftop high enough to catch a signal. I did, and he promised to arrange for me to travel across. But on the Talperu bridge, a helpful policeman told me that it would be a waste of time to ask for permission to cross, because the instructions were quite clear: no one should be allowed.

I spent the night in a school hostel, where the children showed me a path they took to reach villages on the other side of the river. Logically, this path would be safe for me as

well—at least, there would not be any landmines. Before
sunrise, I slipped past the guards and reached Pusbaka.
I was the first visitor to the village since the start of the Salwa
Judum, except, of course, the NHRC team that crossed
the bridge in anti-landmine vehicles. I was immediately
'arrested'.

The family that extended its 'hospitality' to me during my
week-long captivity had four members. But I could not talk
to them as I did not know their language. My bodyguard,
who was by my side at all times, was the only person who
could translate for me. The villagers refused to release me,
and would not let me return. They would first ask the dadas,
the Naxals, they said.

It was a scary week, akin to entering a foreign country
without a visa. In Pusbaka, there was no electricity, no
school, no hospital and no post office. All the buildings had
been destroyed. The distant lights crowning the Bailadila
hills became my only connection with 'India'. I would watch
the lights every night as I lay under a mosquito net on my
charpoy, with my bodyguard never out of sight. In the few
words he spoke to me, he explained that the buildings had
been blown up to prevent the police from occupying them.
After the Salwa Judum had been stopped from entering the
village, he said, the people had begun cultivation. Indeed,
green stalks of paddy were standing tall in the village.

One day, an old man conveyed to me that the NHRC
team had been accompanied by the same SPOs who had
raped the girls. 'Everyone ran away and they caught hold
of two of us. We were trembling with fear and blurted out
that no rapes had taken place here.' He said that though the

figure of twenty was incorrect, it was true that women had been raped, and named eight girls who had been subjected to it over a period of time.

I was horrified to know that one of them was the daughter of the very family in whose house I was being held hostage.

After what seemed like an eternity, I got the news that the dadas would allow me to go back. Back in 'India', I went to the same police camp on Talperu bridge and told them of my imprisonment. 'You are very lucky to have returned alive; they are savages!' was the response. I had a warm welcome: a good lunch from the community kitchen. It was Janmashtami, a Hindu festival, and some local villagers had also been invited to celebrate. I asked the officer in charge, deputy commandant Vijay Shankar Singh of the CRPF, if I could meet Commander Dhariwal. My interest had been piqued ever since the villagers mistook me for him. He laughed and explained that Dhariwal wore spectacles and sported a beard just like me. Dhariwal, he said, had been transferred some time ago.

We got talking over lunch and I asked him how he would compare Chhattisgarh to the North-East, where he had been posted.

'The local support for rebels is much stronger here than it is in the North-East.'

'And what about Kashmir?'

He took a while to answer. 'In Kashmir, the fight is direct, face-to-face. Here, there is so much forest cover. And the Naxals have mastered the art of explosives, which is deadly. Also, they attack in large numbers.'

I asked him what, to his mind, could be the solution to this problem.

'There is no military solution. You have seen how thick the forest is. It is impossible to surround it from all sides. And anyway, it is a government-created problem: most jobs are held by outsiders and the administration is geared to serve the businessmen rather than the tribals. These poor people sell tamarind for Rs 2–3 a kilo, but have to shell out Rs 15–20 for the same amount when they go to buy it in the market after just a few months. If the CRPF were to leave, the state police would be unable to defend itself, let alone take any action against the rebels. The solution has to be a mix of military, political and administrative action.'

Some wisdom here, I thought. I asked him if he was speaking on record and he was happy to confirm that he was. But was anybody listening in 'India'?

***

For the tribals, the political situation could not pose a greater dilemma: the Naxals wanted them to stay away from the roadside camps, while the Salwa Judum wanted to herd them there. The only thing they were sure of, was that their misery would only deepen.

By early 2007, the Salwa Judum had lost steam.

In March, the police launched another attack on villages near Basaguda. One of these, Lingagiri, refused to take the help of the Naxals to ward off the police. The villagers were too frightened to take sides.

In that village, I met Ghantal Raju, who lost his parents and his sister—she was raped before she was murdered—in the attack. He told me of four others who had died. The remaining villagers decided to walk across the border into Andhra Pradesh. It was a five-day journey. One woman in the group, Ghantal Baby, was pregnant and gave birth to a boy on the third day. They named the baby Adi Ramudu, king of the forest.

Thousands of villagers migrated to the forests of Andhra and Orissa that border Chhattisgarh, to the chagrin of the police and forest officials of those states. They even burnt down the temporary homes; one of the forest settlements I visited in Andhra had been razed more than a dozen times. The crops that the migrants had cultivated after clearing forest land were destroyed. The objective was to somehow push these people back, but the situation in their home state was even worse. Initially, the state refused to acknowledge the existence of any internally displaced people. Their exact number has never been estimated. They are the nowhere people, neither here nor there.

On 15 March, the Naxals drove the last nail in the Salwa Judum coffin at Ranibodli, killing fifty-five policemen, including thirty-nine SPOs. The police had been camping in some rooms of a hostel for tribal girls when the Naxals attacked. The dadas say they lost six of their comrades in an attempt to ensure that no civilian was harmed.

In a retaliatory attack on 9 April, the police attacked Ponjer and Santoshpur and killed twelve villagers without provocation. I reached Santoshpur the day after, to find people fleeing the village in fear. When I wrote about my interviews with the villagers, the police refuted it with a press release stating that people had died in the crossfire.

Then, a citizen journalist on CGNet posted a video

interview with the head of the SPOs' team, a former sarpanch
of Santoshpur. He admitted to having led the attack and
gave graphic details. The police response was to send out
another press release claiming that the interview with the
sarpanch had been taken at gunpoint! The case attracted
public attention and an inquiry was ordered. The inquiry,
however, concluded that the villagers had been killed by
'unidentified gunmen'.

In May 2007, Dr Binayak Sen was arrested. His supporters
claimed it was a punitive action by the state for exposing the
killings of Santoshpur and Ponjer.

The CPI, meanwhile, continued to resist the Salwa Judum
and organized its first rally against it in Cherla in Andhra
Pradesh in May 2007. More than 40,000 people took part.

I had wrapped up the documentary for Channel 4
around this time, and gave a copy of the film to a senior
representative of the largest newspaper in Chhattisgarh. He
kept his promise to get the story of the wrongdoings of the
Salwa Judum into their local edition, although this could not
have been easy. The morning that the article was published,
the Chhattisgarh police chief O.P. Rathor succumbed to a
massive heart attack. A coincidence, of course.

It had become obvious that the Naxals gained support
in far greater numbers because they were a foil to the Salwa
Judum, a force the tribals had grown to loathe. The CPI
organized another anti-Salwa Judum rally in Dantewada,
Mahendra Karma's home town. More than 50,000 people
attended—a success for which the Naxals take credit. People
turned up for the meeting at the behest of the dadas, they
maintain.

On 9 July, the Salwa Judum, backed by the CRPF, started marching from Errabore, burning one village after another. A villager from Gompad, who managed to elude the pillaging group and run to Regadgatta, found Ramanna chairing a Party meeting there. Ramanna and his men gave chase and caught up with the CRPF team. They hid behind trees, and the CRPF had no cover. Twenty-four CRPF men were killed in that incident. A boy named Dulal from Gaganpalli was so furious, that when he had no bullets left, he charged at the CRPF jawans with his knife. He was the only casualty on the Naxal side.

Every Party success boosted the confidence of the people. On 29 August, eleven policemen were killed in Tadmetla. Two months later, ten Mizo jawans died in Bande. Eleven policemen were killed in November in Tongguda, and twelve in Battiguda the following month. And the list goes on.

When the CPI called an anti-Salwa Judum rally at the headquarters in Jagdalpur, more than 1,50,000 people attended.

The meeting was significant not only as a show of strength against the Judum, but also as the beginning of the end of the newly forged alliance between the CPI and the Naxals. So far, the CPI had lent its name to the rallies. But this time, the Naxals wanted it to be held under the banner of the Anti-Displacement Front. They say that not only did the CPI refuse, but they also did not allow anyone from the Party to address the public. Many attendees had walked for over a week to reach Jagdalpur. The Naxals claim that not even 10,000 people at the rally were CPI supporters. If the CPI could independently garner public support on this scale, why would their candidate get fewer than 80,000 votes in the elections just a few months later, ask the Naxals.

More than 80 per cent of the people left the camps by 2007, but it seemed that the rest would not be able to go back home for a long time. That was the sense I got from Ajay Singh, the second in command in the Salwa Judum, after Mahendra Karma. Singh used to supply rice to the Naxals. But after the Salwa Judum came into the picture, he quickly decided on which side he would be. He became a contractor and built a palatial house for himself. 'We are trapped. We started the movement with the assurance of full support. But the government has ditched us halfway,' he said.

Another person who gained from his association with the Salwa Judum, is Sunnam Nagesh. Driving around in his new SUV, Sunnam began to enjoy a life of comfort. He bagged a contract to build a nine-kilometre road for over Rs 18 crore. He complained, 'Most of the people I brought to the camps have gone back to their villages and apologized to the Naxals. But we cannot go home. We are neither here nor there.' He did, however, devise a way to enrich his coffers—selling most of the rations meant for the camp in the market.

The Naxal hit list comprised twenty-five Salwa Judum leaders, including Sunnam, Muka and Ajay Singh. Nine of them have been executed already. The rest will not be spared, they told me.

Recruitment had never been so steady for the Naxals. In 2005, they had planned to form their second military company in December 2006. But by March 2006, they had seven such companies.

The tract of the Bailadila, where the mines of the Tatas

and Essar are coming up, and where the first attacks by the Salwa Judum took place, more than 500 comrades were recruited in the six months between January and July 2006. In February 2006, they formed a civil army—the Koya Bhumkal militia—with 6000 people and at the time of this interview, its numbers had more than doubled.

Whenever I visited a village, I put one question to the residents: 'How many of you worked full-time for the Party before the start of the Salwa Judum and how many after?' My calculations indicate that the ranks of the Naxals grew at least threefold, if not more, since the start of the Salwa Judum.

The Naxals say as many as 996 tribals died since the start of the Salwa Judum. Of them, 200 remain unidentified. They claim that only around 200 of the dead were sangham members, the rest were innocent villagers. The casualties on their own side since 2005, they say, number less than fifty. More than 2000 houses in over 700 villages have been burnt.

Vasu told me, 'Though we called the movement People's War, it was the Salwa Judum that made it a real people's war. The Salwa Judum left no room for fence-sitters.'

Sonu even wrote an article in their magazine with a telling title—'Thank You, Salwa Judum.'

***

I have heard that many SPOs used to be Maoist commanders before joining the police—stories that the Naxals rubbish. They claim that only one full-time Party member, Madkam

Mudraj, succumbed to the SPO recruitment campaign during the time of the Salwa Judum. But they hasten to add that though the Party gave him a weapon, he worked from home and was not strictly a member of the operational armed cadre. I had heard about him in Singaram, the village where SPOs had killed nineteen 'innocent villagers'. The villagers had told me that it was Madkam who identified the villagers to be killed, and that his only motivation was to settle personal scores.

Madkam was on my list of people to interview, so I asked the police chief of Dantewada, Rahul Sharma, if he would introduce me to him. Madkam was in Sukma, a couple of hours away and he offered to get him to come down to the station to meet me. I agreed readily, never loath to accept a cup of tea and a chance for a conversation. Over tea, Sharma said, 'The main problem is that the tribals are not greedy. If they were, finding a solution would have been easy.' Before I could explore the statement further, he added, 'We need to bring TV to villages to solve this problem.'

This sounded familiar. I remembered that John Rettie, my journalism guru, who was an expert on Latin America, would say, 'What all the American forces could not do in so many years, TV has done. It has destroyed the Latin American tribal culture and its strength to fight back together.'

Sharma's words brought to mind what Gondi professor Hiralal Shukla told the Intelligence Bureau when it sought his suggestions to end the Naxal problem. He said that the tribals needed to be kept busy. 'You start a cultural university in Bastar. I will wean the tribal away from Maoists with his culture.' I could not help but notice that none of them spoke of justice. The solutions are about how to manage the problem for the rest of society, while the injustice continues.

Madkam arrived in a few hours. Sharma was happy to let me meet him on my own, but Madkam, a thin young man, wanted two of his colleagues to be present during the interview. They too were SPOs. He introduced one of them as Kichche Nanda, the leader of the team which attacked Singaram. Kichche's 'coup' in Singaram had made him a name to reckon with.

But I wanted to talk to Madkam first. I asked him why he had left the dadas.

'The dadas did not pay me any money. When I did not work at home, my parents gave me a earful and when I did not deliver to the dadas, they shouted at me.'

I did not tell him that I had met his father at the Maraigudem Salwa Judum camp on the Andhra-Chhattisgarh border. The inmates of the camp told me that he had lost his mental balance after his son killed so many people in Singaram. I wanted to know why he had joined the dadas in the first place.

'There were no police in my area. Since childhood, I had seen only the dadas. But when the Salwa Judum arrived, I joined them.'

'And what were you fighting for when you were with the dadas?'

'They said this government was not good and that they would bring Mao's government,' Madkam offered, rather like a child repeating a lesson learned by heart. And then, collecting himself, he added, 'They may not kill you unless you work for the police, but if you have more than five acres of land, then you are in trouble with them anyway.'

'So why did you kill so many innocent people in Singaram?' I asked.

'They were not innocent,' he insisted. 'Site was my deputy in the Party and she was holding a meeting there. It is possible, though, that when we fired, innocent people may also have died.'

'Are you the only one who has switched over from their side?'

'Yes,' he nodded. 'I am the only one with a gun who has surrendered. But more will surrender in the days to come.'

I turned to Kichche Nanda next. He had led the attacking party that day in Singaram. I started by asking him his reasons for joining the Salwa Judum.

'My brother, Kartam Bhima, was killed by the Party in 2004. He was the headman of the village. I ran away to Orissa after his murder and worked as a driver there. But when the Salwa Judum started, Soyam Erra, who is the head of Dornapal camp, took me to DGP Rathor in Raipur. Rathor sahib asked me to join Salwa Judum.'

The third boy, Bhupendra Koli, looked more like an innocent child than a special police officer. He said softly, 'One day, the police came to my village in Chintalnar and asked me to show them the way. I did, and was instantly on the Naxal hit list. I had no choice but to be an SPO.'

Not a very unusual story.

As we talked, the trio felt more at ease and offered to introduce me to some policemen who were on sentry duty in plain clothes. One of them, an Adivasi from north Bastar, said, 'We must be thankful to the Maoists. We have our jobs because of them. But they want to keep us Adivasis as slaves. As soon as you raise your voice, they kill you. That's why I want to finish them.'

Another said, 'Activists only want to talk about the human rights of Maoists. Don't we policemen have any rights?'

'Can I take pictures of you?' I asked.

Only Kichche agreed to let himself be photographed.

They had ordered tea for me and, as we waited, they started talking amongst themselves about a Maoist who had been released from jail a day earlier.

Kichche said, 'Do you know the name of the lawyer who fought the case for the motherfucker? Let's sort him out.' He noted down the name of the lawyer in his diary. I was amazed to see them do this in front of a journalist. But that is the reality of an ill-trained force.

Madkam is now a married man; a father, in fact. He has a baby daughter. He keeps calling me from time to time and only recently shared with me the news of his promotion. He is now part of the regular police force and earns Rs 9000 a month. The Rs 1500 he used to get as an SPO was meagre, he says. He lives inside the Sukma jail complex, which is now being used to lodge security forces. He is happy, he keeps telling me.

Madkam and SPOs like him might have given some much-needed intelligence to the state's security forces. But was it worth the mayhem that the Salwa Judum has caused in Bastar? And how long will he survive?

8

THE MILITARY MAN

I went back to a Maoist camp in the eastern division of the Party's Dandakaranya 'state' to connect with my old friend, Vasu. This was near the proposed Bodhghat Dam, where we had met earlier. His camp was a half day's walk from the road, in a village, next to a big house. The setting was odd for a hideout, but Vasu assured me that this was sufficiently far from the road to be safe for a short stay.

I would be staying in a house this time, and the first thing I noticed was an oil lamp at the altar of a tulsi shrub on the veranda. This was, after all, Bihari Das's area. A neighbouring house blared out a bawdy Hindi song, and though the homes were spaced apart, the volume was loud enough for me to catch every word. Like Hinduism, Bollywood too had penetrated quite deep.

The courtyard had a hand pump under which some people were hunched, washing clothes. In the garden, a man squatted on a jhilli, surrounded by a few other people, who also sat on their jhillis. Clearly, they had spent the night there.

'That is Rajanna, he is in charge of manufacturing arms for the Party,' Vasu said.

I tried to contain myself. This was a man I would give anything to have an interview with—one the Naxals would hardly want me to talk to. Which army would like to reveal the military secrets behind the manufacture of its arms! But fearing an outright 'no', I dared not ask to speak to him. I simply said that I would like to stay at the camp for a few days to understand its workings.

'Stay as many days as you like,' Vasu said.

The next morning, I woke up early, but lay in bed thinking of ways to reach Rajanna. I heard the other comrades outside. The sound of dishes clanking told me that work in the kitchen had already begun. Others were filling up water. From the window, I could see that neither Rajanna nor Vasu had gone out for their morning exercises.

Over breakfast, I approached Rajanna, trying to appear as casual as I could. He looked too old to be in charge of anything in a Naxal squad. With his grey hair set in smooth waves and thick glasses in rectangular black frames, he looked like an eccentric professor. The army fatigues and the casually slung Sten gun contrasted peculiarly with his face.

Rajanna, whom I preferred to think of as 'the Professor', was happy to talk. 'My father was a carpenter in Hyderabad. We were so poor that I used to work with him every day after school to make ends meet. Still, he could not afford to buy me new shoes, even for festivals. Our neighbours, though, had everything. It made me angry, and those memories stayed with me. Recently, I was in Kolkata to inspect some work in one of our arms manufacturing units. I would take the bus, and every day, it would pass by a big sweet shop. I saw so many cars parked outside that shop and so many bright lights all around that I could not bear it. I would shut my eyes tight when the bus crossed that spot. The imbalance of income in society has disturbed me since childhood.' He paused and drank some water. Clearly, he was still struggling with the memories.

'The Telangana movement for a separate state in 1969 was my first exposure to politics. Some boys in my area hurled a crude bomb at a CRPF team. My neighbour was a chemistry student and used to make bombs while I watched carefully. Soon I started to assist him. After I finished school, I started working in factories, like Kirloskar, Alwyn and Andhra Electricals, but was never appointed as a permanent employee. I was active in trade unions and would invariably get thrown out after three to six months. My father died of jaundice at this time, and my mother wanted me to stay away from trade unions.

'It was around this time that the Naxal movement was crushed in Bengal. Charu Mazumdar had died and Kondapalli Sitaramaiyyah was trying to organize the Party in Andhra. He was a visionary, much like Mao himself. He was very self-confident and used to take impossible tasks upon himself.

'Sitaramaiyyah bought a plot of land in Laksatipetta in Karimnagar, Andhra Pradesh, and began farming. In reality, it was a cover for the anti-feudal struggle he wanted to get started. He bought a second tract of land in Rajnandgaon district in Chhattisgarh, with the intention of making the forest between Karimnagar and Rajnandgaon a safe zone for the Party. The singer Gadar was part of the group started by KS in 1972, a group that later turned into the Jana Natya Manch and played a very important role in the Party.

'KS was not in favour of Charu Mazumdar's line that called for total annihilation, but Charu was so powerful that it was impossible to go against him. In 1972, they killed a landlord in Andhra, for which two of our comrades, Bomayya and Kishtagauda, were sentenced to death three years later. In 1979, when a zamindar's goons killed two of our organizers, Posetty and Laxmi Rajan, KS asked us not to retaliate till the Party grew in strength. I was impressed by his methods and started working in the city as a Party organizer. Later, in 1983, the Party moved me to the technical wing and I started looking after arms and ammunition.

'Only about a third of our Party is armed, and at first, we used to buy all the arms we needed. But now, we purchase only 5 per cent of our arms; around 15 per cent is looted from the police, and we make 80 per cent ourselves.'

It was a substantial amount to manufacture in the circumstances, I thought. I was pleasantly surprised that Vasu did not seem to mind my talking to Rajanna. We had been chatting all morning, and were settled comfortably under a shady tree in the afternoon sun. Rajanna's radio was on, in time for the news report. The newsreader announced that Patel Sudhakar Reddy, one of the Party's Central Committee members, had died. Rajanna turned it off without a word. His face betrayed no emotion.

'Patel Sudhakar Reddy, who has just died—in a fake encounter, I think—was arrested in 1991 in Bangalore. That was the time we used to buy arms. An arms dealer had invited Patel Sudhakar to negotiate a deal with the police, but had come under police pressure and betrayed him. That was how he was arrested and jailed for five years. After this fiasco, the Party started thinking about making our own weapons, but no action was taken until a State Committee member, Saket, was arrested the same way. Also, one of our consignments was intercepted. Finally, the Party decided to make a concerted effort to manufacture our own arms.

'Three couples were moved to one location—my first wife and I were one of them. Padma and her first husband were the second couple and we began to manufacture weapons from scratch. Padma is now married to me.' Sitting next to him, chopping mangoes plucked from the garden, Padma might have been any housewife. This tribal woman from Gadchiroli in Maharashtra did not match any image I had of a Naxal arms manufacturer. She quickly explained, 'In Balaghat, Madhya Pradesh, we both lost our partners in police raids within the space of a month. We decided to marry each other.'

Rajanna said, 'As you know, women are the main force of our movement today. Have you heard of the blouse struggle? It drove many girls to the Party.'

Padma explained. 'By the 1980s, girls from my tribe had started wearing blouses. But when a bride entered her new home, she had to throw away her blouse, never to wear it again. Many girls objected to this custom and the Party supported them.

'But that was not my only reason for joining the Party. My parents never wanted me to join the Naxals and thought it better to get me married off. But one day, a forest guard slapped my father in front of me just because he had collected some wood from the forest to build our house. That was the turning point for me and I decided to join the Party. Two of my brothers were in the police. I persuaded them to quit. They decided to turn to farming instead, but the police began to harass them. Things have come to such a head that they cannot live in our village any more. My mother does not intend to leave as she wants to spend her last days there. My brothers have been put behind bars repeatedly since I joined the Party. It has been twenty years since I last went home. Now that there is a police camp in my village, it has become all the more difficult. Last year, I asked my brothers and my mother to meet me at a secret location. It was the only way I could see them.

'Forest officials used to harass the girls in my village,' Padma continued. 'They raped so many of them. It was risky to even go to fairs—wherever you went, the forest guards could pick you up.

'That wasn't the only kind of exploitation. I used to go into the forest to cut bamboo. They paid a single rupee for a whole day's work, but we needed the money. With the Party's support, we fought for a hike in wages. It was a long fight.

'I have been part of eight attacks so far, in which we lost five of our comrades. I had never seen death up close before. Even now, when I think about them, I cannot help but cry. The Party asked me if I would like to marry Somaru and I said yes.' Rajanna fished out a picture of Somaru from his bag. 'Somaru was my best friend,' he said. He had two more pictures in his bag—one of Che Guevara and the other of a Telugu poet, a cutout from a newspaper. This constituted the sum of the Professor's hard-earned property.

It was a long but useful deviation, for I did not want to talk only about arms.

Rajanna continued his story. 'I was educated only till class ten, but I manage to read English books. My background in carpentry has been very helpful in putting weapons together. In places like Munger in Bihar, gun manufacturing is a cottage industry. The Indo-Nepal border is another good place to get these weapons. You see the machine gun I carry? It is locally made.'

I noticed that the others were also listening, while Padma served us mangoes. I wondered if the Maoists really share their military stories, or if they were just feeding me lies. I supposed I had to take it or leave it. I bit into a slice of mango and listened.

'The Party bought its first AK-47 in 1987,' Rajanna said, speaking through a mouthful of pulpy mango. 'Earlier, we used to buy an AK-47 for Rs 1.5 lakh, but they cost Rs 5 lakh each now. So we cannot buy them any more.'

'Don't you buy crates of AKs as Kashmiris and guerrillas in the North-East do?' I asked.

Rajanna laughed. 'You need at least Rs 100 crore to deal in the international arms market. The revolutionaries in the North-East and Kashmir are horrified by our measly budget.'

I wanted to know where the Naxals get ammunition from.

'The ammunition comes via dealers between us and the police. The police are very greedy, and such deals take place in every police station in India. Policemen at all levels, from the lowest ranks through the top, are involved. India does not produce any ammunition for the AK series of rifles anyway; it has to be imported by the government. There are some private factories that make ammunition of the basic kind for 12-bore rifles. But for more sophisticated weapons, like the .303, SLR, Insas and the Sten gun, ammunition is made only in the government factory in Khadki, Pune. Our major expense is on cartridges. For example, in Manpur, where SP Choube and twenty-eight policemen were killed, we used up about 1200 cartridges in just three and a half hours. Each roughly costs us Rs 150–200. But then, we buy only one-fourth of our ammunition. The rest is looted from the police!'

'Wasn't a consignment of rocket launchers meant for you confiscated in Chennai some time ago?'

'Yes, that was when Madhu was caught, and he turned approver. He had been working with us since 1995, but thanks to him, our factories in Rourkela and Bhopal were busted. We were working on the .303 and Sten gun project at those factories and had even successfully tested some consignments in the forest. We had also sent some consignments of rocket launchers to the forest before the rest were captured. His arrest was a big blow, but in Andhra, the Party just does not have the strength to punish people like Madhu any more.'

'How do you train people to use rocket launchers?' I could tell from Rajanna's smile that he found it to be a pertinent question.

'It needs a lot of practice. But, as Mao has said, a guerrilla can only practise in war. Rocket launchers have a range of 300–700 metres. We tried it one at night in Kistenar near Narayanpur in 2006, but it went haywire. When we tried during the day, the rocket hit the kitchen of a police camp and injured two people. One needs far too much practice to master their use, so I have decided to abandon that project.'

Rajanna is not one to give up, though.

'In 2005, we experimented with a cannon to fire an iron ball into the Daula police station in Abujhmad. It was similar to the cannons that kings used in the past, but that too misfired. We lost four of our comrades when the cannon burst. After those two failed experiments, I started considering how we could improvise a cannon. I cut a water pipe to size and soldered it close at one end, leaving a small hole in the back to induct a detonator. I packed the pipe with gunpowder and shards of iron.'

So that is what the heavy pipes that many comrades carry around these days are—pipes that they call tope!

'Yes, it is a crude device but it works wonders. So many people have now joined the Party after the Salwa Judum that we are not able to arm all of them. Operating this improvised cannon needs a three-member team. So it also helps to keep our people employed.'

Some employment, I thought to myself.

'This cannon releases a cloud of smoke when it is fired. Visibility is impaired for up to five minutes in a 100 square metre radius. In the forest, this works very well, giving our people time to escape. The result is as good as ten rifles put together. I need fifteen days to deliver one rifle if all the materials are ready, but fifty improvised cannons can be delivered in a day.'

I could see why he was so proud—fifty cannons a day is no small number. Rajanna, with his talent and ability, has had a visible impact on this conflict. I have seen militant groups in Kashmir and the North-East, as well as the LTTE. Their weapons have the gleam of new metal. In Chhattisgarh, however, I do not recall seeing a single rifle that looked like it had been freshly unpacked from a box. Also, they cannot count on infrastructure like electricity and basic machinery—for the assembly or manufacturing process. There is only so much that the Naxals of Chhattisgarh can expect, given that their main area of operation is the forest.

'Do you also make automatic weapons?' I asked him.

'We cannot make any automatic or semi-automatic rifles. Whatever semi- or automatic rifles we have are either seized or bought. We cannot even make magazines for our rifles. We only make single-shot rifles inside the forest. But yes, we can make bombs. We do not have large moulds to make proper shells, but we use pipes and sanitary equipment. We can make grenades equivalent to the Indian army's M36 range, only a bit heavier.'

'Wasn't one of your operations in Rajnandgaon closed down recently?'

'Yes. We had been operating that factory for quite some time. One fine morning, the headman of the village disappeared, and we guessed he had gone to the police. It was very sudden and we could not go very far, but we took away the most valuable of our belongings. The police found only some broken generators and pipes.

'We are very good at repairing rifles. In fact, that is my area of expertise. You give me any automatic rifle, and no matter how many pieces it is in, I will get it working. The government's rifle repair unit is in Jabalpur; it recently celebrated its golden jubilee. We heard them claim on the radio that in these fifty glorious years, they have made so much progress that they can now repair any type of rifle. My boys found it very funny—they had managed the same feat in less than a decade.' Rajanna, clearly, does not think much of the factory. He says that though he does not have an education to speak of, and must face hostility at every step, he has managed to set up an effective team of trained weapon makers.

'We keep reading that you get maximum police casualties in road blasts. Wasn't it your truck of gelatin that was caught in Jashpur on the Jharkhand-Chhattisgarh border?'

'Yes, but we had several other consignments of gelatin. One truck did not make a difference. Improvised Explosive Devices (IEDs) comprise our main weapons now and they are very easy to use: you just need gelatin and a detonator.'

'The attack on the NMDC mines must have yielded a substantial loot of explosives,' I said.

'But we also need detonators,' Rajanna explained. 'They are made only at Indian Detonators Ltd in Hyderabad. Gelatin is like wet flour. You need to link it with a detonator and as soon as you provide a spark, the gelatin explodes. It is not too difficult to organize this. We allow some of the mines and quarries in our area to work only because they supply detonators and gelatin to us.

'Sometimes we also have to contend with technical failures. Recently, we were unsuccessful in carrying out some blasts, so we stole a truckload of gelatin in Manpur, Rajnandgaon, and abducted a group of technicians from the mines. Their advice to us was to place gelatin of superior quality in the centre and surround it with cheaper, inferior gelatin. Gelatin also attracts moisture, so if we place it under the surface of the road, we need to waterproof it first.'

It was a lot of information, but fascinating, nevertheless.

Rajanna continued, 'Our latest advancement is the use of walkie-talkies to detonate bombs from a distance. Chandrababu Naidu suggested that Indian Detonators Ltd should produce detonators that would only respond belatedly, and they have been successful in their research. These detonators are useless to us because we need ones that act in a fraction of a second. Only then can we cause damage as and when we like. Both types are available in the market, so now we need to check each detonator before we use it.'

'Do you use RDX?'

'To procure RDX, we need connections with international weapons dealers—the kind that the Kashmiri and North-East groups have. We have yet to forge those ties. The government uses TNT in its weapons but we have not reached that far either. TNT is one and a half times as powerful as an IED, and RDX is ten times so.'

As we talked, a BBC radio newscast mentioned Sri Lanka. Perhaps it reminded Rajanna of Prabhakaran. He said, 'Dhanu used RDX to kill Rajiv Gandhi. Had she used an IED, she would have had to carry ten times the amount of explosives, which would have been detected easily. I had a lot of respect for Prabhakaran though I did not condone many of his acts. Some of the comrades are in deep depression over the collapse of the LTTE. But I tell them that the situation in Sri Lanka is different from ours. The LTTE had transformed itself into a regular army with a fixed base. When you have a fixed base, it is easier to bomb you and demolish you. But we do not have a fixed base. Bastar is a guerrilla zone and it is very difficult for a conventional army to defeat guerrilla troops.'

'How do you rate the Adivasis here as fighters?'

'I would not call the local Adivasis a martial race. They are not like the Nagas in that respect. But they do have a culture of hunting. So gunpowder is easily available in the market here. Some of our comrades who used to be in the LTTE earlier have taught us how to mix sulphur in gunpowder to make it more potent.'

I asked him if he had observed a difference in the way the various tribes of Bastar nurtured their fighting spirit.

'I find that the Koyas are very adventurous, unlike the Dorlas, who are more educated and settled in life now.'

I had noticed Rajanna was carrying a Party magazine in Telugu; the article he was reading had pictures of tunnels and bunkers. I wanted to know if they had permanent bunkers in Abujhmad.

'Not yet, but we may need them soon. Attacks are not very far off. These, here, are translations from a German magazine on how to build bunkers.'

'If the army is coming, have you prepared yourselves for it? Have you set up booby traps?'

'Not yet. That just takes a night.'

'So will there be a war in the forest?'

Rajanna did not want to dwell on the incipient confrontation. It could hardly be easy to consider the consequences of a situation where the Indian army finally decides to engage with the Maoists. 'The main war should be fought outside the jungle, in cities. There is more emphasis now in the Party to develop the cities than ever before. Let's see how far that goes. Struggle in the jungle can at best support the wars being fought outside, like in Nandigram.'

My lesson was interrupted by the sound of a whistle: it was lunchtime. 'Let's meet again after lunch,' said Rajanna. He also needed his afternoon nap.

Refreshed after the siesta, Rajanna rejoined me, and I quizzed him on gathering intelligence. I had heard about the preparation before the Ranibodli attack from Rajman.

'The most important part of these operations is the recce. It takes a long time to gather intelligence. It took us nearly three months to prepare for Ranibodli. If the recce is flawless, the final operation becomes easy. The Ranibodli attack was a great success for our State Military Commission (SMC). We killed fifty-five policemen, and even though the police had camped in a girls' hostel where students were staying, we made sure no civilians were harmed. After Ranibodli, we were flooded with requests from villagers who were fed up with police camps near their villages. They said they would help us with whatever information we needed if we agreed to attack.

'The main policy of the Party now is to seize automatic arms from the police. Our militia, armed mainly with axes, carries out surprise attacks on individual policemen in public places, and makes off with their weapons. That is how we acquired as many as fifty weapons in six months.'

I was not surprised by what Rajanna said. I had been wondering about these attacks myself. I had always thought of the Bastar tribals as timid beings who would tremble at the sight of a forest guard. Their transformation into a weapon-snatching militia is a miracle, in whichever way it has been made possible. I had read a story about a member of the cadre had surrendered in a police station with a .303, and then made off with two automatic rifles.

I asked Rajanna if that was a new strategy too.

Rajanna denied it. 'That story was planted by the police in an effort to place someone in our midst as a covert operator. That man had been one of us long ago. The police roped him in to infiltrate our ranks, but we caught on to the plan and killed him. See, intelligence is the main thing in this war. The state is deploying a Cobra force here, but it cannot do much if you don't give it eyes. That is intelligence. The Andhra police planted many coverts in our Party, and they managed to strike at the top and hurt us gravely. They are smarter than the Chhattisgarh police. They learnt these tactics from the USA's Low Intensity Conflict document, based on the American experience in Vietnam and Malaya. The Indian army came up with a sub-conventional war operations document in 2006 on the same lines, and applied it in the North-East. Our Party is studying these documents and we have come out with counter-documents that are yet to be ratified by our Central Committee.'

Continuing with his explanation, Rajanna said, 'We give different responsibilities, like military operations, supplies, arms procurement and so on, to different people in our State Military Commission. The commission has eight members and they meet at least thrice a year. One of us reports to the Central Military Commission, which plans big operations, like Nayagarh, Koraput and Balimela.'

I asked Rajanna if he thought the movement in Andhra could be revived.

'The revolutionary tradition in Andhra goes much deeper than you realize. Whomever I talk to is ready for revolt, but no one speaks up because of state repression. In Andhra, the Party will have to start from scratch. It may take five to ten years. There will be defeats but leaders will come forth. This movement will not die; it will rise again.'

I could hear the confidence in Rajanna's words, though I am not sure it is rooted in reality. The people of Andhra have moved on. They now possess land, and are in need of better seeds, electricity, improved irrigation. The Party needs to do a lot of catching up to remain relevant to the population of small landholders. The Andhra government has been saying that there are no more than a hundred Naxalite leaders left, and that the movement will die with them. But from what I learned about the Naxals from their stories, a hundred leaders like Rajanna—scattered though they may be—have the ability to stage a comeback.

In the evening, I was invited to a meeting in a village nearby. Before we set off, Rajanna addressed everyone at the camp as they stood in a line like disciplined schoolboys. He spoke of 'RV1' and 'RV2' and explained for my benefit, 'These are the places to reassemble at if we come under enemy attack. This is not a Party stronghold, so we need to be cautious. Reassemble Venue 1 is the place where we assemble within twenty-four hours of the attack, and Reassemble Venue 2 is where we regroup within three days.'

On the way, he pointed to a school building. 'You won't find any teacher in this school. Though it is meant to be a school, it has employed military architecture.' I could not follow what he meant, so he explained, 'They have positioned the windows in such a manner that you can fire in every direction from within. Can you tell me why a village in this remote area needs that?' Indeed, the building was unlike any village school I had seen. The windows were at such an angle to the walls that the occupants could fire on enemy groups approaching from any direction.

At the meeting, Rajanna spoke about the struggle against the Bodhghat Dam in the village. His listeners were rich Oriya Brahmins who had been brought to the area by the king more than a century ago; all of them owned hundreds of acres of fertile land on the banks of the Indravati.

'In the New Democratic Revolution, we can work with rich farmers. At this stage, we are only against the zamindar,' he said.

I have heard many sermons about the New Democratic Revolution, all of which claim that it is a step towards socialism, from which communism will follow. But what is the difference between a zamindar and a rich farmer?

'A zamindar is an absentee landlord. A rich farmer may employ people to work for him, but he too works on the farm along with his family. The rich people from this area, who are more likely to have opposed us, are now seeking us out because they see no other way to protect themselves from this dam.'

I could hear the sound of drums in the village. It seemed as if a wedding ceremony was in progress, but Rajanna did not want me to venture there. It would attract attention, he explained. It was dark already, and the meeting, like all Naxal programmes, went on and on. I don't know when I dropped off to sleep, but it was past midnight when Rajanna shook me awake. 'We will have to walk a bit now,' he said. 'As a strategy, we do not stay on after meetings in case people who have gone back from here tell the police where they met us.'

We walked through the darkness, a small torch lighting our way. Now that I was awake and refreshed, I was ready to toss more questions at Rajanna.

'How did you manage to form the military companies?' I started off.

'The companies are our primary military force; each has seventy-five members. At the next level, we have 3500 people in military uniform; most of them do not carry arms, and work primarily on supply and logistics. We also have militia in the villages—thousands of villagers armed with traditional weapons. We have not been able to form a battalion yet—that is our next task.

'When we move through villages as a company, we get only about 25 per cent support in terms of food from the people. It is not easy to feed large numbers, and we understand that. But in the platoon formation, where we have squads of twenty-five each, we get up to 75 per cent support from the people. We have made it our policy now that smaller formations will depend entirely on the people's support for food.

'In Nepal, the Party used to give each guerrilla fighter Rs 100 a month, but we do not have such a system. The comrades do not get any money—there is no concept of personal income here. But there can be no revolution if your very survival is threatened. The Party takes care of basic necessities, like soap, oil and clothes—we spend around Rs 450 a month on each comrade. The Military Commission has decided that the companies can eat non-vegetarian food once a month, and we usually kill cattle.

'Revolution is not possible without a middle class. The Party has addressed, and to an extent alleviated, excessive poverty in Dandakaranya, though this does not mean that these people are comparable to the middle class as we know it. Still, one cannot deny that the Party's intervention has considerably improved their lives. People have access to the forest and the land now. A single mahua tree yields an income of Rs 5000 a year; the people are not starving any more. Now, a tribal in Bastar has some surplus money, and the mind space to consider a better life. People encourage their children to join the Party to attain higher goals—though it must be said that when one of the children joins the Party, there is less pressure on the land to divide it further.

'In my opinion, the fight in Bastar should transform itself into a fight for tribal autonomy. We should demand that all of Dandakaranya be able to decide its fate without interference from outsiders. Schedule Five of the Constitution gives these rights in theory, but the Party should work towards making that a reality.

'The Salwa Judum has given the tribals an immediate tangible enemy, which will help create consciousness. But the Salwa Judum may not be around for much longer, and the younger generation should have a goal to fight for, an objective. Some of my colleagues disagree with me, saying that if we convert the struggle into a war of nationality, it will dilute the class war. But I feel that the nationality struggle is a prelude to the class war, just as the New Democratic Revolution is to socialism.'

I have often wondered whether the Naxal movement will ever really be led by Adivasis, and said so aloud.

'It will never happen,' said Rajanna. 'Yes, we can bring the best of them to the fore by promoting them, but they have not seen the outside world. They have no comprehension of the games being played there. It will never happen, unless there is some mammoth change that we cannot predict.'

'Do you think talks will help achieve a solution?'

'Talks will not solve anything. In a fight for power, how can anything be "solved"? In the Andhra talks, the main demand we had put forward was for land reform. Other technical demands like relief to arrested comrades were secondary, and yet those were the things the media highlighted to divert attention from the main issue. We had given them a list of eighty firms that held land illegally in Hyderabad. The government could not deliver even on those small demands—what can talks achieve? In our last congress in 2007, a majority voted against any talks in the future, calling it a waste of time. And, as you know, the congress is our highest decision-making body. A decision taken by our congress can only be altered by the next congress, whatever opinion individuals members may have. You must understand that we are a disciplined party.'

It was a complicated lesson, but the night was so tranquil that I felt I could really listen to Rajanna, not just hear the words he uttered. I found him simple and open, unlike others in power who are often too clever with their words, too diplomatic to allow deep questioning. I may not have liked everything that he said, but the interaction seemed meaningful, sincere.

I was not sure where Rajanna was headed. As though he could hear my confusion, Rajanna said, 'This is a complex war. Military might is not the most important thing.'

9

FILLING THE BLANKS

Sifting through my notes on my return, many questions cropped up. Unfortunately, in this story, there are no phone numbers to dial for clarifications.

Sometime in 2010, I heard of a meeting being organized by the Naxals in Abujhmad, and was keen to meet the younger leaders, who were expected to be there. I felt it would help me get a sense of where the movement was headed. But more than anything else, I wanted to spend some time with Vasu. In all our meetings, he had directed me to the right places and the right people, but I had not had an opportunity to spend time with him.

The state had opened up Abujhmad after thirty years. Until then, one had to take special permission from the government for entry. Now, it seemed to be testing the waters for a future in Abujhmad where a huge area has been given to the army to establish a training centre. There had hardly been any police presence there earlier, but some police stations had been set up on the periphery.

What was surprising was that the government had opened up Abujhmad in the middle of their latest Operation Green Hunt. Though the name remained the same, this particular mission of the Centre was especially designed for a situation that affected an area spread over multiple states. A new name would have been more appropriate, I thought, but then, the importance of names has been overlooked repeatedly.

Names do have relevance, after all. It was thanks to his uncommon name that I found Moti Ravan, a Gondi scholar and a tribal himself. I noticed the name in a news report: Ravan, the demon king, whose effigy is burnt by Hindus on Dussehra, is a curious choice of name.

'There is a story behind my name,' he explained. 'My father named me Moti Ram, but I felt it was an attack on our very identity. As you know, Ravan, killed by the Hindu god Ram, was revered by us, the tribals of Dandakaranya. So I changed my name to Moti Ravan. I cannot understand why any civilized society must burn someone else's god. That is not what Hinduism decrees. It was right wing extremists who popularized the burning of Ravan back in the 1930s as part of their politics. Left wing extremism also started in India around that time—in the late 1920s. The political history of India has been rife with wars between these two extremist groups. And what is happening in Dandakaranya is an extension of that very war.'

It was a year after the start of the Salwa Judum that an effigy of Ravan was burnt on Dussehra in Dantewada town for the first time. Mahendra Karma was the chief guest at that function. If Moti Ravan's understanding is accurate, then what had started in India in the 1930s reached Dantewada in 2006 through the Salwa Judum.

Moti Ravan said, 'If you try to understand Adivasis from your urban and Hindu perspectives, the consequences will be similar to what is happening in Chhattisgarh.'

In government documents, the name Abujhmad is translated as 'the plateau not understood', because in Hindi, 'abujh' means 'not understood'. The forest is so dense and the tribes so primitive that they have remained untouched by civilization. No one has been able to reach them or understand them. Moti Ravan, though, enlightened me, 'Abujhmad is a Gondi word. "Abujh" means sal and "mada", forest.' Abujhmad is a forest of sal trees, like Salboni in West Bengal.

'The entire region of Dandakaranya should have been carved out as a state of tribal Gondi speakers when the Indian states were created in 1956 on the basis of language,' Ravan continued. 'But Gondi speakers were divided across five states. Gondi is an ancient language, and through it, I have tried to decipher the scripts of the Harappan civilization. They are contemporary scripts, you see. If Gondi disappears, so will our chances of unravelling the mysteries of our ancient civilizations. Every new census shows fewer and fewer Gondi speakers. There are no government-run schools where the medium of instruction is Gondi, and the state-run All India Radio does not broadcast any news in the language.'

Moti Ravan's explanations helped me appreciate the Maoist demand for an integrated Dandakaranya and their strategic choice of Gondi as the lingua franca of their movement today. However, amongst the people who are trying to solve the problems of these Gondi-speaking areas, very few actually understand Gondi.

The problems themselves are rather basic. Abujhmad in Chhattisgarh is one of the blocks of Narayanpur district. It has not yet been surveyed for administrative purposes, although the Geological Survey of India has worked enough on it to know what minerals lie beneath its surface. It is believed to be the second densest forest in the world, spread over an area of 4000 square kilometres, with a population of at least 16,000. The Abujhmad Development Authority, a government body, says there are 237 villages in Abujhmad. Most of these are in Chhattisgarh, while some are in the Gadchiroli district of Maharashtra. Rajman, the Maoists' secretary for Abujhmad, however, pegs the number at 480—more than double the official figure. He ought to know, because for all intents and purposes, the Maoists have been functioning as the administration in Abujhmad, the heart of India, where the Indian government has admitted its own failure.

Mad, as the Maoists like to call Abujhmad, has 120 panchayats, but all the government-appointed panchayat secretaries live elsewhere. More than a third of the sarpanchs also live in the towns. Each panchayat gets Rs 5–8 lakh a year for development projects, though not even a third of it is spent on the villages. Almost every village has schools, but teachers don't turn up. There are five hospitals, but not a single doctor holds an MBBS degree. Health conditions are appallingly poor: the Maoists told me that more than two hundred people die of diarrhoea each year. Villagers have no option but to walk thirty or forty kilometres to the towns to collect their rations. Around 250 villages have electricity poles, but the power supply is uncertain and erratic. Almost every village has hand pumps, but most are in a state of disrepair. Only 150 villages are part of a road network. People prefer to farm on their own land, but have to work as daily wage labourers outside their villages whenever there is a drought. Around 700–800 people work full-time for the Party and help in the administration of the region.

On the Chhattisgarh side of Abujhmad, the only functional schools and hospitals are run by the Ramakrishna Mission. At the other end, in Maharashtra, social worker Baba Amte's organization, Maharogi Sewa Samiti, does the same. My next task was to do a round trip of sorts, to cover Abujhmad from Chhattisgarh to Maharashtra.

As I walked around the sprawling campus of the Ramakrishna Mission in Narayanpur, now the district headquarters, I was impressed by the dedication of the monks to the welfare of the tribals, especially in the fields of health care and education. My room in the ashram was a spartan affair. I picked up a book on the table and found in it a quote by Swami Atmanand, the founder of the ashram.

When I came to Abujhmad for the first time, I was shocked to see the deprivation around. I kept asking people how I could help, but no one would answer. Then finally, one man, who was probably a little educated because he addressed me as sahib, said, 'If you want to help us then do something so that police and forest people do not come to our village and, secondly, you can open a shop where we can get proper rates for our forest produce.' The answer stayed with

me, and when we started the school and hospital in
1984, we also started a fair price shop.

The Maoist understanding of the situation could not have
been better aligned with the Swami's.

For the tribal students here, the day began with a prayer
to the spiritual leader, Ramakrishna Paramhamsa. I did
wonder if this was entirely appropriate in a government-
funded institution, which is expected to be secular. The
missionaries talked to me freely, but avoided any political
questions, including my query about whether any of their
students had turned out to be Naxals.

I had arranged to meet Ramu, my Maoist contact for the
trip, at a spot not far from the Ramakrishna Mission, so that
he could take me into the Naxal-dominated pockets. Driving
over to meet him, I saw a young man dressed in city clothes,
and stopped to ask him the way. He knew Ramu's house and
offered to take me there. As we chatted in Hindi, I learned
that he was a teacher in a government-run school in the
village; a tribal who held an MA degree in political science.
He lived in Orchha, the nearest town, and came to work on
his motorbike. I suspected he had mistaken me for a Maoist
leader—who else would go into the forest with a rucksack?

'There was only one teacher for eight classes before
I joined last year,' he said.

'How do you teach if you do not know Gondi?'

'Yes, language is a big problem. Even though it is
a roadside village, the children do not speak any Hindi.'

He appeared to be grappling with possible clues to who
I really was, because he said, a little tentatively, 'The dadas

are helpful.' He searched my face for a reaction. 'They have promised to make a playground for the children in my school. I mean, they haven't promised me, but they have promised it to the other teacher who has been here for a long time.'

I asked him if he had ever met the dadas.

He nodded and added, 'But I am frightened of them.'

I asked if they had harmed any teachers, but he did not answer.

Ramu was not at home; he was away for the harvest. The teacher was surprised. 'There is no sign of harvest in my village even though Dussehra is almost here. Tradition says we must eat freshly harvested rice on Dussehra. These people must be growing the local variety of rice—that would explain why he is already harvesting.'

The teacher had to leave, but Ramu was back soon, and we set off. As he spoke no Hindi, our journey was a silent one.

At our first destination, I met three boys. Only one of them, Ramesh, spoke Hindi. He said he was a platoon commander in Company 1. He was from a privileged village near Narayanpur—it had a residential government school, and even electricity, by virtue of its being located close to a road. He had been able to study only up to class three, he said. The Party's cultural shows drew him to it, and he started working for it at a very early age. Some villagers informed the police, who relentlessly harassed his family. 'Every time the police visited the village, my whole family would have to run away into the forest for days. I am the eldest of four brothers, and when I turned sixteen in 2000, the Party suggested it would be better if I joined it full-time in order to avoid the police.'

In 2006, Ramesh married a comrade from Mad. 'She is a soldier in the 6th company and is working in the east division of Dandakaranya. There are ten divisions in Dandakaranya now. We have twelve companies and more than thirty platoons. Each company costs the Party Rs 4 lakh a year. There are sixty to seventy soldiers in a company and twenty to thirty in a platoon. About fifty-odd boys and girls join our divisions each year.'

Divisions are like administrative districts, and the figures this foot soldier gave me matched the ones I had from his leaders.

On the way, we passed a group of children walking with an old woman. The children looked scared, and the woman stopped to talk to Ramesh. I wondered what had made them so wary. It was our clothes, explained Ramesh. 'They thought we were the police because we were in plain clothes, but as soon as they saw the comrades in fatigues behind us, they were reassured.'

Much is upside down here, I thought.

When darkness fell, Ramesh announced that we would spend the night in a ghotul—ghotuls serve as dormitories for guests, especially for men. This one had a good many people gathered around a fire, chatting and weaving bamboo baskets. Ramesh and I sat with the group while the other comrades got busy preparing the evening meal. The villagers joined them, helping to fetch water, wood and utensils.

Ramesh told me our ghotul was in a village called Padapur. It has a primary school that has been running with a single teacher for the last ten years. The teacher lives in Muriapara in Narayanpur and comes to school twice or thrice a year, including national holidays like 15 August and 26 January. Not a single student has passed class five—the highest level it offers—ever since it started. In fact, no child has even learned to write his or her name. It was the same story in every village in the area, I was told.

I mused on how much the government has spent to yield zero results in ten years!

I asked them about ration cards next, and someone replied that of the thirty-six families in the village, only five or six have not got them. That wasn't so bad, I thought, until someone piped up that the last rations they got was three months ago, and that their assigned shop was forty kilometres away in Narayanpur. It takes over a day to walk that distance, and it is routine to be told on reaching there that stocks have run out. The shop has now been shifted to the police camp. The village panchayat secretary, Shyam Singh, was in the village recently—his only visit in three years. The closest hospital is in Orchha, but the doctor is hardly ever on duty. Though the hospital has nine sanctioned posts, only one doctor has been appointed. I met him in the town of Kondagaon, where he lives, and all he did was complain about not having the money to pay the bribe required for a transfer.

The Ramakrishna Mission runs five primary schools in the neighbouring villages. The Maoists had started a school in the village in 2005, but the teacher quit after six months. The story is an oft-repeated one. Maoist leaders acknowledge their inability to run schools in the villages under their control. Education is their weak point—there is far too much attention on military issues in the party strategy, as many junior Maoist leaders have complained to me in hushed tones. Nearby, there is a government residential school with eight sanctioned teachers and twenty-five students. It is primarily run by a cook who had been hired to prepare meals for the children.

As I sat there listening to the group around the fire, it seemed as if the picture Rajman, the Maoist secretary for Abujhmad, had painted for me in words, had come alive.

Sukhram, a villager who spoke Hindi, picked up the thread as Ramesh excused himself to go and help the comrades.

'We have what we call "tricolour teachers" here,' said Sukhram. 'They come to school only to hoist the national flag on Independence Day and Republic Day. Since the dadas came here, we do not allow the teachers to hoist the tricolour, and unfurl a black flag instead, but they come to school on those days nevertheless. We even built a hut for the school and requested the teacher to live there—the dadas did too—but he never turns up. The only other day we see him is when the board examinations for class five are held. He takes some children to the examination centre, but no one has yet passed from our village as they have never really studied anything.'

Having found a listener who took an interest in their lives, Sukhram chatted on. 'June to November, till the crop is ready, is the most difficult period for us. We have had no rations since June this year, so we are surviving on roots and on the little money we make selling these bamboo baskets. We also sell some amla and buy rice with the money that comes from it. No one comes to collect tendu here.'

The dadas do not allow tendu traders into this part of Abujhmad, even though it means a loss in revenue for them. No one wants to let outsiders into their headquarters, I thought.

'So how is it that rice is being cooked tonight?' I asked, looking at the makeshift kitchen.

'You are a guest, and the Party keeps reserve food in villages that are on our routes.'

Ramesh had returned by then, and added, 'Besides, the PLGA helps with the cultivation of rice.' He was careful to ensure that I did not go back with a wrong impression of the Party. Even while he went about his chores in the kitchen, he had been listening to our conversation intently.

Sukhram, though, was not as wary as Ramesh, and said, 'I have heard that the dadas distributed land and cattle in the nearby villages, but they have not given us anything.' Grudgingly, he went on, 'But yes, thanks to them, people from the forest department do not come here any more and we can cut as much bamboo as we want.' Sukhram has not had to experience the terror unleashed by forest officials as others before him have.

I saw some boys helping each other read and write, while others were teaching basket-making. Soon, the boys and girls started singing and dancing. Sukhram explained, 'According to our custom, unmarried men and women used to spend the night in ghotuls but ever since the Party came here, the girls go back home after the dance, and only the boys spend the night in the ghotul.'

With outsiders having entered Abujhmad, 'civilization' appears to have invaded the region.

Sukhram pointed to my bag: 'Everyone wants to know if you have a gun from the Party.'

I opened my bag to reveal notebooks, a towel and a few clothes, and resumed our chat.

I asked Sukhram why people supported the dadas. 'They are people like us,' he laughed.

The dance seemed to be out of rhythm after a while. It was because the music to which they were dancing had changed, explained Sukhram. These were Maoist songs. It was a metaphor hard to ignore. While bringing in the 'revolution', the Maoists should not rob the tribals of the natural rhythm of their lives. Our mainstream 'development' has disturbed it quite enough anyway.

***

The girls left, and the food was ready soon after. Ramesh joined us. He told me he had not gone home for five years. 'If I go back, the police will bother my family again. This way, everyone is happy.' And then, in an unwavering voice, he added, 'It will be a long battle. It may take many generations. Slowly, people from the cities will also join us and we will form a real people's government. I know the Indian army is very powerful and I have heard about our mistakes in Russia and China. We do not want to repeat them. What has happened in Andhra can also happen here, but we will fight till the finish.'

The maturity of his thoughts struck me—Ramesh had worked out the progress of the movement in his head. He was not merely parroting what he had been told, as had been my experience with other tribal comrades his age.

Maybe something in his voice inspired the others, because Bhaskar opened up, asking Ramesh to translate. 'Even if someone is not with the Party, he or she is still bothered by

the police. If they are in the police force, they should serve
the people; why are they harassing and looting the tribals?'
He pointed to the third comrade in the team. 'This is Shivaji;
he is from Pusalvay village, a two-hour walk from Kutru
area, where the Salwa Judum started. He joined the Party
in 2006 to fight the Salwa Judum because his whole village
was herded to a camp in 2005. He was spared because he
was away at the time. All the villagers came back last year
and now, four boys like him, and a girl, have joined the Party.
They are all uneducated. Before the Salwa Judum, no one
from Pusalvay worked for the Party. Five boys from that
village have also become SPOs.'

Split right down the middle, I thought. 'You must have
been friends with the boys who have become SPOs.'

'Yes, but I will kill them if I find them.'

I wanted to know how the Adivasis were faring in the
Party hierarchy. Doing a quick head count of the composition
of the companies with Ramesh, I found that eleven of twelve
company commanders were tribals, but all the secretaries
were from Andhra. So the fighting force is now almost
completely tribal, though they are still being managed by
the Maoists from Andhra.

The next morning we set off early. We must have walked
for quite a few hours. The heat was oppressive. I was tired,
and when Ramesh said we would have to wait for a while, I
dozed off almost as soon as I sat down. When I opened my
eyes, I saw Vasu limping towards us. I knew this would be my
last trip before I got down to writing the book, and wanted to
make sure I could tick as many items off my list as possible.
Driven by the familiarity of our old association, both of us

instinctively took out our notebooks to make lists of tasks still to be completed, people still to be met.

I told Vasu that I had met Jeet Guha Niyogi, and that he had denied having any links with the Party or with Vasu, though he said that Dr Sen was associated with him and attended almost all his programmes. I wanted to know about Jeet's association with the Party. How did it start? Did Jeet approach them or was it the other way round? Where did things stand now?

'It was our initiative to form a legal organization, though Jeet came to us first, proposing to work together. I wrote the constitution for his organization, Jan Mukti Morcha. I was also present at their inaugural meeting, not in the open or in the day, of course, but at night. Denying it is his choice. Dr Binayak Sen was also present at that meeting. Now, Jeet is collecting money from tendu traders, calling himself a front for the Party. We have issued a pamphlet clarifying that he has no connection with us any more and have also warned Jeet that he must stop.' He scribbled a reminder to himself to find a copy of the pamphlet for me.

I told Vasu I was keen to meet some local tribal leaders in the Party, maybe Venkitesh, the head of the south Bastar division, or Ramder, the only tribal in the state committee, and Vasu said he would try to arrange a meeting. I also wanted to meet some college-educated tribals in the Party, but Vasu shook his head ruefully, saying, 'That is our weakness. We fail to attract educated Adivasis. In Dandakaranya, the Party has just one Adivasi comrade who is a graduate—Pahad Singh. He was a teacher in Ambagarh Chowki in Rajnandgaon and quit his job to join us. A dozen tribals have left their jobs to join the Party. But they have studied only up to school, no further.'

Also on my list was a visit to some of the villages on the other side of the Bailadila hills, those that had been attacked repeatedly during the first Operation Green Hunt in 2005. Especially Vechapal, because of reports of beheadings there by security forces. But the hills can be very difficult terrain, impossible to negotiate without local help—help which I had not yet managed to get. There is a single road that leads to those villages, and it is closely guarded by the police. I asked Vasu if he could find me someone from those villages to interview. He noted that down too.

All through my travels in Bastar, I have been confronted with events centring on the mines. Vasu now heads the Party in the area where the Tata Steel plant is coming up, and still speaks of not allowing it to happen. The Bailadila range is the curse of Bastar. It contains the purest form of iron ore—69 per cent—in the world, and many corporations have had their eyes on it since its discovery in 1900. More than a century later, it still dictates the politics of Bastar.

I remember that KS, Vasu's former leader, had led a successful movement in the 1970s to move a government steel plant planned for Bastar to Visakhapatnam. I found it strange that a steel plant was acceptable in Visakhapatnam but not in Bastar.

Vasu explained the logic. 'In the 1960s, the Party believed that national steel plants could benefit the people, as they had done in Russia. But in Dandakaranya, where there is no educated middle class to speak of, the Party has realized that small-scale industry under the leadership of the village-level Jantana Sarkar, and not enormous steel plants, is the path to development. A steel plant will not help the uneducated tribals in Bastar.'

'So you concur with the CPI, who are in agreement with the king and the many activists who are against the Tata plant?'

He reacted immediately. 'They are frauds. The CPI is not fighting against the Tata plant. See what they did in West Bengal.' Vasu conceded, however, that the one man who has worked the hardest to expose the Salwa Judum is Manish Kunjam of the CPI. The CPI, he said, has also done the most to counter them.

***

My checklist for the book was lengthy, but by evening, I felt I had got most of what I needed.

I had known Vasu for more than twenty years now, but I had never asked him any personal questions. I remembered he had once said at one of our coffee house meetings that he was from Medak. 'Is that right?' I asked him now.

'I am from Karimnagar district,' he said. Karimnagar is where the movement started in the 1970s, the same place that Kosa, Ramji and Sonu hail from. He also told me his name—at least I believe that was his real name.

I asked him why he had joined the Party.

'As a child, I was influenced by my grandmother's fight against the landlord to save her tiny plot of land. Our landlord was a terror. His sons used to pick up any girl they wanted from the village. I formed a small team of village boys to fight them, but they beat us up. I felt completely helpless and realized that we would have to form a larger group to fight them. I had heard about the Party but did not know how to contact them. Then, one night, we wrote a warning to the landlord on the walls of the village, making it seem like the handiwork of the Party. It served our purpose, and scared the landlord for a while. Slowly, the news of the writing on the walls reached the local dalam. One night, they came to the Dalit basti (settlement) of my village and inquired about the graffiti. There was a Dalit boy in our group who told them the whole story and that's how I came in contact with the dadas.

'The people of the villages that were going to be relocated because of the new Chhattisgarh capital project tried the same strategy. They did not want to give up their land but lacked the means to fight back. They too wrote on their walls in the name of the Party but, by that time, the Party had collapsed in Raipur. We could not even contact them.'

'Why did the Party collapse in Raipur?'

'Because of Sumit's betrayal.' He spoke of how the Party had been following Sumit's interaction with the superintendent of police, Choube. Vasu had the mobile number that the police had given Sumit, as well as the details of his bank account in the State Bank of India, Rajnandgaon, where the police deposited money for him. I wondered why the Party could not prevent the arrests if they knew so much already.

I had already heard this from Anil on our first meeting at the Indian Coffee House in Delhi.

But Vasu was on a nostalgia trip, something I had never seen before, so I let him go on. 'You must have read in the papers that most of our overground workers, including my wife, have been arrested. My wife is in Raipur jail now. She was sentenced to ten years of imprisonment for the offence of circulating a CD that had photographic evidence of the atrocities of the Salwa Judum!'

I too had received a copy of it by post, I recalled.

'I first worked as a part-time organizer in the Singereni coal field area, where I had a full-time teacher's job. I was also part of the teachers' union affiliated to the Party. In 1989, the Party asked me to join full-time and go to Raipur, and I accepted. I had not even heard of Raipur at the time. That's when I met you.

'I have two children. My daughter should be in engineering college now. They live with my brother. If you ever meet them, please tell them that I am sorry I have not been able to give them a normal childhood, but whatever I am doing is for the uplift of humanity and that is what they too should work for.'

I told him that the police chief of Chhattisgarh had recently spoken to the press alleging that Gudsa Usendi sends his own children to private schools, but he blows up schools for tribal children. Gudsa Usendi is the alias used by the Maoist spokesperson in Dandakaranya.

'My children have had to change twelve schools in eight years. They have also had to change their names and hide their parents' identities; but, yes, they did go to private schools when they lived with us in cities.'

'By the way, I thought you were not Gudsa Usendi any more. But the police claims that you are!'

'You are right. I have not been the spokesperson since 2006. Sanjeev, whom you met in 2004, is the spokesperson now. So he is Gudsa Usendi now, but the police still call me by that name. That is the level of their intelligence.'

'Is it the same Sanjeev who told me that not firing at former Chief Minister Chandrababu Naidu after blowing up his car was the biggest mistake of his life?'

Vasu nodded.

I asked him if he was aware of a debate in the papers triggered by a column I had written. The police chief had responded with a series of articles, and Gudsa Usendi had joined in too. Vasu nodded again. 'But the responses from Usendi stopped quite abruptly. Do you know why?' I asked.

'Our last two replies were not published. Whenever we sent a response, the newspaper would send it to the police chief first. He did not approve of the last two of our responses, so they were not published. This is yet another example of your free press,' he said. 'Your weekly column was also pulled off for the same reason. The police chief did not approve of it.'

Vasu, perhaps, had more inside information than I did.

'We had also issued a press release challenging the BBC for its report that claimed we had chopped off the fingers of those tribals who voted during the election in 2009. No one carried it, not even the BBC. Can they produce a single person who was subjected to that torture?'

Vasu's words were scathing, and he clearly still regarded me as a representative of the BBC. So I decided to distract him a bit. 'Why has the Party not taken any action against the teachers who do not attend school?' I asked him. After all, everyone agreed on the importance of education.

'Imagine what you reporters would write if I were to slap a teacher! We publish leaflets and take out rallies every year, demanding that teachers attend schools. But no one reports them, and teachers do not feel compelled to do their duties.'

I asked him to give me a copy of those leaflets, and Vasu made a note of it.

Our conversation was interrupted by the arrival of a CD. It was accompanied by a note in English, addressing me as Shu and listing the contents. It contained much of the information and evidence for which I had requested Vasu. Who could possibly know my nickname here? There was more to it than met the eye!

We ate dinner by the fireside and talked well into the night. As Vasu chatted on, I discreetly tried to cross-check the facts I had collected from other leaders. Finally, he decided to call it a night. He had set up meetings with some senior leaders, and also arranged for guides—Vinod, Manas and Aitu from the Bailadila area—to take me to the next destination. I wondered whom I would meet this time, but there was little point in asking. If Vasu had wanted to tell me, he would have. For now, I was satisfied that I would be able to talk to villagers from Bailadila, no matter where my path led.

The tall grass flanking our route was wet with dew and my clothes were soon damp. As we trudged on, my thoughts wandered to the name of the place through which I was passing. I wondered how much the process of replacing old names with new ones would help the state erode tribal identities. Moti Ravan had told me that the original Gondi name for Bailadila is Konda Mendol ('konda' meaning ox and 'mendol', body), but not many know it today. That included my young guides. Sabyasachi had spoken of how, over the years, the Kondh tribals of Orissa had forgotten that they were originally known as Kui. Kondh is a derogatory term coined for people who have their brains in their 'kandh' or shoulders.

Vinod, who was from Vechapal, led the way. His village is ten kilometres from Bailadila's mine No. 3, which has been allotted to Essar. That is where the second Jan Jagran started; the same place that was attacked by Naga troops at the beginning of the Salwa Judum. Those villages have borne the brunt of many more attacks since. Though they are only a short distance from the road, access is jealously guarded by the police.

Vinod set the ball rolling. 'Sannu Karma, a relative of Mahendra Karma's, was the landlord and sarpanch of my village; he owned forty acres of land. Three villagers, Badru, Jagdish and Rama, held thirty acres each, while my father, Aitu Oyam, had ten acres. The rest had landholdings of less than five acres. Sannu Karma was a terror. He would force people to work on his field all day in exchange for Rs 10 or a kilogram of rice. In 2004, Ganesh Uike dada came to our village and held a meeting, where he asked these five landowners to distribute land from their holdings.

'Four of them, including my father, agreed, but Sannu Karma refused. It was the peak of summer, and the hot-headed Ganesh was in no mood for negotiation. He arose, picked up a stick, and beat up Sannu,' Vinod said gesticulating animatedly to enact the beating. 'The other four families, including mine, were allowed to keep five acres for themselves. Though we gave up half our land,

I appreciated the idea of redistribution of land and joined the Party soon after.

'Sannu never forgot that humiliation. When the Salwa Judum started the next year, he moved to Faraspal, Mahendra Karma's village, along with his five sons, who then became leading figures in the Salwa Judum. The Party distributed Sannu's land to the people after they moved away. When the Salwa Judum attacked our village, Sannu's sons came too. They captured ten families and carried them off to Mirtur camp. Those villagers managed to escape from the camp after a few days.'

I was entranced by the scenery: its serenity was in such contrast to the events Vinod was narrating. We crossed a verdant valley with a patchwork of farms on the hill slopes surrounding it. In better times, this could have been the Switzerland of central India.

Aitu, a native of Hurepal, a village under the same gram panchayat as Vechapal, was walking behind me. He said, 'My village has a similar story. Twelve people have been killed there by the Salwa Judum. My elder brother, Ichchhami, was one of them. Like Sannu, Madkam Kopa was the manjhi from our village. (Manjhi is a traditional title for the unofficial head of the village.) Madkam owned sixty acres of land. Just like in Vechapal, there were three more families in my village who owned land, about fifteen or sixteen acres each. The Party distributed their land in 1998 after the second Jan Jagran. Those three families are still with the Party.

'Madkam was the only one who resisted and refused to give up his land. But after the start of the Salwa Judum, Madkam ran away and the Party distributed his sixty acres of land amongst the people. The dadas killed him in 2006 in Bhansi near the NMDC mines.'

I asked Aitu what happened during the second Jan Jagran.

'There was a retaliation against the land distribution which had been started by the Party. I joined the Party after that Jan Jagran. My village had been attacked fifteen times by the Salwa Judum. All sixty-two houses were burnt. There are now fifteen full-time members from Hurepal in the Party. Before the Salwa Judum, there were only three, including me.'

We had reached another ghotul, just outside a village— our resting place for the night. Nearby, I could hear a rising chant. It was the local priest, chanting in a trance to cure an ailing man. While the others occupied themselves with collecting utensils, water and food for the night, I began to follow the sound. It led me to a hut. Inside was the priest, clad in a loincloth, reciting mantras to the sick man seated in front of him. I sat there for a long time watching them, but no one seemed to notice.

When I went back, I decided to try and talk to Manas, the third boy Vasu had sent with me. Manas was the youngest in the team and had been quiet all the while, much like Bhime on my earlier trip. He said he was from a village called Timenar, also near Vechapal. 'I was in class five when the Salwa Judum started, after which the school closed down, and I joined the Party in 2007.'

He could not have been even sixteen at that time, I thought.

And then Manas dropped a bombshell. 'I am from Mahendra Karma's family.' My expression of utter disbelief amused him and he laughed out loud. 'My grandfather is Mahendra Karma's cousin. During the Salwa Judum's first attack on Vechapal, Mahendra Karma himself came to the village with five jeeps and ten truckloads of people. I was in the classroom then.

'Karma entered our class and held an AK-47 to my chest. He knew who I was. He asked me about Santosh, the Party leader from our village. When I said I did not know, he started asking the others. I ran out of the classroom and hid till he left. The Salwa Judum camped in Vechapal for two days and burnt the whole village down.

'That day, there must have been a thousand-strong mob with Karma. They marched into the nearby villages and managed to catch ten people—the rest had fled into the forest. At Cherli Harial village nearby, Naga forces bound the hands of their captives and shot them at point-blank range. After that, they beheaded eight of them. Two heads were found some distance away, but six were never found.'

I had heard about this before, but had never met anyone who had been present in the village during the attack. It was the first massacre after the start of the Salwa Judum. The press had reported it as the killing of ten Maoists in an encounter.

Manas went on, 'Fifteen days later, the Salwa Judum attacked my village once again, at 5 a.m. This time, Karma was not in the team. They could not catch anyone, but looted and burnt all 110 houses and killed our animals. That is when I decided to join the Party, and my only mission now is to kill Karma.'

'Isn't he your grandfather?'

'Yes, he is, but he has become a man-eater now and must be finished. That is why I have come to the Party.'

Vinod was back, having collected enough rice for our dinner. He heard the tail end of Manas's story and chipped in: 'When Manas came to our unit, he was a child. Vasu dada wrote an angry letter to Ganesh dada asking why he was sending children to the Party. Ganesh wrote back to say that he had no choice. The children simply wanted to join the Party. He said he did not want them to do something stupid, and so he was sending them far away. All of them want to kill Karma.'

I was surprised by this explanation. Why would the Naxals want to save Mahendra Karma? 'How many members from your extended family are in the Party?' I asked Manas.

'I do not know how many of us are there in all, but five people from my family in my village are in the Party: Kishor, Somli, Raju, Kranti and I. My family is quite large. That is why we have been allowed to retain the ten acres of land that we own, unlike the others.' Manas added enthusiastically, 'I have heard that nine people from Faraspal have also joined the Party.'

Faraspal is Mahendra Karma's village.

'Unga was the first to join from Faraspal. Mahendra Karma is his bade pitaji (uncle).'

Aitu joined in, 'Unga was a good singer and poet. He was a very good comrade. He had become an area committee member and was about to be promoted as a divisional committee member. He tried to attack Mahendra Karma thrice, but did not succeed. He died near Singaram where the Salwa Judum killed nineteen people in 2009. He was only twenty-five.'

I had heard about the rape of four girls from Vechapal who were in Jagdalpur jail; did anyone know of that, I asked.

'Yes, it happened during one of the attacks. There are so many of them that we have lost count. I suppose that is why I forgot to tell you,' said Vinod, a little apologetically. 'They were raped, and their clothes were replaced with military uniforms. Their hair was cut short and they were presented to the media as Maoists.'

'What is the situation now?' I asked.

'We have not gone home for a long time, so we do not know the latest news, but the last we heard was that the villagers were still living in the forest. They come to the village to tend to the crops and go back. But the Salwa Judum has repeatedly burnt the crops.'

'Do you know why your village is being attacked so many times?'

'Yes, they want to take our land to give it to the Tatas and Essar,' Vinod replied. 'But we are resisting their moves. What can we expect from the Tatas and from Essar if the government-run NMDC can be so callous? Bacheli, the NMDC township, is a three-hour walk from our village. We used to go to the market there to sell our forest produce and buy rice. No one from the other side of Bailadila has got a job in the NMDC in the last fifty years. Have you seen the colour of the river? We call it the "red river" now. Clouds of iron dust blow into it every day from the NMDC mines. We don't have electricity, roads, schools or hospitals.'

I checked my notes and told them that the NMDC had made a profit of Rs 6648 crore last year, before deduction of taxes. A study called 'Impact of Industrialization on

Tribals from Bailadila' by the National Labour Institute, dating from the 1970s, had found that apart from affecting agricultural life, water pollution on account of the NMDC plant has disturbed the social and cultural life of the area. Thousands of people living in the villages have been facing starvation. The study by Ram Sharan Joshi further said: 'In some of the villages, it was found during the survey that their per capita consumption of paddy and kodon has drastically come down from 500–600 grams to 150–200 grams a day. Some of the families were managing with less than two meals a day.'

Vinod asked, 'Does the home minister not read any reports? Why is he surprised that the Naxals killed four security men in NMDC?' He was referring to a report about the minister in an old newspaper he was carrying. 'NMDC has made life unbearable for us; why won't we kill the people who represent them? Does he not understand that? You call it development. Whose development is this?'

There was no dancing in the ghotul that night, but quite a few young boys had turned up. The ghotul, I was told, was where they slept every night. I remembered Hiralal Shukla's book on the history of Bastar where he talked about ghotuls being the centres of the Bhumkal rebellion in 1910. Many of them had been destroyed by the British after they crushed the rebellion. The more I heard the young men talk, the more I realized that in these ghotuls, conversation is still predominantly political.

I shared with them the reply I got after putting a query to the government under the Right to Information Act: NMDC causes no pollution in the area. A case in Bilaspur High Court

challenging the NMDC for the pollution it causes has not
come up for hearing for several years.

'How much does the state earn from Bastar?' Vinod
asked me.

'I do not know the figures, but recently, I was reading an old
speech made by a former Bastar MLA, Mankuram Sodhi, in
the Madhya Pradesh Assembly on 19 February 1969. He said
that at the time, the government earned Rs 1 crore 60 lakh
a day from Bailadila alone. The state officially spent Rs 3 crore
on the district. So roughly, it was an earning of Rs 600 crore
in a year, against an expenditure of Rs 3 crore. According to a
study by the Centre for Science and Environment, the NMDC
made a profit of more than Rs 4000 crore by selling iron ore
from Dantewada district last year.'

Sodhi also said in the same speech that the state had spent
Rs 9 crore on irrigation in smaller districts like Raipur and Rs
11 crore on Bilaspur, but had allotted only Rs 28 lakh for a
district as large as Bastar. The area covered under irrigation
in the district is just above 2 per cent now.

He had further said, 'A team of the Tribal Policy
Commission has recently toured the region and they have
accepted that there was no work done for the welfare of
Adivasis in the last three Five-Year Plans in Bastar. But many
individuals who came here four or five years ago with nothing
in their hands have become millionaires.' He had also
warned in that speech, forty-odd years ago, 'Like Mizoram
and Nagaland have created a problem for you, Bastar will
do the same one day unless you spend on it at least 10 per
cent of what you earn from there.'

Things have not changed much for the tribals since 1969.

Although the boys were keen to talk, I announced that this was the end of my story. I was tired and we had a long way to go the next morning.

***

I knew we had reached our destination when I saw a girl in fatigues keeping watch from atop a tree. A whistle went off, and a row of people in green fatigues greeted me with a Laal Salaam. This was a fairly large camp.

Someone introduced me to an old man—GS.

It took me a moment to figure out what GS stood for. I was shaking hands with Ganapathy, the general secretary. He looked completely unlike the man in the photograph that newspapers keep printing. Perhaps that is the only image available with the government, outdated enough for his face to have lost most of its resemblance to it.

So this was the senior leader I had been assured of a meeting with—the 'biggest internal terrorist' wanted by the government. 'The last time I met a journalist was before 2000,' he told me as we had a cup of tea together. In uniform, he looked young—like a man in his early forties—but I knew he would be about sixty. Only when I looked at his eyes could I make out that he was past his prime—distant, dreamy, darting here and there as if in search of something.

As we were to spend some time together, he suggested I rest while he wrapped up some meetings. I was not to know that, over the next couple of days, I would spend the most frustrating hours of my entire journey with him.

We had very long interview sessions; he gave me all the

time I could have asked for. But Comrade Ganapathy avoided answering almost all the questions I asked him. He spoke at length, but handled everything so diplomatically that there was not much information one could take away from the interactions.

I asked him, 'Is there a successful model you follow?'

In response, Ganapathy posed a question of his own. 'Was there anything to follow in 1917, before the Russian Revolution?'

'But these tribals who are fighting with you, what will they get out of following your dreams of a red flag on the Red Fort? They need something here; will you make sure they get something out of this fight?'

Ganapathy rejected my perspective. 'It is wrong to think that the tribals are fighting for anything less than the highest Party aim. We want to bring communism to the world, and they are contributing to it.'

I pointed out that I had met hundreds of tribals over the last few years, and had seen the change in their attitude to the government and their understanding of their own situation. They had turned into fighters but would still need some small but tangible growth, some progress, to justify their struggle. Most people here had never travelled by train, or even visited the capital city of Raipur. What was their identification with the Red Fort, really? I wondered whether Ganapathy was in fact living in a world of his own, a world cut off from reality.

Smiling somewhat arrogantly, he said that the home ministry was not far off the mark when it noted that the Maoists had a presence in as many as twenty states.

I countered it with another home ministry figure that says their presence is restricted to as low as 2 per cent of the total number of police stations in the country.

Ganapathy negated all my observations, making no secret of his disdain for the information I had gathered from the other leaders.

'Many of your leaders have told me that getting autonomy for tribals will be an achievable aim,' I said.

'Nobody in the Central Committee thinks that way.'

It was hopeless trying to get any truth out of him. He is as seasoned a politician as any. But would his dreams fructify if he remained as removed from reality as he appeared to be?

***

I stayed at the camp for a few days more. A stream of crystal clear water flowed next to it—it became my favourite spot as I sat chatting with the dadas. One day, I was pleasantly surprised to hear someone address me in Chhattisgarhiya. I had not expected a Chhattisgarhi to side with the Maoists in Bastar. Chhattisgarh is a divided state; many in tribal Bastar still say they are 'going to Chhattisgarh' when they go towards Raipur. The Maoist movement in Chhattisgarh has so far been confined to the tribal region alone. Though Chhattisgarh is the epicentre of the movement today, I did not know of any non-tribal Chhattisgarhis joining it. In the eyes of Chhattisgarhis from the plains, Maoists are no better than thugs or murderers. Why, then, had this man joined the Party?

He was a short, stout, middle-aged man with thinning hair. He introduced himself as Srikant, the head of the Party in Maharashtra. He became the Party's first non-Telugu state committee member in 2003. Three years later, he became the secretary for Gadchiroli, again the first non-Telugu to head any 'state'. He is the only non-tribal, non-Andhra member of the Dandakaranya state committee. Srikant puffed on bidis for as long as we talked. The only other Maoist I have met who smokes is Kosa, though only occasionally.

'I know you won't tell me to which village you belong, but please tell me which district you are from, and whatever else you can share,' I told him.

He said he was from Raipur, and that he belonged to the 'milkman' caste, 'rout'. His family owned about four acres of land there. His father, he said, worked in Bhilai Steel Plant, as did one of his three brothers. His other brothers are farmers. Though Srikant is the head of Maharashtra, I wanted to talk to him about Chhattisgarh. I wanted to know why he was not posted in Chhattisgarh.

'I started off in Chhattisgarh, working alongside Ramesh. He was the first comrade dispatched to the urban areas of Bhilai around 1985, before Vasu. But he surrendered in 1996, and I had to go underground quickly. In the tribal areas, no one understood Hindi and I did not know Gondi. Marathi was easier for me to learn, so I was sent to Gadchiroli.

'My first introduction to the Party was indirect. In 1982, there was a rally of tribals in Manpur, near Rajnandgaon, which I attended. I was a student, then. I heard tribal leader Lal Sham Sai, a former zamindar of Panabaras, tell the people that all the political parties had betrayed the tribals. He said a party called the People's War had entered Bastar and advised the villagers to help them when they came to

Manpur. Only they could be our saviours, he said. His words remained with me.

'In 1983, I met a cultural team from the People's War at Shankar Guha Niyogi's house in Dalli Rajhara, and that was it: I was hooked. I quit university and started working in a manufacturing company called Simplex (the owner of Simplex was accused of murdering Niyogi) as a labourer in an ancillary unit outside Bhilai. My salary was Rs 400. It was my intention to gauge the condition of the workers there, and I found that there were no labour laws in place. The situation has still not changed, of course.'

'But neither you nor your Party is there to help them,' I countered.

Srikant admitted that it was a lapse. 'Our work in the urban and non-tribal areas of Chhattisgarh was not our priority earlier, which was a mistake. Chhattisgarh has been getting one jolt after another of late. After I left, Vasu was doing substantial work, but he had to leave too. But give us five years and see how we change things in the plains of Chhattisgarh.'

'What makes you so confident?'

'I am not going to discuss that with you, but let me tell you that in five years' time, we will be going from south to north Chhattisgarh undetected.'

'A tall claim when the Party doesn't have a single sympathizer in all of Chhattisgarh's plains today,' I said.

'Well, I think the Sumit fiasco was a temporary setback. My teams from Gadchiroli have been working on distant locations, like Kawardha, the chief minister's home district in Chhattisgarh, though nothing newsworthy has happened yet.' He implied that since they had not killed or attacked anyone yet, journalists would not know of Maoists making progress there.

'Gopanna and I surveyed the Manpur area in December 2004, and see how fast we developed it.' He was referring to the attack in Manpur which had left SP Choube and twenty-eight other policemen dead. 'So believe me when I tell you Chhattisgarh will change in five years. We started surveying Dhamtari district in 2006; Gopanna's arrest forced us to go slow, and there was a break. We killed thirteen policemen at one go there too.'

People in Chhattisgarh are deceptively quiet, Srikant said. 'They are simmering within. There were land movements in Chhattisgarh too, though not much has been written or said about them. After Naxalbari, a landlord was killed in 1970 in Bhatapara area. In retaliation, Darasram Sahu, a leader, was killed by landlords in the Lal Khadan area near Bilaspur. Earlier, in the 1960s, Sihawa, which is in Dhamtari district, had witnessed the Lal Topi movement, led by Sukhram Nage. They captured land and set up sixty new villages. The cases are still pending in Dhamtari court. Sukhram Nage was killed in jail. You must have also heard about the movement led by Kangla Majhi where tribals were incited to take over land occupied by non-tribals. They had also demanded a separate state, Gondwana, for the tribals.

'You have seen that Chhattisgarh has the highest rate of farmer suicides. If as many as four farmers commit suicide every day, as official figures state, then why won't villagers join the Party? So far we have made no effort to work with farmers in Maharashtra either. It has been a mistake which we are now rectifying.'

'Yes, the farmers who are committing suicide are like gratis suicide bombers for you,' I said.

'We do not look at them in that light, but you are correct in that there is no shortage of exploited people. Traders in Chhattisgarh have amassed so much money. Earlier, Nagpur used to supply goods to Raipur but it is the other way round now. Let me tell you a story. In 1997–98, a trader called Gupta Seth, a resident of Gotatola village in Mohla block, paid Rs 500 to a number of tribal farmers, and in exchange, took subsidized loans from banks against their names. The government gave a 75 per cent subsidy on those loans. He never paid the remaining 25 per cent and now the tribals are receiving notices for loans they never took. Gupta Seth has since moved out into the town. No one helps the tribals and no journalist reports their stories. No wonder the people are angry.'

I asked Srikant why there was a sudden spurt in attacks on police in Maharashtra.

'In the last two years, the police have killed thirty-four people in fake encounters in Gadchiroli. We were under pressure from the people to retaliate. Hence the attacks. The press should check what happens behind the scenes before reporting police killings.

'In the three years from 1991–94, the police killed eighty people. We could not be silent spectators to that, and had to strike back. Then they stopped their attacks. So we stopped ours, and concentrated on building our organization. The other day, the press reported widely that we killed fifteen policemen in Markanar, on the Maharashtra-Chhattisgarh border. But they did not write that we had stayed in the village for days before the attack. Nor did they think about why the police got no information about us.

'Similarly, when we attacked SP Choube in the same area, we had been hiding there for more than ten days, and many locals saw us, but no one reported us to the police. Go to that village, investigate, and you will know. We could not have done these things without the cooperation of the people. And please verify for yourself why the people are supporting us. Life in that area has changed because of ponds dug by the Jantana Sarkar. Earlier, the villagers used to go outside the state to work as labourers, but they do not need to any more. Their fields are yielding enough to keep them working on their own farms. But the press cannot see all that.'

I wanted to know what his family thought of his work.

Srikant laughed. 'They thought I was in the grip of madness. When I visited home the last time in 1983, my parents brought in a guniya (local priest) for jhad fook (exorcism). They thought I was possessed. My parents have passed away now and I have no connection with the rest of the family. I have married an Adivasi comrade from Gadchiroli.'

A man sat next to him, cleaning his AK-47. His face was disfigured and Srikant caught the curiosity in my eyes. 'A bullet punctured his face during the attack on SP Choube. It entered from one side of the face and exited through the other.'

The conversation ended there, for he suddenly remembered that Venkitesh, the secretary for south Bastar division, whom I wanted to meet, was in the camp. He introduced me to Venkitesh, a dark, short-statured and muscular man. He wanted to talk in Gondi but I insisted that his Hindi was good enough.

I asked Venkitesh if he would become the Laldenga of Dandakaranya. The reference was lost on him, so I explained that Laldenga had led the secessionist movement against the government to become the chief minister of Mizoram many years later. Venkitesh is the first of the new-generation tribal Maoist leaders. Most of the Maoists who came from Andhra are ageing now. If there is a solution at all, it must come from these new leaders.

Venkitesh became a divisional secretary in 2007. Another tribal, Diwakar, also rose to be a secretary of Gadchiroli division in 2008, but is said to have committed suicide. The police say he was killed by the Party because he wanted to surrender. So what was Venkitesh's motivation, I wanted to know.

'I wanted to study,' he said immediately. 'I was very keen, but there was no teacher in the school. I could study only up to class two.

'I was born in a poor family in Pidmel village near Chintagufa in south Bastar and grew up seeing the atrocities of the forest department. They would come and take away our chickens, and we would have to give them milk and ghee, or else, they would file a case against us. I joined the Party in 1990. Until then, I had only travelled up to Sukma. I had not even seen Jagdalpur.' Raipur is still on his wish list, as is a train journey.

It seems bizarre even to think that sometime in the future, the Indian government may have to negotiate with a leader who has never boarded a train, and never travelled to the capital of his state, leave alone the capital of his country.

Venkitesh quickly added that he had seen trains, television sets and cinemas during his stint as a labourer in Andhra. 'The forest department did not allow us to farm. We did begar (forced free labour) in road construction and forest plantations. Government officials misbehaved with our women. Our headmen collected money from us on their behalf and earned a commission. When I was a child, a forest guard beat up my elder brother right before my eyes. I clearly remember him shouting, "I am asking you to do government work and not my personal work. This forest and this land belong to the government, why are you refusing?"

'But the government has never cared for us. I wanted to take revenge. There was only one Party member in my village before me, and now he has returned home. Three more have joined. Initially, ten had signed up, but seven have now gone back. They can fight from the village. This will be a long war and we are preparing people for that. It is a fight for our right to our land and forests.'

Venkitesh was not the first to speak of Party members going back. To me, the Party seemed like an army training camp for youth: train for a few years, and return to your village. I asked him how many local villagers there were in the leadership now.

'In the South Divisional Committee, which I head, we have ten members. All of them are local tribals and four are women.'

'Weren't there more tribals in the State Committee, apart from Ramder?'

'Yes, there were two more Adivasi members in the

State Committee, but both were suspended last year for misbehaviour with female comrades. One more leader was demoted at the same time for sexual misconduct. He was a non-tribal and he later surrendered to the police. But both the Adivasis continue to be under the Party's banner.'

Other non-tribal leaders had avoided my questions on this subject. Venkitesh's reply was guileless and direct. This gives me hope for the future.

He continued, 'My wife is an Area Committee member, a local organizational squad commander. We decided not to have any children. I had a vasectomy in Bhadrachalam but it was not successful. Then, a doctor was brought into the jungle and I underwent another surgery. I have two older brothers who are farmers and live in the village along with my mother. The police keep bothering them from time to time. My only sister is married. My father died when I was very young. The Salwa Judum came to my village but did not burn any houses. They picked up around twenty people and took them to Dornapal camp. I hear that fifteen of them have come back. No one from my village has become an SPO.'

***

The days went by faster than I realized and it was time for yet another farewell. Everyone in the camp stood in a row to shake hands and bid me Laal Salaam. They even sang 'Jaane waale sathiyon ko laal salaam, laal salaam' ('Red salute to departing friends').

Ganapathy came forward to give me a hug; no other Maoist leader had hugged me before, and I hesitated. It did not seem appropriate as a journalist, but it seemed unnatural to refuse. He promised we would meet again. But would we, I wondered. Perhaps outside a negotiation meeting, at a press conference, or in the jungle again. Perhaps never. I was disappointed that my interview with him had not been very fruitful.

We set off, and when it got dark, Venkitesh bid us goodbye—he needed to attend to some work. He put me in the care of his fellow comrades, who would drop me off on a roadside from where I could make my way back. We would spend the night in the jungle. It was not safe to go to any villages so close to the road, they cautioned.

I was glad to be with the foot soldiers of the movement— five of them, all in their late teens. After a while, a young boy got us food from a village. As we ate in complete darkness, he started talking in fluent Hindi. 'We Adivasis will have to fight, we have no choice. Today, we do not have enough to eat. So we are working on increasing productivity through our Jantana Sarkar, but this fight is not for hunger alone. This is a fight for change and it will be a long one. We will fight till the people support us. If the fight dies down here, it will rise again in a new area.'

'Who are you?' I asked. 'I can't see your face.'

'That is not important,' he replied, and left as soon as we finished eating.

Later, sitting around a quickly lit fire, Vetti, one of my guides, fished a picture of a girl out of his wallet. He said she was Kadti Penti, his friend. 'I liked her,' he said. 'She was also the head of the Jantana Sarkar of my village. She was picked up by a team of Salwa Judum goons led by Soyam Erra, head of Dornapal camp. They raped her and cut her into pieces. They packed parts of her body into a sack and threw it into the Sabari river. The sack was later found by a fisherman in Molkisoli village.'

No one spoke. I had met Soyam Erra in Dornapal camp, but I too held my tongue. Do they ever talk to each other about their personal tragedies?

Jitru spoke of his family, the burning of villages, the killing of family members by the Salwa Judum. He said he had studied in class seven in the same ashram school on the banks of the Talperu where I had spent the night before going to Pusbaka. His mind had become too distracted with all the violence he saw around him, and he quit school soon after. In the camp, Jitru asked me hundreds of questions; he was bright, keen to learn about the world of which he had seen so little. He wanted to know about the politics of Kashmir and Palestine. He wanted to know about the moon missions and finding water there—he had heard about it on the radio—just like any child would, anywhere. I wished he could have continued his education, but he was adamant that there was no option but to fight.

Akash is from Maharashtra. He knows he will be fighting his own people in this war—friends and family will be killing each other. A boy and two girls from his class have joined the Party, and two of his cousins have become policemen. He says that in Gadchiroli, it has become very easy for Adivasis to get jobs in the police department; no one needs to bribe anyone and the minimum educational qualification for eligibility has been lowered from class ten to class seven. But Akash sees it as a trap, not a solution, and feels that his friends, who have joined the police, do not understand that.

That night, Akash heard on the radio that the people of Raigarh in Chhattisgarh have written to the government, declaring that they do not want to give up their land to industry. But he feared they would face police repression. 'Instead of the forest department, now the government is the police,' he said, firm in his decision not to side with the police. 'The rallies held by farmers and tribals are brutally repressed. If we do not take up guns, the government will not listen to us.'

Sarium Irma is from Palamadagu village. He worshipped his teacher, Rambaran Patel, who saw much promise in Sarium. Sarium wanted to be a teacher himself. But when the Salwa Judum attacked his village, they forced Rambaran to beat him up and torch his home. That day, Sarium decided to join the Party. 'I too am a human being. I too can fight. I must resist injustice. The boys who have become SPOs know that their life is limited. They have no future. So they have turned into beasts. They will come to my village and loot whatever they can and take away whomever they can catch. Then the women of the village will organize a rally and march to the police station and bring the arrested people back. This is routine for us. It must stop.'

Next, it was comrade Soni's turn to speak up. She was the only girl amongst us that night. I had met comrade Soni on an earlier trip. I had noticed her at the Martyrs' Day rally, shouting slogans with all the force her lungs could muster. I had shot many pictures of her then—a scrawny girl with a strong voice. I remember that when she took the stage, there was pin-drop silence for the entire half-hour of her speech. I could not follow what she was saying in Gondi, but understood this much—when Soni spoke, people listened. She said she was from Chandraguda village near Kistaram, the eldest of three sisters. Her mother had died when she was young, and the siblings had been brought up single-handedly by their father. 'I knew it must have been difficult for him to take care of my two younger sisters. In my own village and also outside it, everybody was suffering. I understood then, that the problem was bigger than us. I needed to do something which would help everyone. That is why I am here and I am going to fight till the finish.' Soni still speaks passionately.

They are not even adults, some of them. And yet, they carry such heavy burdens without even being able to share their anxieties. Can you talk of peace to people who have suffered so much anguish? They are different from the tribals I met years ago while researching stories for the BBC. They speak of sacrifices and they understand exactly what it means to live through the ups and downs of a protracted war. They see that there is no other way for them. They have heard of similar resistance in other parts of the country—Singur and Nandigram are familiar names to them, even though they have not been even to Jagdalpur, a stone's throw away. It is no longer a revolt; it is a war. These are the first tribal Maoists I met. The comrades from Andhra have worked hard and their theory has penetrated deep here.

Satish and his team joined us around the fire. They were passing by and had camped close to us. We had met before, and I had wanted to talk to him as a representative of young leaders from Andhra.

Satish, who is in his early thirties, is the youngest leader from Andhra I have met. He said he was one of the last to join. 'My father was a contractor, and used to be a Telugu Desam Party worker. But he gave it up after hearing about the politics I am into. My life is not predictable. My brother was in engineering college the last time I got in touch, many years ago. Today, I met my partner by chance for a little while, after six months. Sometimes we do not meet for years.'

'Don't you get tired? What keeps you all going? I am here for just a few days, and yet I find it hard to go on and want to return home.'

Satish looked at me. 'Yes, it is very easy to surrender. Hundreds of our leaders from Andhra have surrendered. These days you don't even need to go to jail. Just give a little information to the police and the state gives you money as well. Do you see those two young boys?' he asked, pointing to a duo sitting around a fire nearby.

I could see them but not their faces; they were too far away.

Satish went on, 'Both were taken to jail and tortured severely, but they did not let slip my name. Another comrade who was with them was killed during interrogation but he did not reveal anything about us. All the leaders experience numerous such instances of loyalty. People have so much faith in us. They want this movement to go on, even at the cost of their lives. These two boys returned to the Party as soon as they were released from jail. That is what drives me.'

I was full of questions, but needed to rest. I was going to have an early start the next day. Would this too become a war, only to end up as fights between small groups fuelled by manipulative funding? Would young people like Venkitesh be able to keep up the rigorous discipline that was at the root of the earlier movement led by the Maoists from Andhra? Will this tribal leadership take the movement to a meaningful destination?

I could see that leaders like Vasu and Venkitesh had no hope of ever receiving any help from the rest of the country. They only looked to their village government for justice. They have a very real understanding of class differences— the electricity that lights up the police station but does not reach their huts is a constant reminder. They are not talking theory, and the defeat of the Salwa Judum has shown them a course of action, however unacceptable it may be in the system that controls all the resources.

The sound of singing and dancing from a nearby village continued till the wee hours of the morning. I wondered how long these songs would survive the onslaught of 'civilization'.

At 4 a.m. I set off for my designated spot by the roadside to catch the bus, which turned up as expected. I was relieved to get a seat and must have dozed off, because I woke up disoriented when the driver slammed on the brakes. He had seen a red flag. He got off, looked at a poster on a tree trunk and declared we would have to turn back as the Maoists had called a strike. I could tell that the posters were fake, but could hardly reveal that I had been with the dadas, and that if they had called a strike, I would have known. The bus went back, dropping some of us in the middle of nowhere.

As suggested by some of my fellow passengers, I walked ahead to the next police station. The police officer refused to send anyone to check the posters out. 'It could be a trap,' he said. He busied himself calling his superiors on his satellite phone. All traffic stayed off that road for the day.

I tried to persuade an old man on a two-wheeler to give me a lift. With the lure of some cash, he agreed to let me ride pillion on his TVS 50 and drop me off at the nearest town, around forty kilometres away. When it broke down midway, I realized that the TVS 50 from the 1980s, though still in use, is not always operational. Money has limited value in this part of India.

Walking on, I reached Hemalkasa at the other end of Abujhmad, where Baba Amte's son, Dr Prakash Amte, runs a school and hospital. Dr Amte was not in town, so I met his deputy, Vilas Manohar. Vilasji came to this area in 1975, a year after Dr Amte, and has lived here since then.

I asked Vilasji what he thought was the solution to the Naxal problem.

'No one wants to know it from us,' was his acidic response. 'Go and ask the leaders, they know it all!'

So I changed my question. 'Why does a tribal become a Naxal supporter?'

Vilasji posed his own question: 'Why wouldn't he? If I had been a tribal, I would have become a Naxal as well. What have they got from the state? In this area, only Naxal pressure causes change rapidly. When we came here, the price of a packet of tendu leaf was Rs 3. This year, it was Rs 154, thanks to the Naxals. In non-Naxal areas, chillies used to sell for Rs 6 a kilogram; now they cost Rs 60—only a tenfold rise in price for the farmer in thirty-five years. We have got roads, electricity and schools, all because of the Maoists.

'I am not saying that there is no progress; the purchasing

power of tribals has gone up, wages are higher and there are many more schools now, but the Naxals have contributed to bring in about 40 per cent of this change. The government's contribution too is 40 per cent, and the remaining 20 per cent has been possible thanks to increased awareness among the tribals. When the percentage of the government's contribution changes, so will its control on the people.'

'What would you say is the contribution of the work that you do?'

'We are very small and operate in a very small area.'

He sounded realistic, not falsely modest.

'Our school has produced five doctors so far. We trained the first tribal doctor from the area, Kanna Madavi. But now he has built a huge private hospital in nearby Ahiri, though he is a government servant. He has become a part of that same exploitative system. When Sonu came to visit me some time ago, he asked me, "You have produced Dr Kanna, who has become part of the system, equally oppressive to his fellow tribals. What did you really achieve?" I thought he had a point. We have produced forty teachers from our school, and forty policemen as well. Four of our students have become Maoists, two of whom are dead.'

Then he recounted a story. 'Two tribals, Zuru Vadde and Pandu, used to be classmates. They were relatives as well. After leaving school, Zuru became a Maoist and Pandu, a policeman. Pandu killed Zuru in an encounter. The Party avenged the death and killed Pandu the same year in a landmine blast. Zuru's daughter joined the Maoists later, and was also killed. His son has gone over to another predator: he has become a Christian priest.'

Vilasji talked openly about the Naxals' visits to their ashram and wanted to know which of them I had met. 'They are such nice people, aren't they? It is hard to believe the horrific stories about them in the press.' As we talked, we seemed to agree that the one to watch for in the coming years was Sonu. He was most likely to be the next general secretary of the Party.

I asked him if people really supported the Maoists or obeyed them out of fear.

Vilasji posed another question in response. 'You have made this long trip in Abujhmad, what have you understood?'

I did not have to think very long. I gave him the example of the last stop of my journey, the roadside village where I had been dropped off by the Maoists. Villagers had come forward with parathas, chicken and milk for the whole team. I realized that one might grudgingly offer food under duress, but never would one serve the best food under such circumstances.

Vilasji was pleased. 'Exactly. You have understood it correctly.'

I asked him once again, 'I know that no leader wants to take advice from social workers like you, who have worked with Adivasis all your life, but what is the solution to this problem?'

'Education,' he said. 'Give them education. Modern education makes you cowardly, selfish and greedy. If the state can give tribals education, the problem will be solved.'

***

I did not want to take the risk of being detained by the police with all the Maoist literature I had collected in the forest.

I also burnt the letter Vasu had given me for his children. I think he knew I might, because he also told me, 'Give them a kiss each on their foreheads, and a big hug from me,' reminding me of Che, who once said that a revolutionary was also the greatest lover. I saw that quality in Vasu. At that moment, I had felt that he was a caring man who believed that whatever he did was for the good of the people. Vasu's politics kills people, something to which I do not subscribe, but he has facts and figures to support his argument that mainstream politics kills more people and equally painfully, though slowly. The civilized world thinks of him as a terrorist, but I think he is one of the best politicians I have met, and in my field of work I have met many. I would not say this of too many Maoist leaders.

I wonder if Vasu will ever head the Maoist Party. Will he ever live a normal life with his children? Or will he travel to a new area when he leaves this forest, just like earlier revolutionaries, who moved from one theatre of rebellion to another? Many have gone from Bengal to Bihar, from Andhra to Chhattisgarh. Will Vasu turn to Orissa next?

AUTHOR'S NOTE

People like Vasu belong to a rare breed. They would not constitute the biggest security threat to the country without their foot soldiers. The cocktail of Adivasi disaffection and the Maoist devotion to their goal is a dangerous mix.

Much has changed since the time I walked the forests with the dadas. Maoist leader Kishenji, whom I had first approached when I decided to write this book, was killed in an encounter. Rahul Sharma, the police chief of Dantewada who was my connection to the side of the security forces, committed suicide. Mahendra Karma, the mighty Salwa Judum leader, lost his seat in the latest election.

In Manendragarh, where I grew up, the dominance of outsiders like myself seems to be complete. The erstwhile tribal constituency has become a general seat. Deepak Patel, a trader, and the relative of a moneyed Gujarati, who heads the association of Chhattisgarhis in the US, is now the MLA of the constituency. He is helping the state 'grow' with foreign investments for power and steel plants.

The state-driven, strategic 'hamleting' experiment of the Salwa Judum, cleared at the highest levels of the government, has proven to be a disaster on all fronts. In fact, in the last five years, the Salwa Judum has ended up strengthening the Maoists as never before. Still, the Maoists have no illusions about being anything but a spare wheel, valued only in an emergency. They say that the main battles will be fought in villages and in cities, and that the forest can play only a supportive role. They also say it is Prime Minister Manmohan Singh and his policies that have created this emergency.

There are no illusions in the corridors of power either. In the Naxal cell of the home ministry in Delhi, the only officer sitting at his desk pointed out cynically that none of the top bosses had turned up at work, though it was past noon. 'Who won the Mahabharata?' he asked. 'Aren't the tribals asking for the equivalent of five villages that the Pandavas wanted? Why are our leaders so arrogant? Why are they sending an army to capture Abujhmad?' I think these are valid questions. A red flag flying aloft the Red Fort is the Maoist dream, and it fuels them. But Venkitesh, the highest-ranking tribal Maoist leader in Chhattisgarh, has not even seen Raipur, let alone the Red Fort in Delhi. If Abujhmad is captured, Maoism and Vasu can simply move to a new area. But many Adivasis who are cannon fodder in the Maoist strategy will die in the crossfire.

On my earlier trips to the forest, I had felt that the Adivasis were simply parroting the Maoist ideology. The work done by people like Vasu has helped a section of them understand some of the systemic shortcomings and converted the docile Adivasi in Chhattisgarh into a fighter. But at the same time, the Adivasis realize that the Maoists cannot solve their problems either. Then why do they support them?

I cannot help but conclude that there is no real concern anywhere about the problems of the Adivasis. The Maoists have never claimed that their fight is for the welfare of the tribals. They clearly state that they came to tribal areas because they are safe there, and I think they are doing whatever is necessary for them to be able to continue to use those as safe zones. And yet, they are called law-breakers, while it is the state that often ignores the Fifth and Sixth Schedules of the Indian Constitution that give special rights to Adivasis to take independent, empowered decisions about their lives and resources. It is not merely a lack of understanding of their needs—perhaps no one even wants to make the effort to find out what those needs are. The elite and the middle class garb their callousness with nationalism. I have heard, more often than I like, their response to the military action in tribal areas: it is seen as a 'sacrifice' that a nation must make for progress.

It is only an accident of history that the tribals have turned to the Maoists. They reached the forests first. Right wing extremists have made recent inroads into the area, and the tribals are looking to them as well. Had the Adivasis turned to the right wing groups to find solutions to their problems, we would have called it a problem of right wing extremism. But the real problem is that of the appropriation of Adivasi rights and resources.

The 'Maoist' problem also stems from a breach in communication between mainstream India and its hundred-million-strong tribal population. I think that a majority of Adivasis—and that is a huge number—are turning to the Maoists because no one else is able to communicate with them. Much needs to be done to solve this problem. We need to bring justice to the table. But first, communication, which is my area of expertise, needs to be democratized. We must create platforms where people can be heard.

Whenever I visited Kashmir as a journalist, I worked with a Kashmiri translator. In Sri Lanka, I had to make sure I worked with a local journalist who knew both Tamil and Sinhala. But when I covered the Maoist problem in Chhattisgarh, I found myself working with a non-tribal outsider like me, who did not know Gondi or any other tribal language. I could not find a single tribal journalist in a place that has a large enough tribal population to have acquired the status of a separate state on that criterion alone. It reminded me of Edward Behr mocking such journalism in his book *Anyone Here Been Raped and Speaks English?* In the tribal villages of Chhattisgarh, I would look for someone who knew Hindi, not realizing that a Hindi speaker there is an upper-class representative and, as the Maoists have very creatively turned this war against the upper class, I was not able to communicate with the 'real' tribals.

I think part of the solution to the problem lies in bridging the communication gap. The experiments in CGNet and CGNet Swara have been an effort in that direction. Some Adivasis are now picking up their mobile phones to tell their stories in their own languages. Trained Adivasis translate the messages, which then reach mainstream journalists and the authorities. I am convinced that this has helped some of the Adivasis to connect with the mainstream.

The public hearing on environmental concerns surrounding the upcoming Tata Steel plant took place in the office of the collector of Bastar, ostensibly for security reasons. People protesting the plant were kept away by the police, and press reports spoke glowingly of the 'success' of the hearing the following day. Later, the state-owned National Mineral Development Corporation tried the same trick in Dantewada. But this time, the people had a voice. A citizen journalist called up CGNet Swara and reported that the people suspected a repeat of the Tata story. A journalist from a national newspaper, who had started taking interest in the story by then, showed up at the 'public hearing' in the Dantewada collector's office. There were 50-odd people in attendance. He asked the landowners amongst them to raise their hands. Not a single hand went up—they were not the people who were going to lose their land to the proposed mines. The NMDC has not yet been able to take the land and I think this has helped keep some of the Adivasis from appealing to the Maoists for solutions to their problems. The Tata area, however, is now completely in the grip of the Maoists. There are no hills or forests there to serve as hideouts, so the Maoists do not roam about in their uniforms, but they can still do as they please.

CGNet has also been instrumental in exposing many instances of human rights violations in the area in the past five years, including the latest one in Tadmetla village, underscoring how open communication can help. In Tadmetla, Adivasi dwellings were torched on 11 March 2011 and the burning of homes continued for the next five days. CGNet Swara received phone calls reporting the incidents on each of those days, but there were no eyewitness accounts. I am sure the villagers also informed the local journalists—Dantewada, after all, has twenty-nine full-time journalists at last count—but not one of them published a report. They did not report it not because they did not want to, but because they could not. It is a structural problem. Our communication platforms are far too dependent on the people who burn houses, and not on those whose houses are burnt. After two incidents of burning, the chief minister of the state was approached with a request to order an investigation. For the next couple of frustrating days, the state's biggest newspaper published banner stories on its front pages, with fictitious pictures undermining the as yet unpublished CGNet Swara story. Finally, on 18 March, a public appeal was made from CGNet Swara to the media and the people to find out more about Tadmetla because it was impossible to confirm the burnings using the state mechanism. All the roads to Tadmetla were blocked. Finally, on 23 March, nearly two weeks after the first incident, the mainstream national media reported that more than 300 homes had been burnt, and that there had been killings and rapes. The Supreme Court intervened, and the Central Bureau of Investigation is now probing the allegations.

Lingaram Kodopi was the first to make public the pictures from Tadmetla that he took using his journalistic training with CGNet and his knowledge of local terrain and language. He is the first trained Adivasi journalist from Chhattisgarh. He studied journalism for a year in Delhi but was arrested soon after he returned home. His aunt, Soni Sori, was brutally tortured in police custody and also remains in jail on charges of helping the Maoists. Fellowships have been arranged to train other tribal citizen journalists. But it is hard to convince them to accept because of the pressure the local police bring to bear on them and their families. Who would want to be in Lingaram's shoes?

Tadmetla is not the only story happening in Chhattisgarh, but it was reported thanks to the small experiment of CGNet Swara. There are many unreported Tadmetlas taking place in tribal India, strengthening the Maoist following. I think a democratic platform for communication linking the Internet, mobile phones and the radio can help solve 'India's biggest internal security threat'.

In the world of communication, people can be classified as the rich, or the Internet people, who live in their own world; the middle class, or the mobile phone people, who aspire to become the Internet class one day; and the poor, whom I call the radio people. The world's largest democracy does not allow private or community-owned news on the radio. As the poor can afford only the radio, they are not in any race at present; they are silenced, like the radio in India. Some of them may have joined the Maoists, but they are too weak to make an impact on a nation as mighty as India; at best, they have only a periodic nuisance value. But the day a sizable number of the mobile phone population loses hope in the current system and joins the radio class, things can change.

June 2012
New Delhi

ACKNOWLEDGEMENTS

So many have helped me investigate and write this book that it is impossible to acknowledge all of them. I do not know the real names of many and many would like to remain unnamed.

I would start by thanking my wife, Smita, without whom I could never have written this book. She allowed me to come into harm's way over and over again, knowing all too well the dangers I could face. She fought like the goddess Durga when I almost died of malaria twice after my trips. My blood platelet count was down to almost zero. Doctors in the best hospitals of Delhi had no clue what to do. (Like the people of Dandakaranya and their problems, malaria from that part of the world too is an unknown entity in places like Delhi.) Smita also polished my words, reworking almost the entire book.

My son, Arjun, read the manuscript several times and came up with useful suggestions. So did my friends Anoop Saha, Nidheesh Tyagi, Daniel Lak, David Loyn, Satyendra Ranjan, Vinod Verma and Rahul Banerjee. Arundhati Roy and Sanjay Kak read it when it was no more than a pile of rough notes, which must have been painful to go through, and gave me very constructive pointers.

Himanshu Kumar of Vanvasi Chetna Ashram hosted me several times when the only hotel in Dantewada did not have room for me. He paid the supreme price for his hospitality when he lost his ashram, a labour of love and two decades of hard work. The government of Chhattisgarh bulldozed it.

My friend Kamlesh Painkra helped me translate from Gondi and took grave risks to accompany me to places fraught with danger. Friends like Manish Kunjam of the CPI and Professor Nandini Sundar were always helpful with contacts and insights. The late Iqbal bhai and Kala were wonderful hosts, patiently tolerating my sudden disappearances into the jungles.

Lalitha Sreedhar nagged and pushed me to write this book and introduced me to the publishers, Penguin.

I can't thank Mustafa enough; he travelled with his bulky cameras to treacherous terrains at the shortest of notices. Naresh Mishra, N.R.K. Pillay, Bappi Ray—all journalists in Bastar—were there for me whenever I needed them. They took personal risks to fulfil my constant and often unjustified demands.

Dr Haneef in Andhra put me in touch with many tribal families living in the jungles on the border of Andhra Pradesh and Chhattisgarh. The late K. Balagopal and Varvara Rao helped me understand the history of the movement in Andhra. Purushottam Thakur, Sampad Mahapatra and K. Sudhakar Patnaik were my go-to persons in Orissa.

The late Professor Surendra Parihar told me many fascinating stories of his association with the overground

Maoists in Chhattisgarh and opened the doors to the Ravi Shankar University library in Raipur. Lalit Surjan, chief editor of *Deshbandhu*, gave me access to their archive of old newspapers.

I also want to thank the late police chief of Dantewada, Rahul Sharma, who helped me with contacts in the police. Mahendra Karma, the Salwa Judum leader, always gave me access to his rallies, even though he knew perfectly well what I was investigating.

I want to thank the drivers who ferried me through uncharted roads, many times ungrudgingly. Many government servants and police officers, who would like to remain nameless, helped with invaluable documents and files.

I could not have walked and worked in that difficult terrain had it not been for numerous young Maoist comrades who carried my luggage, cooked for me and told me their stories. This book could not have been written without them. I want to thank all of them, including the late Kishenji, who first gave me an entry into their world, and of course, my friend, Vasu.

I want to thank all my editors, Ravi Singh, Ranjana Sengupta, Sivapriya, Ameya Nagarajan, Arpita Basu and Renu Agal, who put up with my regular delays.

My mother-in-law very kindly allowed me to go underground in her house for six months, which is when I finally finished the book after many delays.

I want to thank all my friends in the CGNet discussion forum and CGNet Swara as the exchange of ideas on these platforms helped me grasp the big picture as well as the details of the story I was following.

And last but not the least, I want to thank my parents, who always knew I was setting off for dangerous places without ever telling them. This project would never have been completed without their blessings and love.